KU-312-581

ENGINEERING DRAWING

WITH WORKED EXAMPLES 2

ENGINEERING DRAWING
WITH WORKED EXAMPLES 2

F. Pickup, C.Eng., M.I.Prod.E.

*Formerly Chief Examiner for A Level Technical Drawing
at the University of London*

and

M. A. Parker

*Lecturer in Charge of Technical Drawing
Hong Kong Polytechnic*

Hutchinson of London

Hutchinson & Co (Publishers) Ltd
3 Fitzroy Square, London W1

London Melbourne Sydney Auckland
Wellington Johannesburg and agencies
throughout the world

First published March 1960
Second impression September 1961
Third impression June 1962
Fourth impression July 1963
Fifth impression November 1964
Sixth impression February 1966
Second edition, revised and metricated, 1970
Eighth impression 1972
Ninth impression 1973
Tenth impression 1974
Eleventh impression 1975
Twelfth impression 1977
Thirteenth impression 1978

© F. Pickup and M. A. Parker 1960

Printed in Great Britain by litho at The Anchor Press Ltd
and bound by Wm Brendon & Son Ltd
both of Tiptree, Essex

ISBN 0 09 100710 0 (cased)
0 09 100711 9 (paper)

CONTENTS

PREFACE

In view of the change-over to the metric (SI) system this book has been reviewed. The topics discussed remain the fundamentals of the subject and continue to cater for many courses in Engineering Drawing, such as those provided for National Certificate, Mechanical Technicians, Trade and Craft Courses.

Many aspects of change to the metric system are relatively straight-forward—an actual length is still the same, even though the number associated with it may vary from one system to another. Any field in which parts must fit each other is more complex however, probably the most difficult being that of screw threads and the standardization of threads. It is for this reason that existing thread forms such as B.S.F., Whitworth and B.A. threads have again been used throughout Book 2 and data relating to these threads given on pages 247 and 248.

The same method of presenting the subject has been followed as in Book 1. The text has been kept to a minimum sufficient to outline the general principles of the subject, and worked examples have been freely used to enlarge on it. Each example shows the method of obtaining the solution together with additional explanatory notes. For some topics where a solution on one drawing would have been difficult to understand, the solution has been drawn in step-by-step form. Sufficient problems for class use and homework for one year are also given for the lecturer.

The authors' thanks are again due to those of their colleagues at the Rolls Royce Technical College who read and criticised the manuscript and checked the drawings. The British Standards Institution again permitted information form some of their Standards to be reprinted.

AUXILIARY PROJECTION

CASES arise in practice where views of an object projected on to the principal planes of projection are either insufficient to describe the object or are difficult to draw or dimension. Such cases include objects with inclined faces of a complex nature and are best drawn using auxiliary views. An auxiliary view is one which is drawn on a plane other than a principal plane of projection. An auxiliary view which is projected from a normal elevation or plan is called a first auxiliary elevation or plan. Other auxiliary views may be projected from first auxiliary views. These are called second auxiliary elevations or plans. It should be noted that an elevation can only be projected from a plan and vice versa.

First Auxiliary Elevations

Figure 1(a) illustrates the method of projecting these views, using First Angle projection. The standard elevation and plan are first drawn with an XY line or datum line between them. It may be convenient to use the centre line of the plan or the base line of the detail as the XY line. The first auxiliary elevation is required in the direction of arrow Q, so points on the plan view are projected parallel to the arrow to cross the new datum line X^1Y^1 at right angles. This new datum line may be placed in any convenient position. The heights above the XY line, A, B and C, of points in the original elevation, are then transferred to the appropriate projectors above the new X^1Y^1 line and the view is lined in. To avoid confusion between full lines and hidden detail lines it is best to complete first those faces which are seen completely in the auxiliary view.

Figure 1(b) shows the same views drawn in Third Angle projection. The method of using the same heights in both elevations is identical with views drawn in First Angle projection.

First Auxiliary Plan Views

The method for these views is similar to that used for first auxiliary elevations and is shown using First Angle projection, in Figure 2(a). Projectors from points on the normal elevation are drawn parallel to the new direction of viewing, given by arrow Q, and cross the new datum X^1Y^1 at right angles. Depths W and Z, from the XY line to points in the original

AUXILIARY PROJECTION.

FIRST AUXILIARY ELEVATIONS.

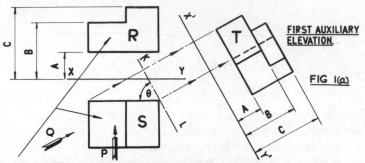

FIRST AUXILIARY ELEVATION.

FIG 1(a)

VIEWS R AND S.— STANDARD ELEVATION AND PLAN VIEW IN FIRST ANGLE ORTHOGRAPHIC PROJECTION.

X,Y. LINE. — RELATIVE TO THE ELEVATION REPRESENTS THE HORIZONTAL PLANE.
RELATIVE TO THE PLAN REPRESENTS THE VERTICAL PLANE.

NOTE — VIEWING GIVEN PLAN IN DIRECTION OF ARROW P WILL PRODUCE THE ELEVATION R.
VIEWING GIVEN PLAN IN DIRECTION OF ARROW Q WILL PRODUCE A NEW ELEVATION T.

THE NEW ELEVATION T IS PROJECTED HAVING VERTICAL HEIGHTS EQUAL TO THE GIVEN HEIGHTS IN ELEVATION R.
THUS THE PROJECTION OF A FIRST AUXILIARY ELEVATION DOES NOT ALTER THE DETAIL'S POSITION RELATIVE TO THE H.P.

THE DETAIL'S POSITION RELATIVE TO THE V.P. HAS BEEN CHANGED SUCH THAT IT IS NOW SET AT AN ANGLE θ TO THE V.P. LINE K.L. PARALLEL TO X.Y. BEING THE NEW GROUND LINE.

VIEWS R AND S.— STANDARD ELEVATION AND PLAN IN THIRD ANGLE ORTHOGRAPHIC PROJECTION.

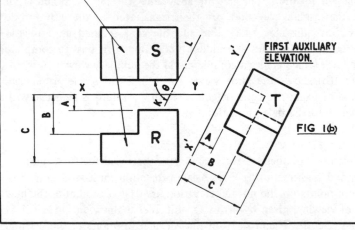

FIRST AUXILIARY ELEVATION.

FIG 1(b)

AUXILIARY PROJECTION.
FIRST AUXILIARY PLANS.

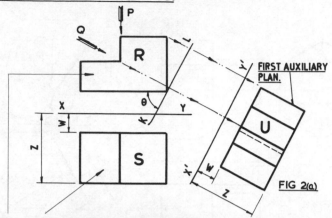

FIRST AUXILIARY PLAN.

FIG 2(a)

VIEWS R AND S — STANDARD ELEVATION AND PLAN VIEW IN FIRST ANGLE ORTHOGRAPHIC PROJECTION.

X,Y. LINE. — RELATIVE TO THE ELEVATION REPRESENTS THE HORIZONTAL PLANE,
RELATIVE TO THE PLAN REPRESENTS THE VERTICAL PLANE.

NOTE — VIEWING GIVEN ELEVATION IN DIRECTION OF ARROW P WILL PRODUCE THE PLAN S.
VIEWING GIVEN ELEVATION IN DIRECTION OF ARROW Q WILL PRODUCE A NEW PLAN U.

THE NEW PLAN U IS PROJECTED HAVING DEPTHS EQUAL TO THE GIVEN DEPTHS IN PLAN S.
THUS THE PROJECTION OF A FIRST AUXILIARY PLAN VIEW DOES NOT ALTER THE DETAIL'S POSITION RELATIVE TO THE V.P.

THE DETAIL'S POSITION RELATIVE TO THE H.P. HAS BEEN CHANGED SUCH THAT IT IS NOW SET AT AN ANGLE θ TO THE H.P. LINE K L PARALLEL TO X Y BEING THE NEW GROUND LINE.

VIEWS R AND S — STANDARD ELEVATION AND PLAN IN THIRD ANGLE ORTHOGRAPHIC PROJECTION.

FIRST AUXILIARY PLAN.

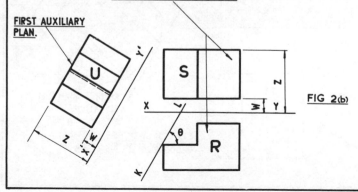

FIG 2(b)

3

AUXILIARY PROJECTION.
SECOND AUXILIARY ELEVATIONS.

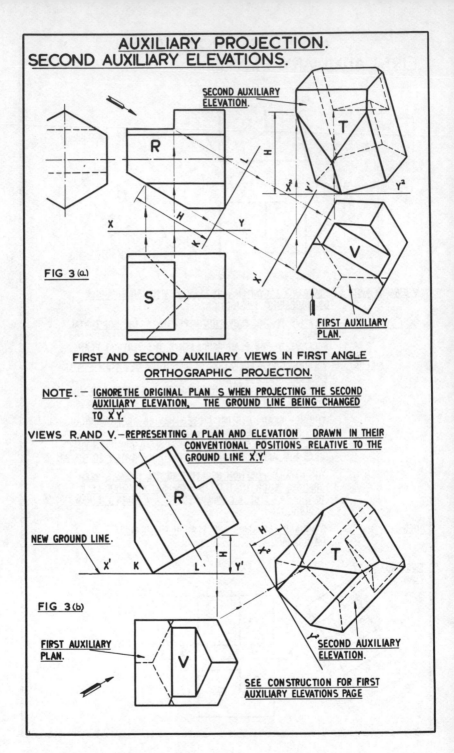

SECOND AUXILIARY ELEVATION.

FIG 3 (a)

FIRST AUXILIARY PLAN.

FIRST AND SECOND AUXILIARY VIEWS IN FIRST ANGLE ORTHOGRAPHIC PROJECTION.

NOTE. — IGNORE THE ORIGINAL PLAN S WHEN PROJECTING THE SECOND AUXILIARY ELEVATION, THE GROUND LINE BEING CHANGED TO X.Y.

VIEWS R. AND V. — REPRESENTING A PLAN AND ELEVATION DRAWN IN THEIR CONVENTIONAL POSITIONS RELATIVE TO THE GROUND LINE X.Y.

NEW GROUND LINE.

FIG 3 (b)

FIRST AUXILIARY PLAN.

SECOND AUXILIARY ELEVATION.

SEE CONSTRUCTION FOR FIRST AUXILIARY ELEVATIONS PAGE

4

AUXILIARY PROJECTION.
SECOND AUXILIARY ELEVATIONS.

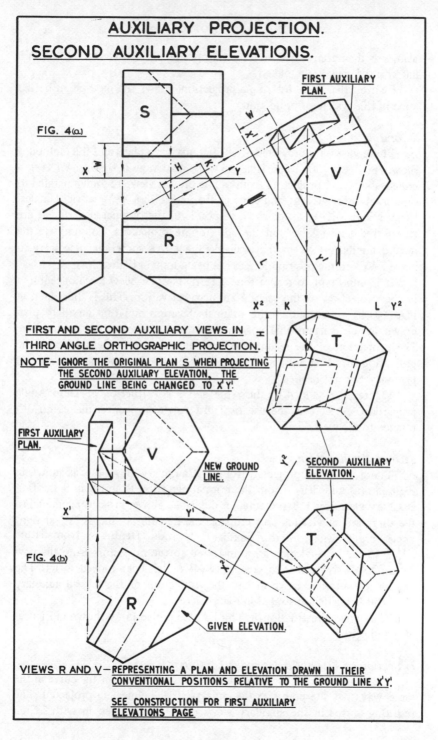

FIRST AUXILIARY PLAN.

FIG. 4(a)

S

W

X

H

K

Y

V

R

FIRST AUXILIARY PLAN.

X^2 K   L Y^2

T

H

FIRST AND SECOND AUXILIARY VIEWS IN THIRD ANGLE ORTHOGRAPHIC PROJECTION.

NOTE— IGNORE THE ORIGINAL PLAN S WHEN PROJECTING THE SECOND AUXILIARY ELEVATION, THE GROUND LINE BEING CHANGED TO X'Y'.

FIRST AUXILIARY PLAN.

V

NEW GROUND LINE.

SECOND AUXILIARY ELEVATION.

X^1 Y^1

Y^2

X^2

FIG. 4(b)

R

T

GIVEN ELEVATION.

VIEWS R AND V— REPRESENTING A PLAN AND ELEVATION DRAWN IN THEIR CONVENTIONAL POSITIONS RELATIVE TO THE GROUND LINE X'Y'.

SEE CONSTRUCTION FOR FIRST AUXILIARY ELEVATIONS PAGE

5

plan, are then transferred to the appropriate projectors from the X^1Y^1 line and the view is completed.

Figure 2(b), in Third Angle projection, shows the method to be the same in this system of projection.

Second Auxiliary Elevations

These views are projected from first auxiliary plans and the method is shown in Figure 3(a). The first auxiliary plan view is first drawn as described above and projectors from points on this view are drawn parallel to the direction of viewing and crossing the new datum X^2Y^2 at right angles. Heights above X^1Y^1, such as H, of points in the original elevation R are transferred above X^2Y^2 on the appropriate projectors. To complete the second auxiliary view in the available space it is sometimes necessary to move X^1Y^1 to the position KL, as has been done in Figure 3(a).

It is important to realise that the original plan view S is not required in the projection of the second auxiliary elevation. This is illustrated in Figure 3(b) which shows the original elevation and first auxiliary plan drawn in the conventional positions relative to a horizontal ground line. The projection of the second auxiliary elevation T is identical with the projection of a first auxiliary elevation as outlined above and the original plan view S is not needed.

Figures 4(a) and 4(b) show the above construction in Third Angle projection. As before, the use of Third Angle projection makes no difference to the method.

Second Auxiliary Plan Views

These views are projected from first auxiliary elevations as shown in Figures 5(a) and 5(b). From the normal elevation R and plan S the first auxiliary elevation T is projected as described above. Projectors parallel to the direction of viewing and crossing the new datum line X^2Y^2 at right angles are drawn from this auxiliary elevation. Depths W from datum X^1Y^1 to the original plan are transferred to the projectors from the new datum X^2Y^2. Note that to save space X^1Y^1 has been moved to KL. The original elevation R is ignored in the projection of the second auxiliary plan, this being demonstrated in Figure 5(b).

The above construction in Third Angle projection is shown in Figures 6(a) and 6(b).

Projection of Arcs of Circles and Other Curves

This is performed by projecting a series of points on the curve in the same way that the points at the ends of straight lines are projected. The resulting curves in the auxiliary views can then be filled in with french

AUXILIARY PROJECTION.

SECOND AUXILIARY PLANS.

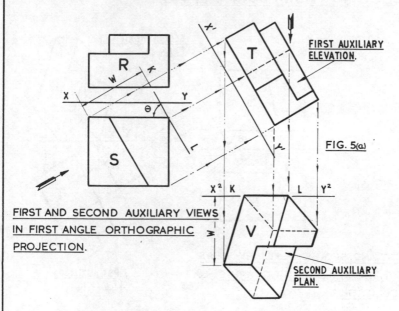

FIRST AUXILIARY ELEVATION.

FIG. 5(a)

FIRST AND SECOND AUXILIARY VIEWS IN FIRST ANGLE ORTHOGRAPHIC PROJECTION.

SECOND AUXILIARY PLAN.

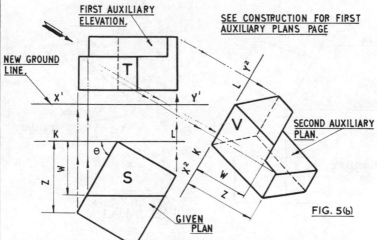

FIRST AUXILIARY ELEVATION.

SEE CONSTRUCTION FOR FIRST AUXILIARY PLANS PAGE

NEW GROUND LINE.

SECOND AUXILIARY PLAN.

GIVEN PLAN

FIG. 5(b)

VIEWS S AND T—REPRESENTING A PLAN AND ELEVATION DRAWN IN THEIR CONVENTIONAL POSITIONS RELATIVE TO THE GROUND LINE X'Y'

NOTE — IGNORE THE ORIGINAL ELEVATION R WHEN PROJECTING THE SECOND AUXILIARY PLAN, THE GROUND LINE BEING CHANGED TO X'Y.'

AUXILIARY PROJECTION.

SECOND AUXILIARY PLANS.

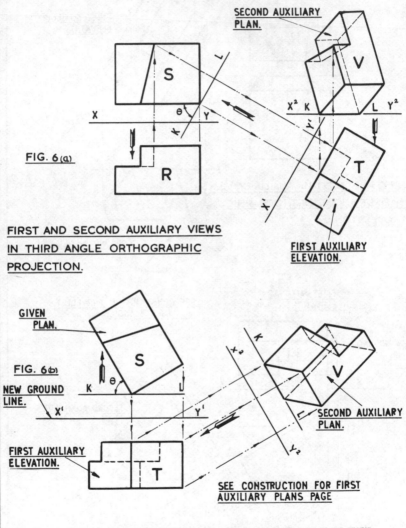

SECOND AUXILIARY PLAN.

FIG. 6(a)

FIRST AND SECOND AUXILIARY VIEWS
IN THIRD ANGLE ORTHOGRAPHIC
PROJECTION.

FIRST AUXILIARY ELEVATION.

GIVEN PLAN.

FIG. 6(b)

NEW GROUND LINE.

FIRST AUXILIARY ELEVATION.

SECOND AUXILIARY PLAN.

SEE CONSTRUCTION FOR FIRST
AUXILIARY PLANS PAGE

VIEWS S AND T—REPRESENTING A PLAN AND ELEVATION DRAWN IN THEIR
CONVENTIONAL POSITIONS RELATIVE TO THE GROUND LINE X Y.

NOTE — IGNORE THE ORIGINAL ELEVATION R WHEN PROJECTING
THE SECOND AUXILIARY PLAN, THE GROUND LINE BEING
CHANGED TO X'Y'.

8

curves. If too many points are projected the work becomes tedious and there is no increase in accuracy.

The Solution of Problems

The solutions of auxiliary projection problems are obtained more easily if the following points are observed:

All XY lines should be marked in some way to distinguish them from each other.

The XY line for the first auxiliary view can be moved to a new position to reduce to a manageable size the distances to points in the second auxiliary view. Also, this will often enable the second auxiliary view to be drawn in the available space. The new position of the XY line must, of course, be parallel to its original position.

Views of symmetrical details are drawn more quickly if centrelines are used as XY lines.

When distances to points on an object are transferred from one XY line to another, they must be laid off in the same direction relative to the linking view. For example, in Figure 5(a) the first auxiliary elevation links the normal plan and the second auxiliary plan. Dimension W on the normal plan is laid off from X^1Y^1 away from the first auxiliary elevation. When it is transferred to X^2Y^2 it is again laid off away from the first auxiliary elevation. Observance of this rule will prevent views being drawn upside down or reversed.

It is unnecessary to project all the points in an auxiliary view since lines which are parallel in the normal elevation and plan remain parallel in the auxiliary views. Thus a few lines can be projected in an auxiliary view and the view completed by making the remainder parallel to them.

Some worked examples follow, and further problems will be found on page 29.

EXAMPLE 12:

The details for a small Jig Assembly are shown in Third Angle projection on page 25. Copy the given elevation and plan of the Base, full size, in First Angle projection, and complete the views with the Inclined Slide and the Holder. Hidden detail may be omitted from the elevation but not from the plan.

EXAMPLE 13:

Views are given in First Angle projection on page 27 of the details for a Setting Block Assembly. When assembled the Support Plate is mounted on the Base Plate as shown in the part sectional view. Draw full size in First Angle projection an elevation and plan of the assembly, corresponding to the given elevation and plan of the Base Plate. The Slide Block

AUXILIARY PROJECTION.

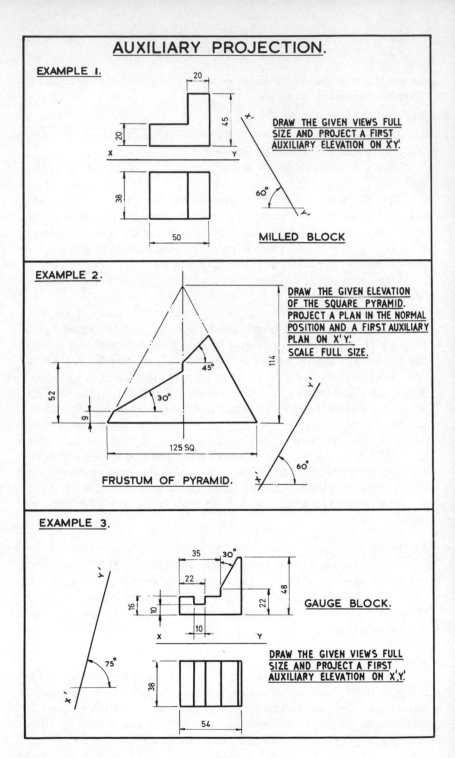

EXAMPLE 1.

20

45

20

X   Y

38

50

x₁

60°

z₁

DRAW THE GIVEN VIEWS FULL
SIZE AND PROJECT A FIRST
AUXILIARY ELEVATION ON X'Y'.

MILLED BLOCK

EXAMPLE 2.

114

45°

52

30°

9

125 SQ.

y'

60°

x'

DRAW THE GIVEN ELEVATION
OF THE SQUARE PYRAMID.
PROJECT A PLAN IN THE NORMAL
POSITION AND A FIRST AUXILIARY
PLAN ON X'Y'.
SCALE FULL SIZE.

FRUSTUM OF PYRAMID.

EXAMPLE 3.

Y'

75°

X'

35

30°

22

16

10

10

X   Y

48

22

GAUGE BLOCK.

38

54

DRAW THE GIVEN VIEWS FULL
SIZE AND PROJECT A FIRST
AUXILIARY ELEVATION ON X'Y'.

10

AUXILIARY PROJECTION.

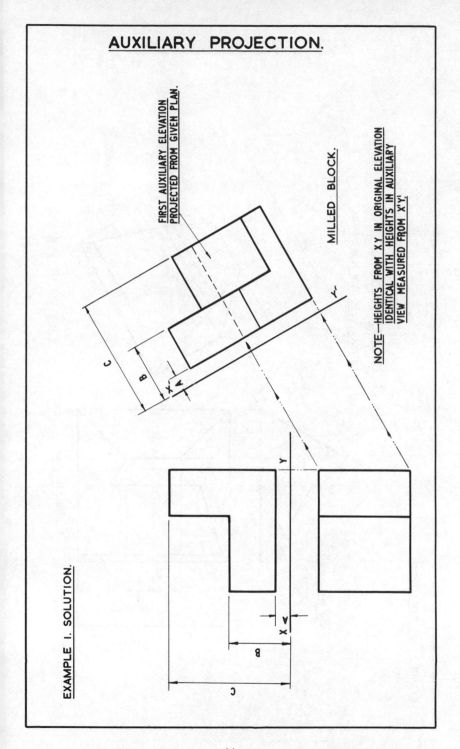

EXAMPLE I. SOLUTION.

FIRST AUXILIARY ELEVATION PROJECTED FROM GIVEN PLAN.

MILLED BLOCK.

NOTE—HEIGHTS FROM XY IN ORIGINAL ELEVATION IDENTICAL WITH HEIGHTS IN AUXILIARY VIEW MEASURED FROM X'Y'

AUXILIARY PROJECTION.

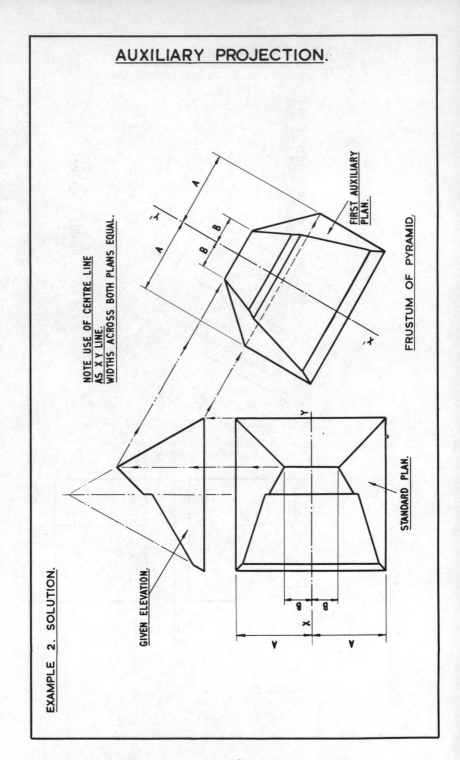

EXAMPLE 2. SOLUTION.

NOTE USE OF CENTRE LINE AS X Y LINE.
WIDTHS ACROSS BOTH PLANS EQUAL.

FIRST AUXILIARY PLAN.

FRUSTUM OF PYRAMID.

GIVEN ELEVATION.

STANDARD PLAN.

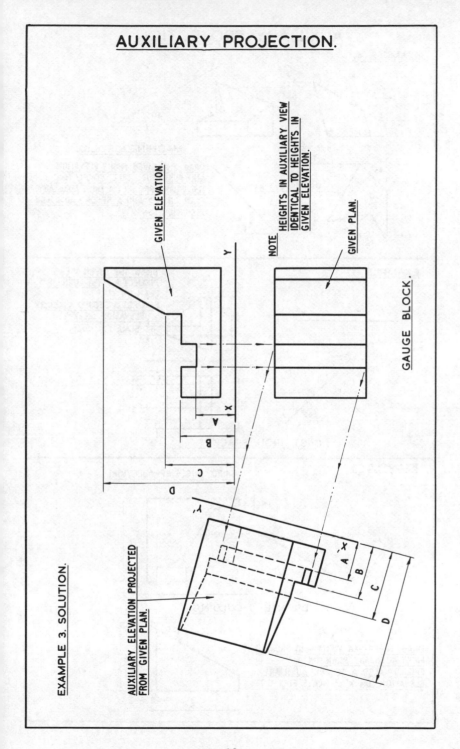

AUXILIARY PROJECTION.

EXAMPLE 3. SOLUTION.

GIVEN ELEVATION.

NOTE. HEIGHTS IN AUXILIARY VIEW IDENTICAL TO HEIGHTS IN GIVEN ELEVATION.

GIVEN PLAN.

GAUGE BLOCK.

AUXILIARY ELEVATION PROJECTED FROM GIVEN PLAN.

13

AUXILIARY PROJECTION

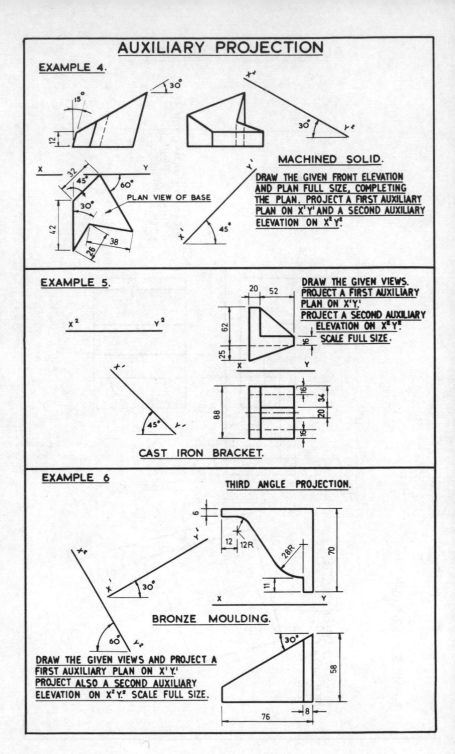

EXAMPLE 4.

15°
30°
12

x²
30°
y²

MACHINED SOLID.

DRAW THE GIVEN FRONT ELEVATION
AND PLAN FULL SIZE, COMPLETING
THE PLAN. PROJECT A FIRST AUXILIARY
PLAN ON X'Y' AND A SECOND AUXILIARY
ELEVATION ON X²Y².

X
Y
32
45°
60°
30°
PLAN VIEW OF BASE
42
26
38

Y'
X'
45°

EXAMPLE 5.

X²
Y²

X'
45°
Y'

DRAW THE GIVEN VIEWS.
PROJECT A FIRST AUXILIARY
PLAN ON X'Y.'
PROJECT A SECOND AUXILIARY
ELEVATION ON X²Y².
SCALE FULL SIZE.

20   52
62
25
16
X
Y

88
16
34
20
16

CAST IRON BRACKET.

EXAMPLE 6

THIRD ANGLE PROJECTION.

Y'
X'
30°

6
12   12R
28R
70
11
X
Y

BRONZE MOULDING.

X²
60°
Y²

DRAW THE GIVEN VIEWS AND PROJECT A
FIRST AUXILIARY PLAN ON X'Y.'
PROJECT ALSO A SECOND AUXILIARY
ELEVATION ON X²Y². SCALE FULL SIZE.

30°
58
76   8

14

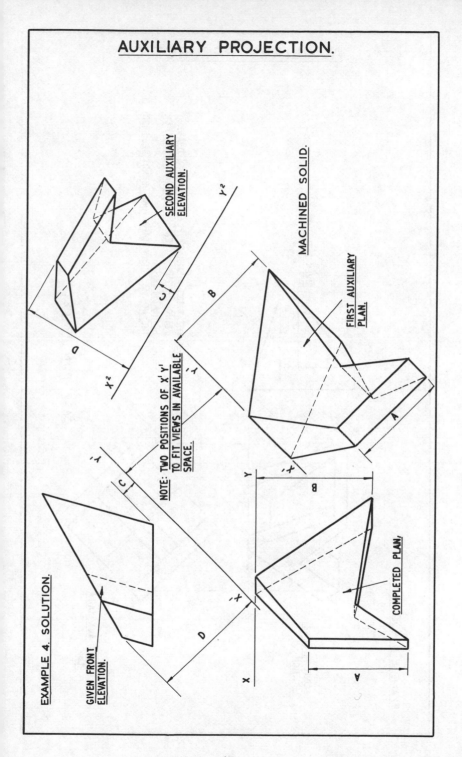

AUXILIARY PROJECTION.

SECOND AUXILIARY ELEVATION.

MACHINED SOLID.

FIRST AUXILIARY PLAN.

NOTE: TWO POSITIONS OF X' Y' TO FIT VIEWS IN AVAILABLE SPACE.

EXAMPLE 4. SOLUTION.

GIVEN FRONT ELEVATION.

COMPLETED PLAN.

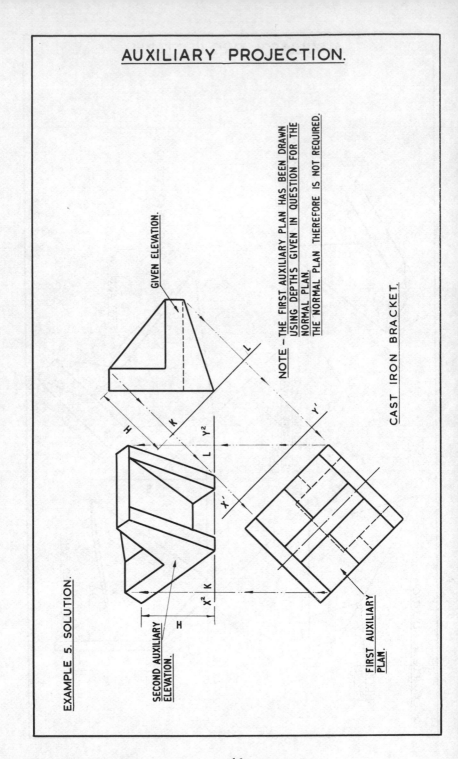

AUXILIARY PROJECTION.

EXAMPLE 5. SOLUTION.

GIVEN ELEVATION.

SECOND AUXILIARY ELEVATION.

FIRST AUXILIARY PLAN.

NOTE — THE FIRST AUXILIARY PLAN HAS BEEN DRAWN USING DEPTHS GIVEN IN QUESTION FOR THE NORMAL PLAN.
THE NORMAL PLAN THEREFORE IS NOT REQUIRED.

CAST IRON BRACKET.

AUXILIARY PROJECTION.

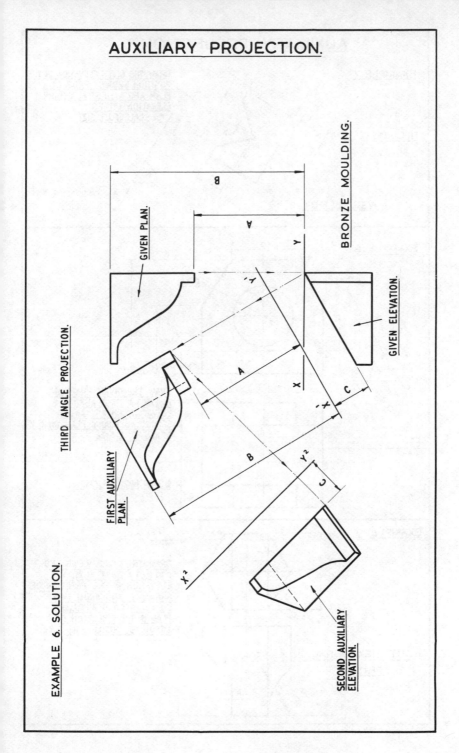

EXAMPLE 6. SOLUTION.

THIRD ANGLE PROJECTION.

GIVEN PLAN.

BRONZE MOULDING.

GIVEN ELEVATION.

FIRST AUXILIARY PLAN.

SECOND AUXILIARY ELEVATION.

17

AUXILIARY PROJECTION.

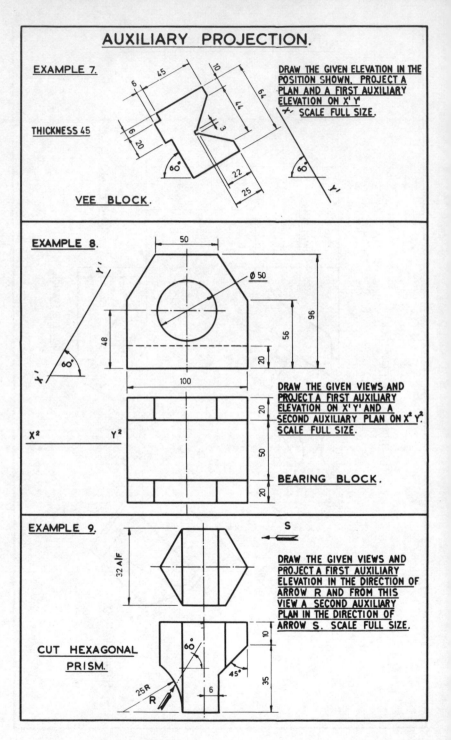

EXAMPLE 7.

THICKNESS 45

45

6

10

64

44

3

6

20

60°

22

25

VEE BLOCK.

DRAW THE GIVEN ELEVATION IN THE POSITION SHOWN. PROJECT A PLAN AND A FIRST AUXILIARY ELEVATION ON X' Y'. SCALE FULL SIZE.

60°

Y'

EXAMPLE 8.

50

Ø 50

96

56

48

20

60°

100

20

50

20

X²   Y²

DRAW THE GIVEN VIEWS AND PROJECT A FIRST AUXILIARY ELEVATION ON X' Y' AND A SECOND AUXILIARY PLAN ON X² Y². SCALE FULL SIZE.

BEARING BLOCK.

EXAMPLE 9.

S

32 A/F

CUT HEXAGONAL PRISM.

60°

45°

10

35

25R

R

6

DRAW THE GIVEN VIEWS AND PROJECT A FIRST AUXILIARY ELEVATION IN THE DIRECTION OF ARROW R AND FROM THIS VIEW A SECOND AUXILIARY PLAN IN THE DIRECTION OF ARROW S. SCALE FULL SIZE.

18

AUXILIARY PROJECTION.

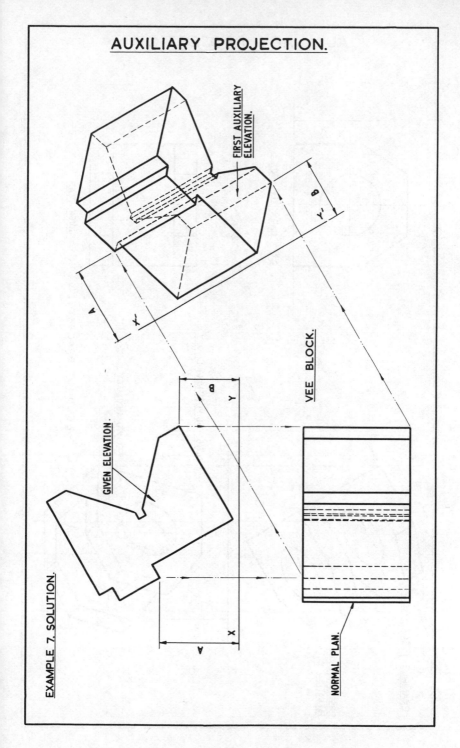

FIRST AUXILIARY ELEVATION.

VEE BLOCK.

GIVEN ELEVATION.

NORMAL PLAN.

EXAMPLE 7. SOLUTION.

19

AUXILIARY PROJECTION.

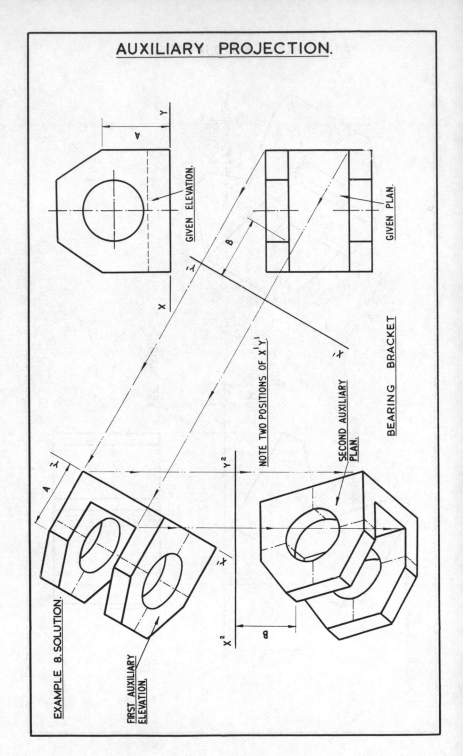

GIVEN ELEVATION.

GIVEN PLAN.

BEARING BRACKET

NOTE TWO POSITIONS OF X¹Y¹.

SECOND AUXILIARY PLAN.

FIRST AUXILIARY ELEVATION.

EXAMPLE 8. SOLUTION.

20

AUXILIARY PROJECTION.

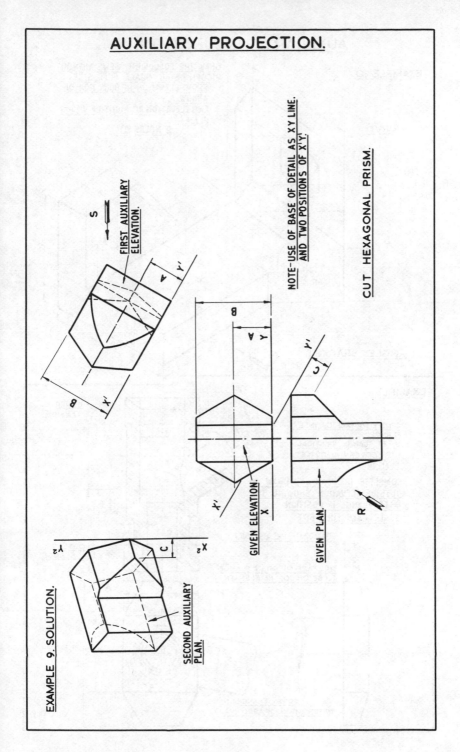

FIRST AUXILIARY ELEVATION.

S

NOTE – USE OF BASE OF DETAIL AS XY LINE. AND TWO POSITIONS OF X'Y'.

CUT HEXAGONAL PRISM.

GIVEN ELEVATION.

GIVEN PLAN.

R

EXAMPLE 9. SOLUTION.

SECOND AUXILIARY PLAN.

AUXILIARY PROJECTION.

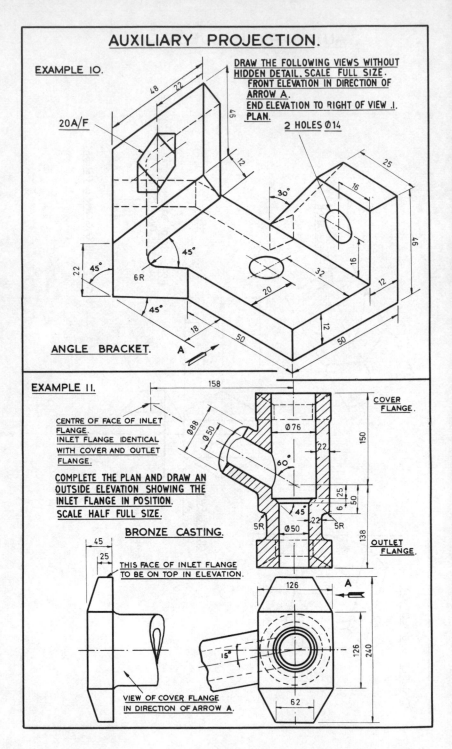

EXAMPLE 10.

DRAW THE FOLLOWING VIEWS WITHOUT HIDDEN DETAIL. SCALE FULL SIZE.
FRONT ELEVATION IN DIRECTION OF ARROW A.
END ELEVATION TO RIGHT OF VIEW .1.
PLAN.

2 HOLES Ø14

20A/F

48   22

45

12

30°

25

16

97

45°   22   45°

6R

45°

18   50

16

32

20

12

50

12

ANGLE BRACKET.   A

EXAMPLE 11.

158

CENTRE OF FACE OF INLET FLANGE.
INLET FLANGE IDENTICAL WITH COVER AND OUTLET FLANGE.

COMPLETE THE PLAN AND DRAW AN OUTSIDE ELEVATION SHOWING THE INLET FLANGE IN POSITION.
SCALE HALF FULL SIZE.

BRONZE CASTING.

Ø88   Ø50

Ø76

22

60°

45

5R   Ø50   22   5R

COVER FLANGE.

150

25
50
6

138

OUTLET FLANGE.

45
25

THIS FACE OF INLET FLANGE TO BE ON TOP IN ELEVATION.

VIEW OF COVER FLANGE IN DIRECTION OF ARROW A.

126

A

126   240

15°

62

22

AUXILIARY PROJECTION.

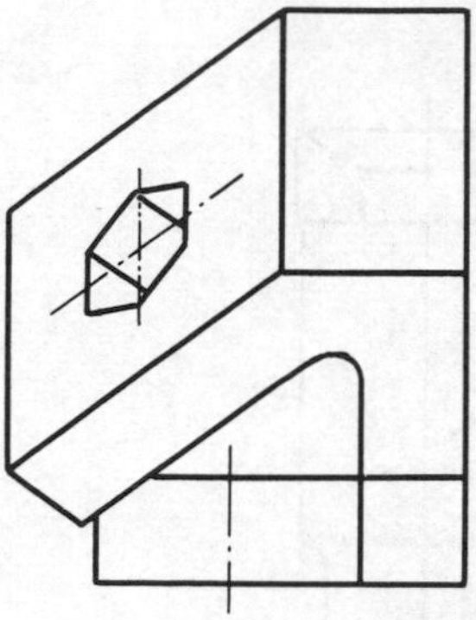

END ELEVATION.

PROJECT AN AUXILIARY ELEVATION IN DIRECTION OF ARROW Q IN ORDER TO OBTAIN HEIGHTS IN ELEVATION A.

ANGLE BRACKET

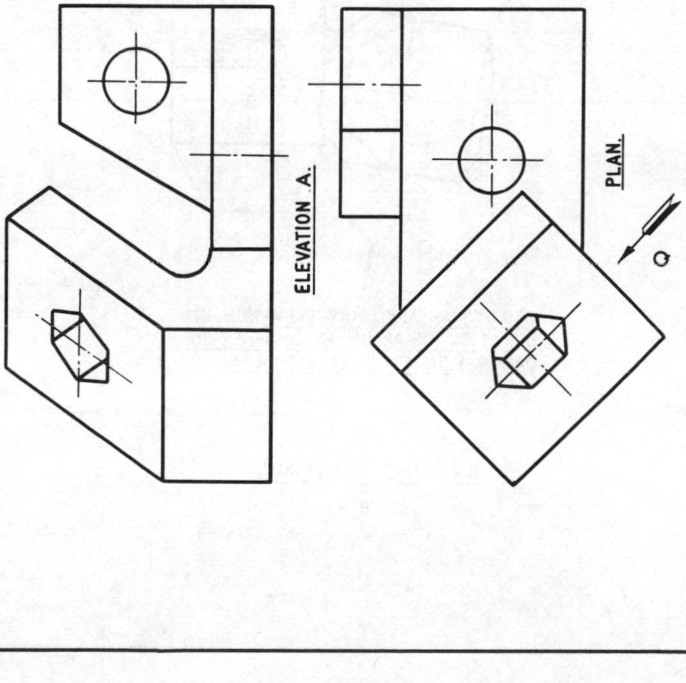

ELEVATION A.

PLAN.

EXAMPLE IO. SOLUTION.

23

AUXILIARY PROJECTION.

EXAMPLE II. SOLUTION.

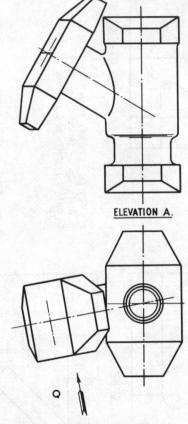

ELEVATION A.

Q

PROJECT AN AUXILIARY ELEVATION IN
DIRECTION OF ARROW Q IN ORDER TO
OBTAIN HEIGHTS IN ELEVATION A.

BRONZE CASTING.

AUXILIARY PROJECTION.

EXAMPLE 12.

THIRD ANGLE PROJECTION.

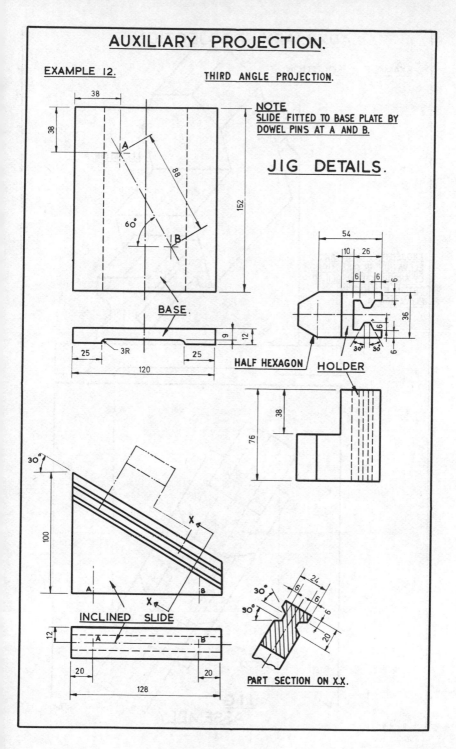

NOTE
SLIDE FITTED TO BASE PLATE BY
DOWEL PINS AT A AND B.

JIG DETAILS.

BASE.

HALF HEXAGON   HOLDER

INCLINED SLIDE

PART SECTION ON X.X.

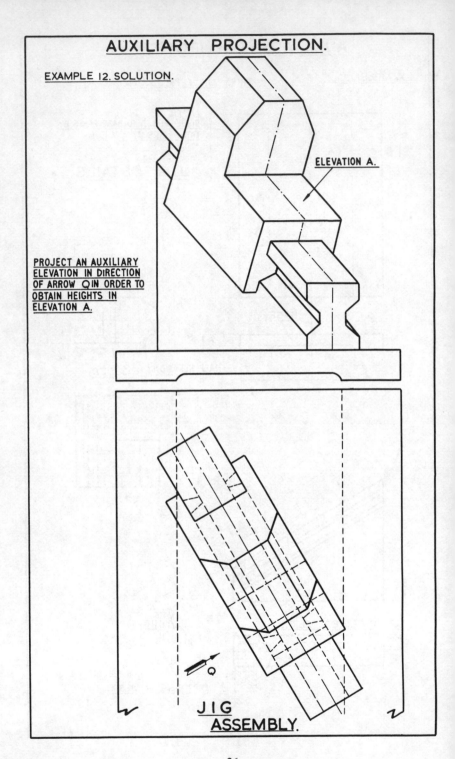

AUXILIARY PROJECTION.

EXAMPLE 12. SOLUTION.

ELEVATION A.

PROJECT AN AUXILIARY
ELEVATION IN DIRECTION
OF ARROW Q IN ORDER TO
OBTAIN HEIGHTS IN
ELEVATION A.

Q

JIG
ASSEMBLY.

26

AUXILIARY PROJECTION.

EXAMPLE 13.

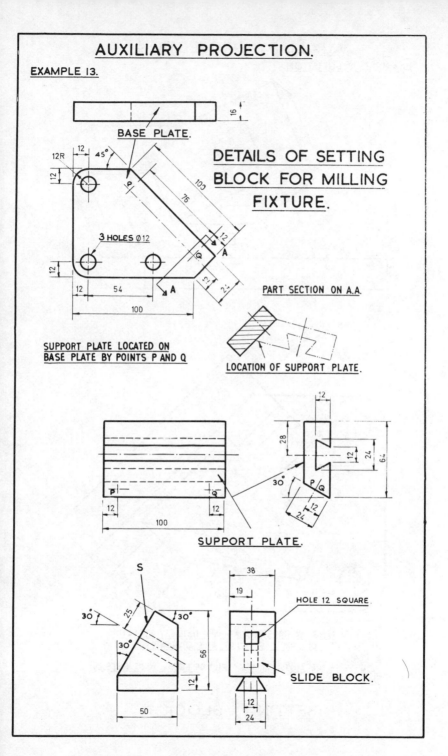

BASE PLATE.

16

12R · 12 · 45°

12

P

3 HOLES Ø12

12

12 · 54

100

DETAILS OF SETTING BLOCK FOR MILLING FIXTURE.

100 · 76 · 12

A

Q

A

PART SECTION ON A.A.

SUPPORT PLATE LOCATED ON
BASE PLATE BY POINTS P AND Q

LOCATION OF SUPPORT PLATE.

28 · 12 · 24 · 64

12

P · Q

12 · 100 · 12

P · Q

30°

12 · 24

SUPPORT PLATE.

S

30° · 25 · 30°

30°

56

12

50

38

19

HOLE 12 SQUARE.

SLIDE BLOCK.

12 · 24

27

AUXILIARY PROJECTION.

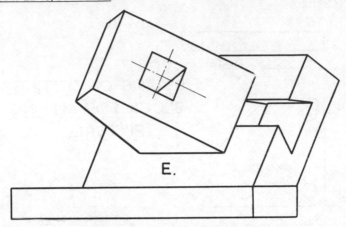

E.

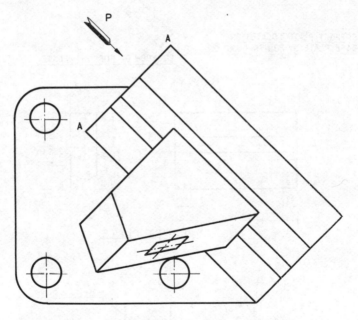

P

A

A

START DRAWING BY CONSTRUCTING AN AUXILIARY ELEVATION
IN DIRECTION OF ARROW P. THIS WILL GIVE WIDTHS A.A.
IN PLAN.
HEIGHTS IN THE AUXILIARY VIEW WILL BE EQUAL TO HEIGHTS IN
ELEVATION E.

SETTING BLOCK.

is to be positioned in the centre of the Support Plate with the face S visible in the elevation.

AUXILIARY PROJECTION PROBLEMS

Scale full size and First Angle Projection to be used unless otherwise stated. Hidden details to be shown in first auxiliary views only.

1. Draw the given views of the hexagonal prism shown in Figure 1 and project a first auxiliary plan on X^1Y^1 and a first auxiliary elevation on X^2Y^2.

2. Views are given in Figure 2 of a small cast iron bracket. Draw the given elevation and plan and project a first auxiliary plan on X^1Y^1 and a first auxiliary elevation on X^2Y^2.

3. Figure 3 shows a right hexagonal pyramid which is cut by the plane SS. Draw the lower portion of the elevation below the plane and project from it a plan. From these views project a first auxiliary plan to show the true shape of the cut face and a first auxiliary elevation on X^1Y^1.

4. A length of $\mathbf{I}$ section bar is shown in Figure 4. It is inclined at 45° to the horizontal plane with the face F parallel to the vertical plane. Draw in Third Angle projection the given elevation, a plan projected from it and a first auxiliary elevation on X^1Y^1.

5. The elevation and plan of a machined block are given in Figure 5. Draw these views and project from them a first auxiliary plan on X^1Y^1 and a first auxiliary elevation on X^2Y^2.

6. Draw in Third Angle projection the given views of the slide illustrated in Figure 6. Use these views to project a first auxiliary elevation on X^1Y^1, viewing the plan in the direction of the arrow.

7. Figure 7 shows the elevation and plan of a machined detail. Draw these views and project a first auxiliary plan on X^1Y^1 and a first auxiliary elevation on X^2Y^2.

8. A length of extruded bar is shown in plan and elevation in Figure 8. Draw the given views and project from them a first auxiliary sectional elevation on the plane SS using the new ground line X^1Y^1.

9. Figure 9 gives the elevation and plan of a slide block in Third Angle projection. Copy these views in Third Angle projection and project a first

AUXILIARY PROJECTION PROBLEMS.

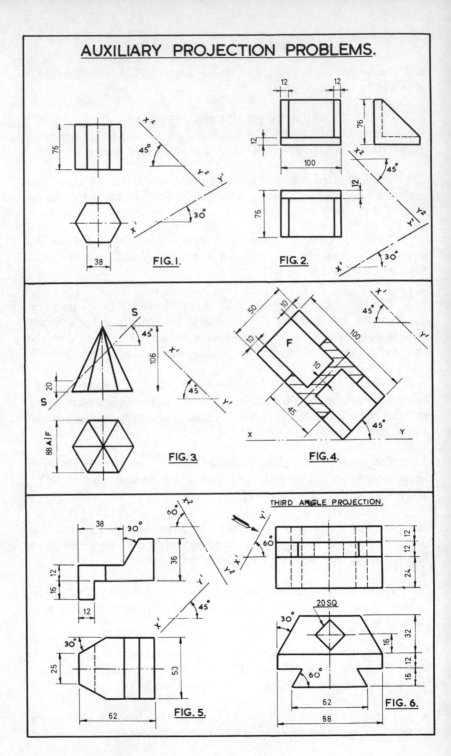

FIG. 1.

FIG. 2.

FIG. 3.

FIG. 4.

THIRD ANGLE PROJECTION.

FIG. 5.

FIG. 6.

AUXILIARY PROJECTION PROBLEMS.

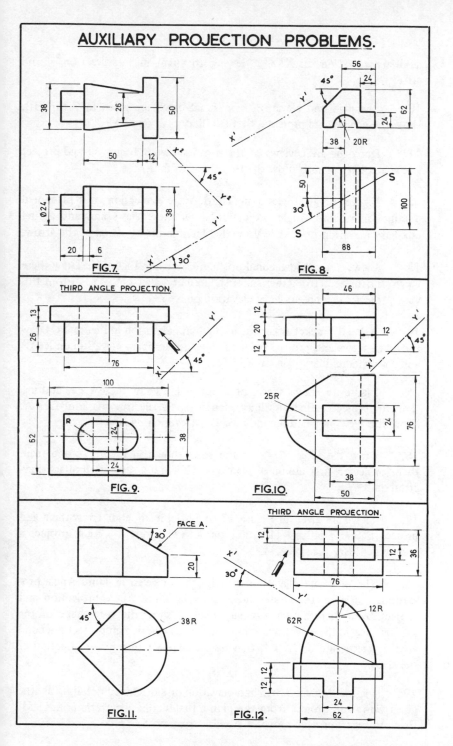

FIG.7.

FIG.8.

THIRD ANGLE PROJECTION.

FIG.9.

FIG.10.

FACE A.

THIRD ANGLE PROJECTION.

FIG.II.

FIG.12.

auxiliary elevation on X^1Y^1, viewing the plan in the direction of the arrow.

10. The plan and elevation of a small block are given in Figure 10. Draw these views and project a first auxiliary plan on X^1Y^1.

11. Draw the given views of the prism shown in Figure 11 and project a first auxiliary plan to show the true shape of face A.

12. Figure 12 gives views in Third Angle projection of a machined detail. Using Third Angle projection draw these views and add a first auxiliary elevation on X^1Y^1. View the detail in the direction of the arrow.

13. Views of a cut hexagonal prism are shown in Figure 13. Draw these views and project from them a first auxiliary plan on X^1Y^1. From this view project a second auxiliary elevation on X^2Y^2.

14. A small bracket is shown in plan and elevation in Figure 14. Draw the given views and project from them a first auxiliary elevation on X^1Y^1 and a second auxiliary plan on X^2Y^2.

15. Figure 15 shows views of a cut prism. Draw these views and use them to project a first auxiliary plan to show the true shape of face A. From this view project a second auxiliary elevation on X^2Y^2.

16. Draw the given views of the solid shown in Figure 16 and from them project a first auxiliary plan on X^1Y^1 and a second auxiliary elevation on X^2Y^2.

17. Views are given in Figure 17 of a machined detail. Draw them and project a first auxiliary elevation on X^1Y^1. From this view project a second auxiliary plan on X^2Y^2.

18. The plan and elevation of a block are given in Third Angle projection in Figure 18. Draw these views in Third Angle projection and project from them a first auxiliary plan to show the true shape of the sloping face in the elevation. From the first auxiliary plan project a second auxiliary elevation on X^2Y^2, viewing the auxiliary plan in the direction of the arrow.

19. Figure 19 gives a plan and elevation of a machined detail. Draw the given views and project from the plan a first auxiliary elevation on X^1Y^1. From this view project a second auxiliary plan on X^2Y^2.

AUXILIARY PROJECTION PROBLEMS.

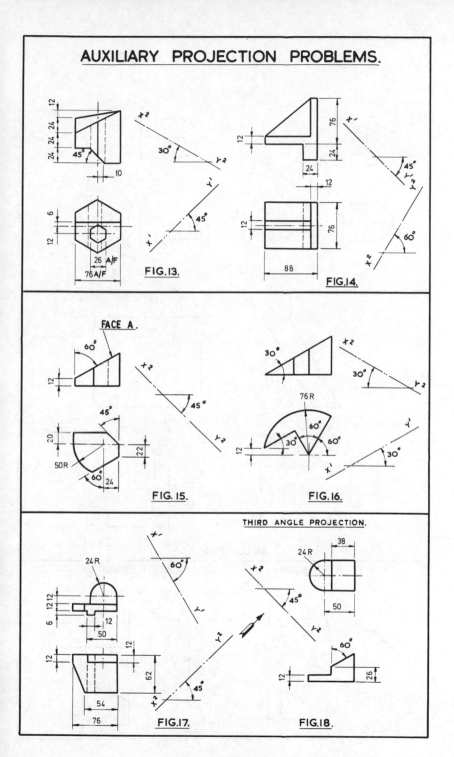

FIG.13.

FIG.14.

FACE A.

FIG.15.

FIG.16.

THIRD ANGLE PROJECTION.

FIG.17.

FIG.18.

AUXILIARY PROJECTION PROBLEMS.

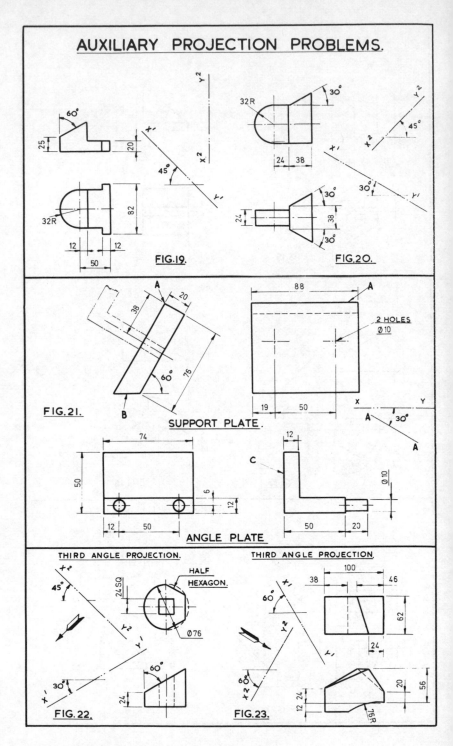

FIG.19.

FIG.20.

FIG.21.

SUPPORT PLATE.

2 HOLES Ø 10

ANGLE PLATE

THIRD ANGLE PROJECTION.

HALF HEXAGON.

Ø76

24 SQ

FIG. 22.

THIRD ANGLE PROJECTION.

FIG.23.

34

20.   A milled block is illustrated in Figure 20. Draw the given views and project a first auxiliary elevation on X^1Y^1, and a second auxiliary plan on X^2Y^2.

21.   Details for a small assembly are shown in Figure 21. Assemble the parts as shown in the end view of the Support Plate and draw an elevation and plan of the assembly. The face B of the Support Plate is to be parallel to the horizontal plane with the edge A positioned relative to the XY line as shown in the Figure. Face C of the Angle Plate is to be visible in the elevation. Hidden detail is not required.

22.   Figure 22 shows the elevation and plan of a cut prism in Third Angle projection. Draw these views in Third Angle projection and project from them a first auxiliary plan on X^1Y^1 and a second auxiliary elevation on X^2Y^2. The arrow shows the direction in which the auxiliary plan is to be viewed to obtain the second auxiliary elevation.

23.   The plan and elevation of a machined block are given in Figure 23 in Third Angle projection. Using Third Angle projection, draw these views and project from them a first auxiliary elevation on X^1Y^1. Viewing this elevation in the direction of the arrow project a second auxiliary plan on X^2Y^2.

INTERPENETRATION OF SURFACES

SURFACE intersections are involved in many orthographic drawings and, in general, the drawing office practice is to approximate curves resulting from them. A simple example of this practice is the chamfer curves of standard hexagonal nuts, such curves in orthographic views being represented by arcs of circles.

Approximation is satisfactory for orthographic drawings provided the approximate curves follow the true curves closely. To avoid inaccurate approximations the draughtsman should understand the principle of simple sections which is used in the geometrical construction of these curves, so that he can plot a few points to determine the general shape of the curve.

In development work any intersection curves must be plotted accurately to obtain accurate patterns.

The plotting of curves of interpenetration appears complex on many drawings, but in fact the constructions are confined to taking simple sections. The choice of section is of vital importance, since as a general rule the simpler the section, the easier the construction becomes.

Simple Sections of Geometrical Solids

RIGHT CYLINDER. Various sections may be taken through the right cylinder as illustrated in Figures 1 to 4, but the problem is to find the section involving the minimum amount of drawing.

Section aa. Any number of sections taken at right angles to the axis of the cylinder would produce one circular section only in the plan view.

Section bb. These are similar to section aa provided the section is viewed along the axis of the cylinder.

Section cc. Sections taken parallel to the axis of the cylinder would require a plan view construction as shown. The resulting sections would be rectangular, the rectangles differing in width as the position of the cutting plane is altered relative to the axis of the cylinder.

INTERPENETRATION.

SIMPLE SECTIONS.

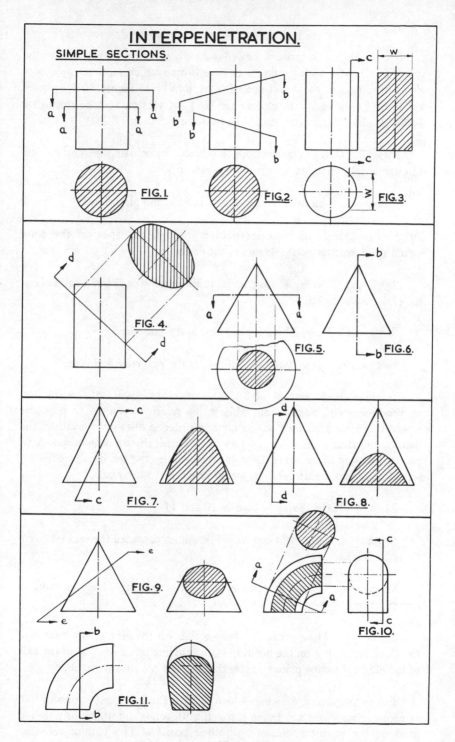

FIG.1.

FIG.2.

FIG.3.

FIG.4.

FIG.5.

FIG.6.

FIG.7.

FIG.8.

FIG.9.

FIG.10.

FIG.11.

Section dd. Such sections viewed normally would produce ellipses, the construction of which would be tedious if many such sections were considered. (Compare these sections with Sections bb in Figure 2.) Therefore, should it be necessary to choose the simplest section to take through a right cylinder, that section should be aa or bb.

RIGHT CONE. The sections produced by cutting planes passing through a right cone are shown in Figures 5 to 9.

Section aa. A circular section is produced in the plan view.

Section bb. Section planes passing through the apex of the cone would produce triangular sections in the end view.

Section cc. The section is parallel to the generator giving a parabola in the end view and plan.

Section dd. A hyperbola is produced in the end view.

Section ee. This section gives ellipses in the end view and plan.

Sections cc, dd and ee require a considerable amount of construction to produce them. Section bb, while being relatively simple to produce, would require a plan view of the cone in order to obtain the width of the base of the triangle for the end view. Therefore, should it be necessary to take a number of sections through a right cone, the sections to consider would be aa, since such sections would be circles in the plan.

ELBOW PIECE. Refer to Figures 10 and 11.

Section aa. Radial sections would be circles provided the sections were viewed normally.

Section bb. These are complex sections requiring a large amount of construction.

Section cc. These sections produce flats on the elbow, the widths of the flats depending on the position of the cutting plane relative to the axis of the elbow. Cutting planes cc give the simplest sections in practice.

For orthographic drawings which involve the interpenetration of two or more solids, a section taken through both solids simultaneously should produce the simplest section on both if possible. This cannot often be arranged, and generally the section taken gives the simplest section on one solid and another not so simple section on the second. The points of intersection of the two simple sections are points on the curve of interpenetration. These points may be projected to complete the interpenetration curves in other views on the drawing. The following worked examples on pages 40-60 illustrate these points.

It is unnecessary to space the simple sections closely except where the interpenetration curve changes direction abruptly.

Before starting to plot an interpenetration curve the views should be examined to determine the limits of the curve. In some cases the limits can be found by direct projection from view to view, as in Examples 1 to 5. In other cases the limits can be positioned by taking appropriate sections. When the limits of the curve have been fixed the curve can be completed by taking additional sections between them. This is illustrated in the solution to Example 7 on page 50.

In this example the lower limits of the curves are reached when the corners of the prism meet the surface of the cone. To find these points in the elevation, draw circles in the plan about the centre of the cone to pass through each corner of the prism. Corner Q has been taken as an example. The circle through Q represents the section produced by a horizontal cutting plane through the elevation. This cutting plane can be positioned in the elevation by projection from the circle in the plan. The limit, Q, of the curve is then the intersection of the plane and the appropriate corner of the prism. The upper limits of the curves, such as P, can be fixed in the elevation from circles in the plan drawn tangential to the sides of the prism.

Finding the limits of an interpenetration curve first, before plotting the curve, gives more accurate results than are obtained by taking random sections.

INTERPENETRATION.

EXAMPLE 1.

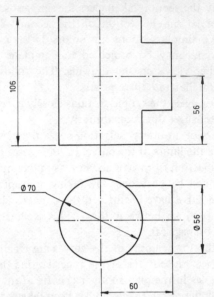

106

56

Ø 70

Ø 56

60

DRAW THE GIVEN VIEWS FULL SIZE AND COMPLETE THE ELEVATION WITH THE CURVE OF INTERPENETRATION.

EXAMPLE 2.

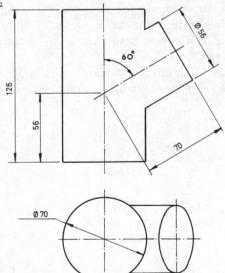

126

56

60°

Ø 56

70

Ø 70

DRAW THE GIVEN VIEWS FULL SIZE AND COMPLETE THE ELEVATION WITH THE CURVE OF INTERPENETRATION.

INTERPENETRATION.

EXAMPLE I. SOLUTION.

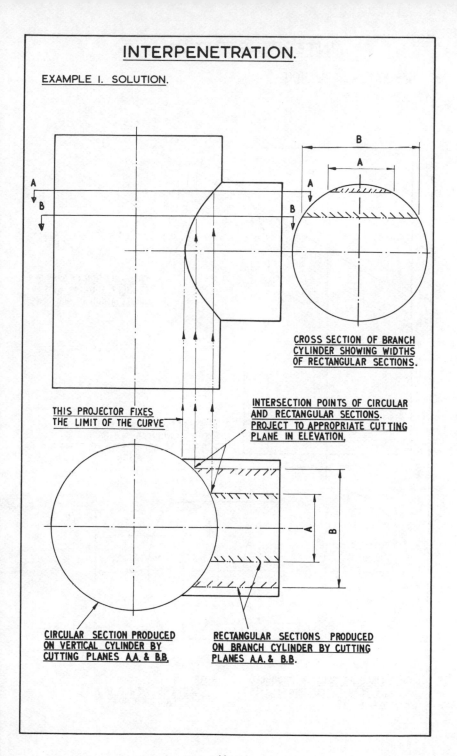

CROSS SECTION OF BRANCH
CYLINDER SHOWING WIDTHS
OF RECTANGULAR SECTIONS.

THIS PROJECTOR FIXES
THE LIMIT OF THE CURVE

INTERSECTION POINTS OF CIRCULAR
AND RECTANGULAR SECTIONS.
PROJECT TO APPROPRIATE CUTTING
PLANE IN ELEVATION,

CIRCULAR SECTION PRODUCED
ON VERTICAL CYLINDER BY
CUTTING PLANES A.A. & B.B.

RECTANGULAR SECTIONS PRODUCED
ON BRANCH CYLINDER BY CUTTING
PLANES A.A. & B.B.

41

INTERPENETRATION.

EXAMPLE 2. SOLUTION.

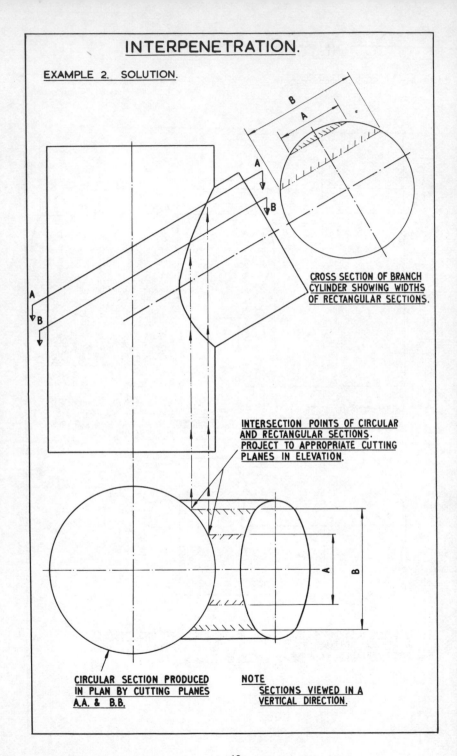

CROSS SECTION OF BRANCH
CYLINDER SHOWING WIDTHS
OF RECTANGULAR SECTIONS.

INTERSECTION POINTS OF CIRCULAR
AND RECTANGULAR SECTIONS.
PROJECT TO APPROPRIATE CUTTING
PLANES IN ELEVATION.

CIRCULAR SECTION PRODUCED
IN PLAN BY CUTTING PLANES
A.A. & B.B.

NOTE
SECTIONS VIEWED IN A
VERTICAL DIRECTION.

INTERPENETRATION.

EXAMPLE 3.

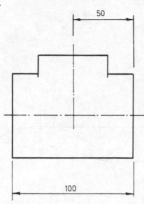
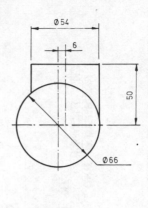

DRAW THE GIVEN VIEWS FULL SIZE AND COMPLETE THE FRONT
ELEVATION WITH THE CURVE OF INTERPENETRATION.

EXAMPLE 4.

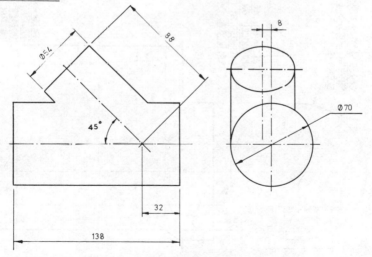

DRAW THE GIVEN VIEWS FULL SIZE AND COMPLETE THE FRONT
ELEVATION WITH THE CURVE OF INTERPENETRATION.

43

INTERPENETRATION.

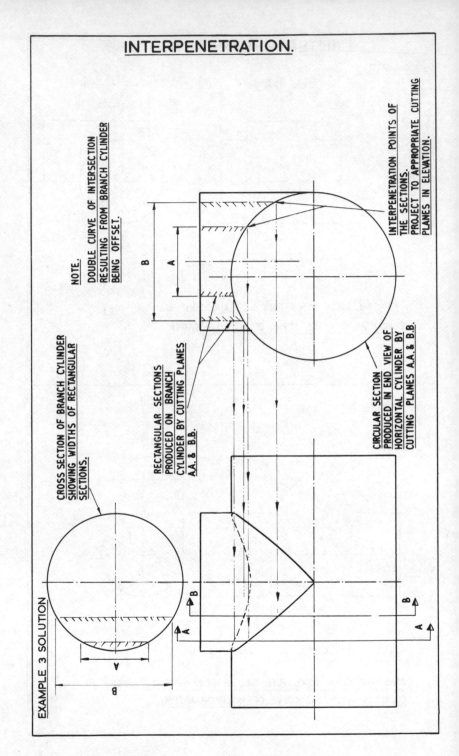

EXAMPLE 3 SOLUTION

CROSS SECTION OF BRANCH CYLINDER
SHOWING WIDTHS OF RECTANGULAR
SECTIONS.

RECTANGULAR SECTIONS
PRODUCED ON BRANCH
CYLINDER BY CUTTING PLANES
A.A. & B.B.

CIRCULAR SECTION
PRODUCED IN END VIEW OF
HORIZONTAL CYLINDER BY
CUTTING PLANES A.A. & B.B.

NOTE.
DOUBLE CURVE OF INTERSECTION
RESULTING FROM BRANCH CYLINDER
BEING OFFSET.

INTERPENETRATION POINTS OF
THE SECTIONS.
PROJECT TO APPROPRIATE CUTTING
PLANES IN ELEVATION.

44

INTERPENETRATION

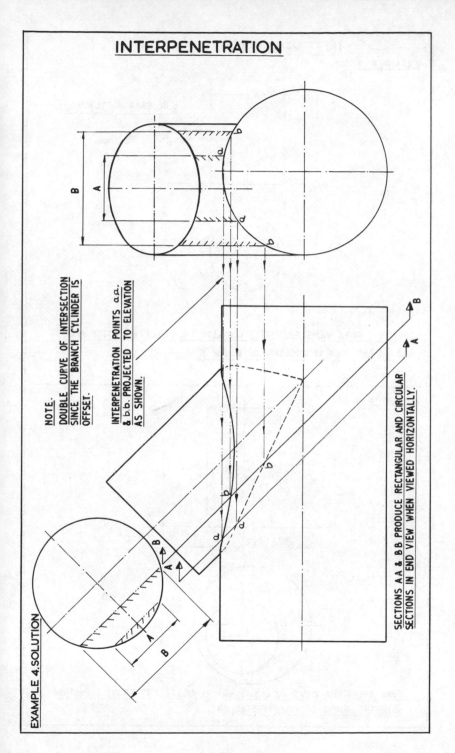

EXAMPLE 4. SOLUTION

NOTE.
DOUBLE CURVE OF INTERSECTION
SINCE THE BRANCH CYLINDER IS
OFFSET.

INTERPENETRATION POINTS a.a.
& b.b. PROJECTED TO ELEVATION
AS SHOWN.

SECTIONS A A & B B PRODUCE RECTANGULAR AND CIRCULAR
SECTIONS IN END VIEW WHEN VIEWED HORIZONTALLY.

45

INTERPENETRATION.

EXAMPLE 5.

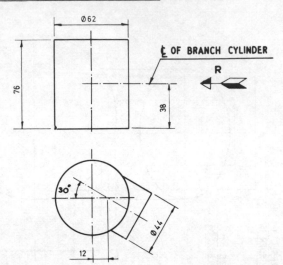

Ø62

76

38

£ OF BRANCH CYLINDER

R

30°

Ø44

12

DRAW THE GIVEN VIEWS FULL SIZE, COMPLETE THE FRONT ELEVATION AND
ADD AN END VIEW IN DIRECTION OF ARROW "R"

EXAMPLE 6.

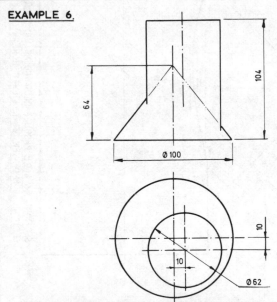

104

64

Ø 100

10

10

Ø62

DRAW THE GIVEN VIEWS FULL SIZE AND COMPLETE THE FRONT ELEVATION
WITH THE CURVE OF INTERPENETRATION.

46

INTERPENETRATION.

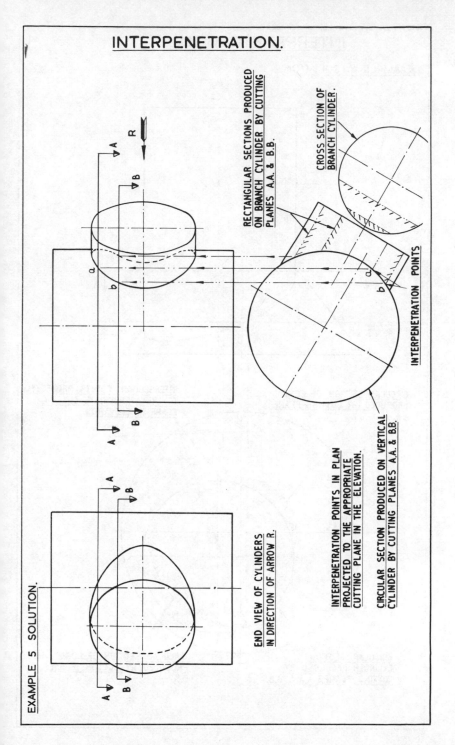

EXAMPLE 5 SOLUTION.

RECTANGULAR SECTIONS PRODUCED
ON BRANCH CYLINDER BY CUTTING
PLANES A.A. & B.B.

CROSS SECTION OF
BRANCH CYLINDER.

INTERPENETRATION POINTS

END VIEW OF CYLINDERS
IN DIRECTION OF ARROW R.

INTERPENETRATION POINTS IN PLAN
PROJECTED TO THE APPROPRIATE
CUTTING PLANE IN THE ELEVATION.

CIRCULAR SECTION PRODUCED ON VERTICAL
CYLINDER BY CUTTING PLANES A.A. & B.B.

47

INTERPENETRATION.

EXAMPLE 6. SOLUTION.

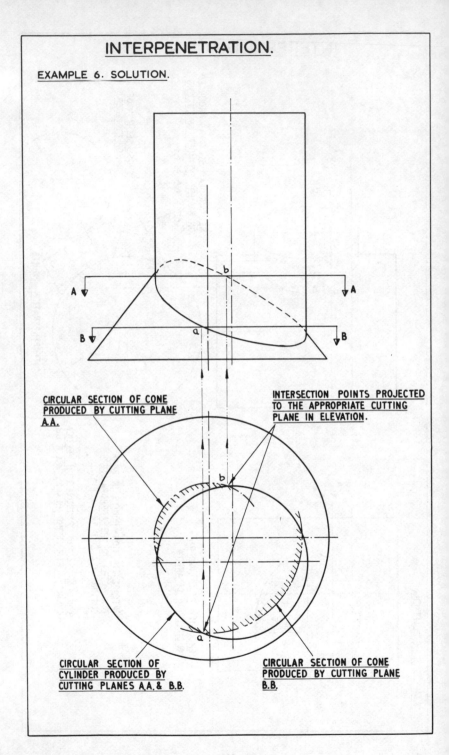

CIRCULAR SECTION OF CONE PRODUCED BY CUTTING PLANE A.A.

INTERSECTION POINTS PROJECTED TO THE APPROPRIATE CUTTING PLANE IN ELEVATION.

CIRCULAR SECTION OF CYLINDER PRODUCED BY CUTTING PLANES A.A. & B.B.

CIRCULAR SECTION OF CONE PRODUCED BY CUTTING PLANE B.B.

INTERPENETRATION.

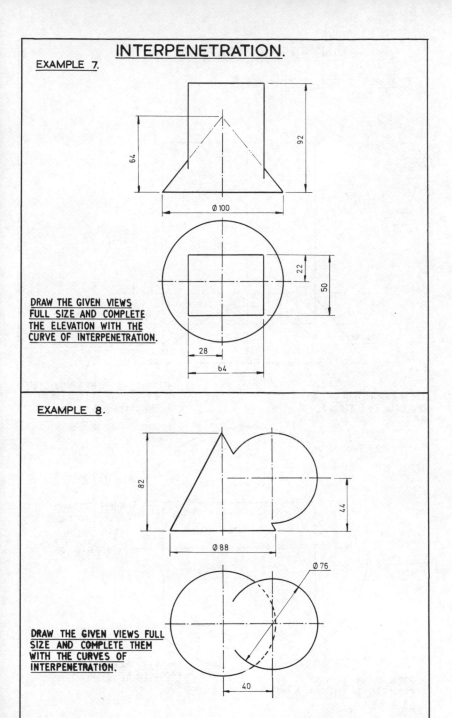

EXAMPLE 7.

92

64

Ø 100

22

50

DRAW THE GIVEN VIEWS
FULL SIZE AND COMPLETE
THE ELEVATION WITH THE
CURVE OF INTERPENETRATION.

28

64

EXAMPLE 8.

82

44

Ø 88

Ø 76

DRAW THE GIVEN VIEWS FULL
SIZE AND COMPLETE THEM
WITH THE CURVES OF
INTERPENETRATION.

40

49

INTERPENETRATION.

EXAMPLE 7. SOLUTION.

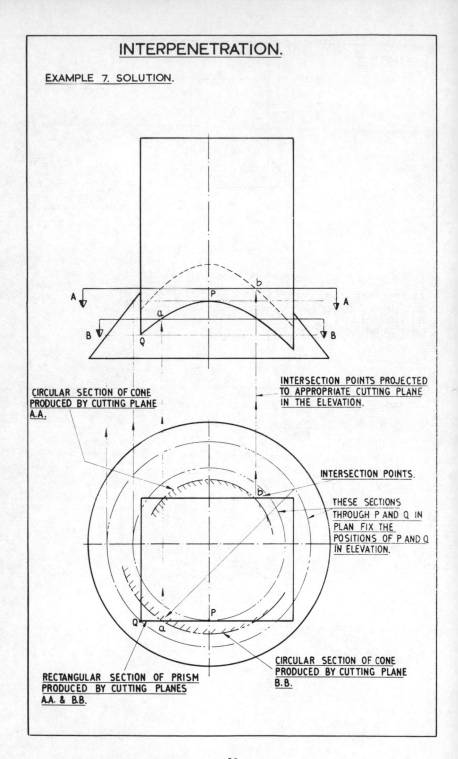

INTERSECTION POINTS PROJECTED TO APPROPRIATE CUTTING PLANE IN THE ELEVATION.

CIRCULAR SECTION OF CONE PRODUCED BY CUTTING PLANE A.A.

INTERSECTION POINTS.

THESE SECTIONS THROUGH P AND Q IN PLAN FIX THE POSITIONS OF P AND Q IN ELEVATION.

CIRCULAR SECTION OF CONE PRODUCED BY CUTTING PLANE B.B.

RECTANGULAR SECTION OF PRISM PRODUCED BY CUTTING PLANES A.A. & B.B.

INTERPENETRATION.

EXAMPLE 8 SOLUTION.

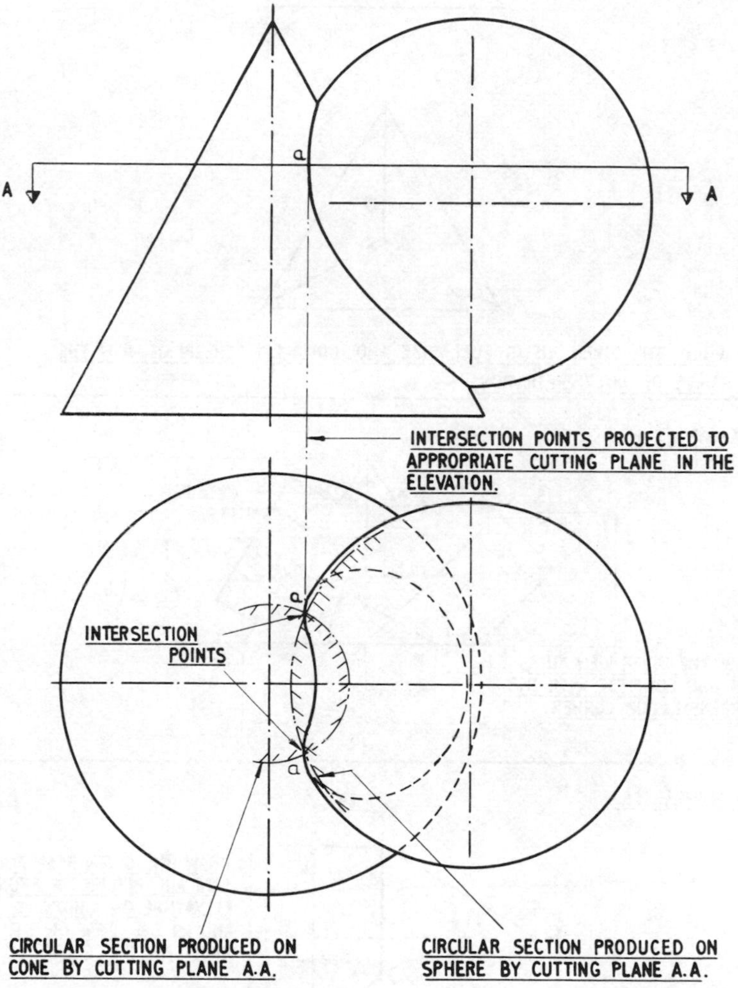

INTERSECTION POINTS PROJECTED TO
APPROPRIATE CUTTING PLANE IN THE
ELEVATION.

INTERSECTION
POINTS

CIRCULAR SECTION PRODUCED ON
CONE BY CUTTING PLANE A.A.

CIRCULAR SECTION PRODUCED ON
SPHERE BY CUTTING PLANE A.A.

51

INTERPENETRATION.

EXAMPLE 9.

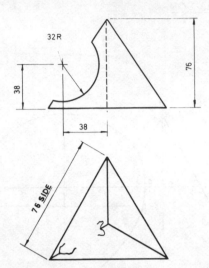

32R

38

76

38

76 SIDE

DRAW THE GIVEN VIEWS FULL SIZE AND COMPLETE THE PLAN WITH THE CURVE OF INTERPENETRATION.

EXAMPLE 10.

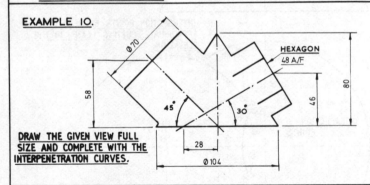

Ø70

58

45°

30°

HEXAGON
48 A/F

46

80

28

Ø104

DRAW THE GIVEN VIEW FULL SIZE AND COMPLETE WITH THE INTERPENETRATION CURVES.

EXAMPLE 11.

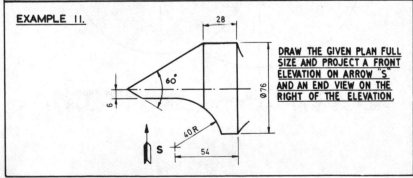

28

60°

6

Ø76

40R

S

54

DRAW THE GIVEN PLAN FULL SIZE AND PROJECT A FRONT ELEVATION ON ARROW "S" AND AN END VIEW ON THE RIGHT OF THE ELEVATION.

INTERPENETRATION.

EXAMPLE 9 SOLUTION.

A ▽   ▽A

PORTION OF RECTANGULAR SECTION
PRODUCED ON CYLINDER BY CUTTING
PLANE A.A.

TRIANGULAR SECTION PRODUCED
ON PYRAMID BY CUTTING PLANE
A.A.

INTERSECTION POINT OF
TRIANGLE & RECTANGLE.

INTERPENETRATION.

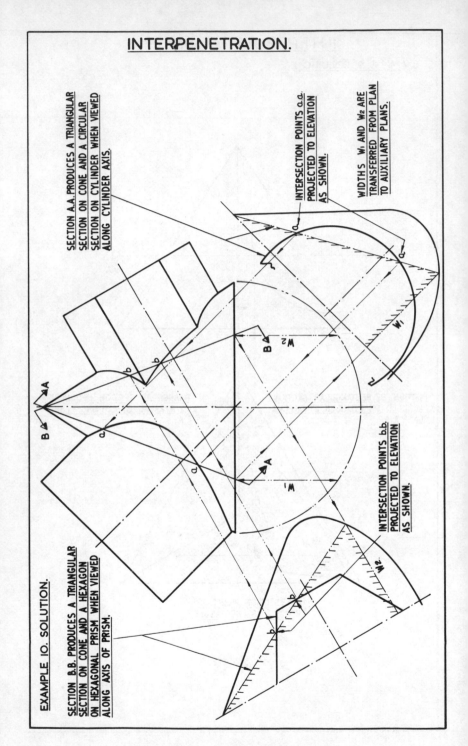

EXAMPLE 10. SOLUTION.

SECTION B.B. PRODUCES A TRIANGULAR SECTION ON CONE AND A HEXAGON ON HEXAGONAL PRISM WHEN VIEWED ALONG AXIS OF PRISM.

SECTION A.A. PRODUCES A TRIANGULAR SECTION ON CONE AND A CIRCULAR SECTION ON CYLINDER WHEN VIEWED ALONG CYLINDER AXIS.

INTERSECTION POINTS a.a. PROJECTED TO ELEVATION AS SHOWN.

WIDTHS W₁ AND W₂ ARE TRANSFERRED FROM PLAN TO AUXILIARY PLANS.

INTERSECTION POINTS b.b. PROJECTED TO ELEVATION AS SHOWN.

INTERPENETRATION.

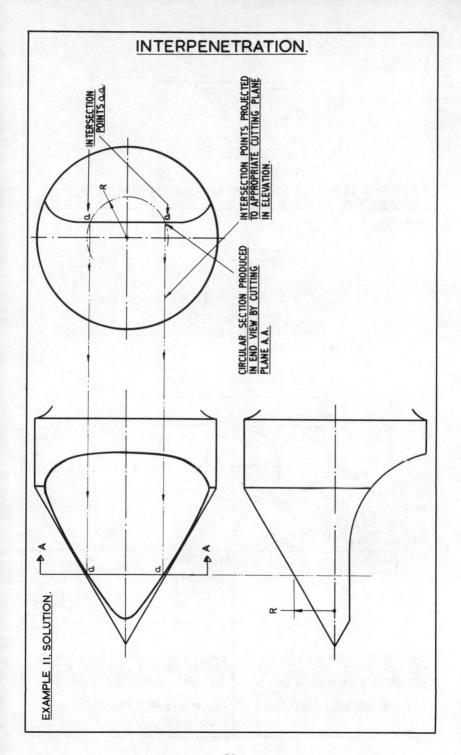

INTERSECTION POINTS a a.

INTERSECTION POINTS PROJECTED TO APPROPRIATE CUTTING PLANE IN ELEVATION.

CIRCULAR SECTION PRODUCED IN END VIEW BY CUTTING PLANE A.A.

R

EXAMPLE II. SOLUTION.

INTERPENETRATION.

EXAMPLE 12.

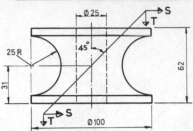

DRAW THE GIVEN VIEW FULL SIZE AND PROJECT A SECTIONAL PLAN ON T.T.
AND A SECTIONAL END VIEW ON S.S.

EXAMPLE 13.

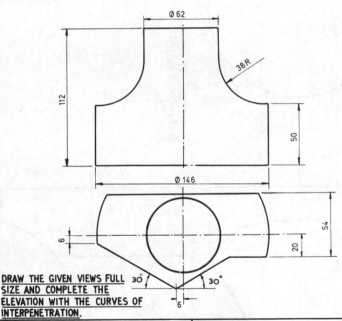

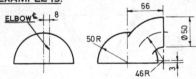

DRAW THE GIVEN VIEWS FULL
SIZE AND COMPLETE THE
ELEVATION WITH THE CURVES OF
INTERPENETRATION.

EXAMPLE 14.	EXAMPLE 15.

EXAMPLE 14.

DRAW THE GIVEN VIEW AND A PLAN FULL
SIZE AND COMPLETE BOTH VIEWS WITH
THE CURVES OF INTERPENETRATION.

DRAW IN THIRD ANGLE PROJECTION.

EXAMPLE 15.

ELBOW

DRAW THE GIVEN ELEVATION AND A PLAN FULL
SIZE AND COMPLETE BOTH VIEWS WITH
THE CURVES OF INTERPENETRATION.

DRAW IN THIRD ANGLE PROJECTION.

INTERPENETRATION.

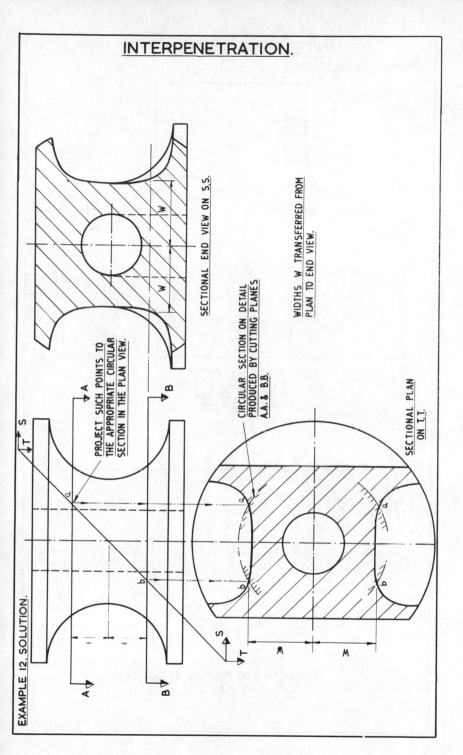

EXAMPLE 12. SOLUTION.

SECTIONAL END VIEW ON S.S.

PROJECT SUCH POINTS TO
THE APPROPRIATE CIRCULAR
SECTION IN THE PLAN VIEW.

CIRCULAR SECTION ON DETAIL
PRODUCED BY CUTTING PLANES
AA. & B.B.

WIDTHS W TRANSFERRED FROM
PLAN TO END VIEW.

SECTIONAL PLAN
ON T.T.

57

INTERPENETRATION.

EXAMPLE 13. SOLUTION.

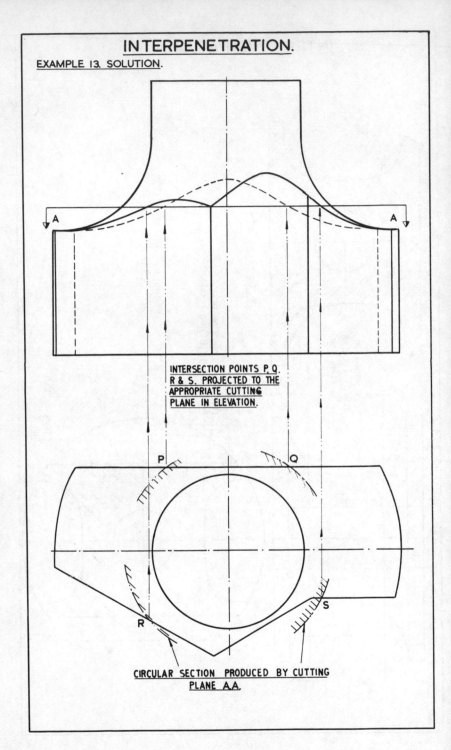

INTERSECTION POINTS P, Q.
R & S. PROJECTED TO THE
APPROPRIATE CUTTING
PLANE IN ELEVATION.

CIRCULAR SECTION PRODUCED BY CUTTING
PLANE A.A.

INTERPENETRATION.

EXAMPLE 14. SOLUTION.

THIRD ANGLE PROJECTION.

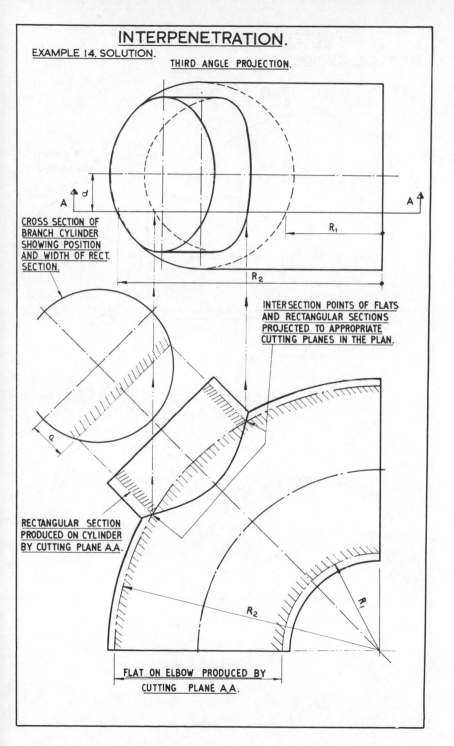

CROSS SECTION OF
BRANCH CYLINDER
SHOWING POSITION
AND WIDTH OF RECT.
SECTION.

R_1

R_2

INTERSECTION POINTS OF FLATS
AND RECTANGULAR SECTIONS
PROJECTED TO APPROPRIATE
CUTTING PLANES IN THE PLAN.

RECTANGULAR SECTION
PRODUCED ON CYLINDER
BY CUTTING PLANE A.A.

R_2

R_1

FLAT ON ELBOW PRODUCED BY
CUTTING PLANE A.A.

INTERPENETRATION.

EXAMPLE 15. SOLUTION.

THIRD ANGLE PROJECTION.

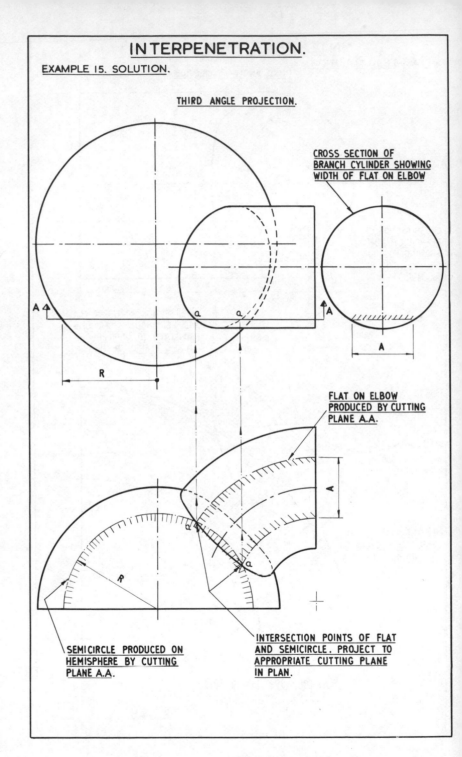

CROSS SECTION OF BRANCH CYLINDER SHOWING WIDTH OF FLAT ON ELBOW

A

FLAT ON ELBOW PRODUCED BY CUTTING PLANE A.A.

SEMICIRCLE PRODUCED ON HEMISPHERE BY CUTTING PLANE A.A.

INTERSECTION POINTS OF FLAT AND SEMICIRCLE. PROJECT TO APPROPRIATE CUTTING PLANE IN PLAN.

INTERPENETRATION PROBLEMS

Scale full size and First Angle projection to be used unless otherwise stated. Hidden detail must be shown.

1. Figure 1 shows a cylinder interpenetrated by a hexagonal prism 60mm across flats. Draw the given views, completing the elevation, and add an end view looking in the direction of arrow R.

2. Figure 2 shows a plan and elevation of a right hexagonal prism penetrated by an oblique cylinder. Draw the given views, constructing the interpenetration curve in the elevation and project an end view in the direction of arrow X.

3. Two interpenetrating oblique cylinders are shown in plan and elevation in Figure 3. Draw these views, and complete them with the interpenetration curves.

4. Complete the elevation given in Figure 4 of the cylinder pierced by a conical hole and project an end view looking in the direction of arrow R. Use Third Angle projection.

5. Figure 5 shows an elevation and plan of the boss for a built-up hand wheel. The boss is to be drilled for four 50mm diameter equally spaced spokes, the centreline of one spoke being given. Complete the given views with the interpenetration curves produced by the hole for this spoke, but do not show the spoke.

6. A front elevation and end view of a barrel-shaped solid of revolution penetrated by a cylinder are given in Figure 6. Construct the curves of interpenetration for both views.

7. Views in Third Angle projection are given in Figure 7 of a hemisphere pierced by a cylinder 38mm diameter. Using Third Angle projection, draw the given views, complete them with the interpenetration curves and add an end view looking in the direction of arrow S.

8. An auxiliary elevation and plan in Third Angle projection of a hemisphere and interpenetrating cylinder are shown in Figure 8. Using Third Angle projection draw these views, completing the plan, and project a front elevation looking in the direction of arrow R and an end view placed on the left of the front elevation.

9. Figure 9 shows in Third Angle projection a plan and elevation of a solid of revolution interpenetrated by a cylinder. Draw these views in

INTERPENETRATION PROBLEMS.

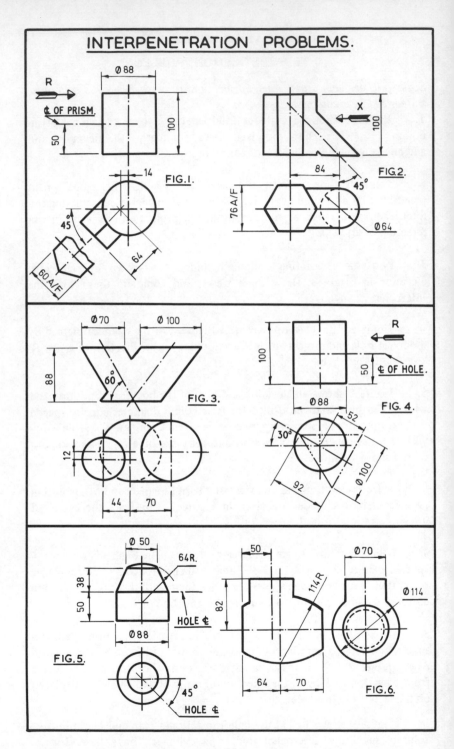

R
¢ OF PRISM.
Ø 88
100
50
14
FIG.1.
45°
64
60 A/F

X
100
84
45°
FIG.2.
76 A/F
Ø 64

Ø 70   Ø 100
88
60°
FIG.3.
12
44   70

R
¢ OF HOLE.
100
50
Ø 88
FIG.4.
30°
52
92
Ø 100

Ø 50
64 R.
38
50
HOLE ¢
Ø 88
FIG.5.
45°
HOLE ¢

50
82
114 R
Ø 70
Ø 114
64   70
FIG.6.

INTERPENETRATION PROBLEMS.

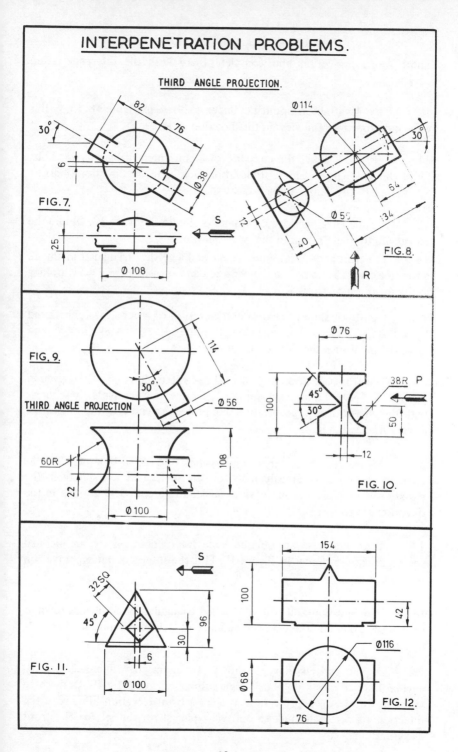

THIRD ANGLE PROJECTION.

FIG. 7.

FIG. 8.

FIG. 9.

THIRD ANGLE PROJECTION

FIG. 10.

FIG. 11.

FIG. 12.

63

Third Angle projection and complete them with the interpenetration curves.

10.   The elevation of a milled cylinder is shown in Figure 10. Copy this view and project an end view in the direction of arrow P.

11.   Figure 11 shows the end view of a cone pierced by a square hole. Draw this view, project a front elevation looking in the direction of arrow S, and a plan. Use Third Angle projection.

12.   A cone enveloped by a cylinder is shown in Figure 12. Obtain the curves of interpenetration in the two given views.

13.   The plan and elevation of a cone and a vertical triangular prism are given in Figure 13. Complete the elevation and project an end view looking in the direction of arrow R.

14.   Figure 14 shows the plan and elevation of a cone interpenetrated by a vertical hexagonal prism. Complete the elevation and draw an end view looking in the direction of arrow S.

15.   The front elevation and plan of two intersecting cones are given in Figure 15. Using Third Angle projection draw and complete these views with the curves of interpenetration and project an end view looking in the direction of arrow R.

16.   Figure 16 shows a sphere interpenetrated by an oblique cone, the apex of the cone apparently being on the surface of the sphere in the elevation. Complete the given views and add an end view looking in the direction of arrow S.

17.   Two views of an oblique cone interpenetrated by an inclined square prism are shown in Figure 17. Plot the interpenetration curves on both views.

18.   The elevation and plan of a milled triangular pyramid are shown in Figure 18. Complete the plan and add an end view looking in the direction of arrow R.

19.   A plan and auxiliary elevation of a hemisphere pierced by a triangular hole are given in Third Angle projection in Figure 19. Draw these views in Third Angle projection, project a front elevation looking in the direction of arrow R and an end view placed on the left of the front elevation.

INTERPENETRATION PROBLEMS.

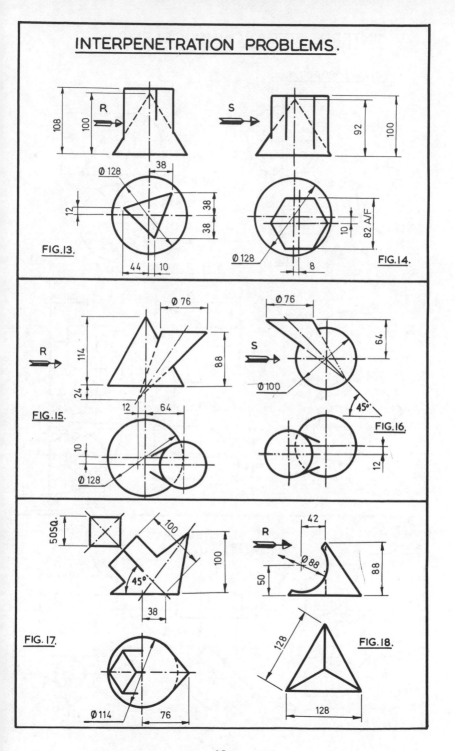

FIG.13.

FIG.14.

FIG.15.

FIG.16.

FIG.17.

FIG.18.

INTERPENETRATION PROBLEMS.

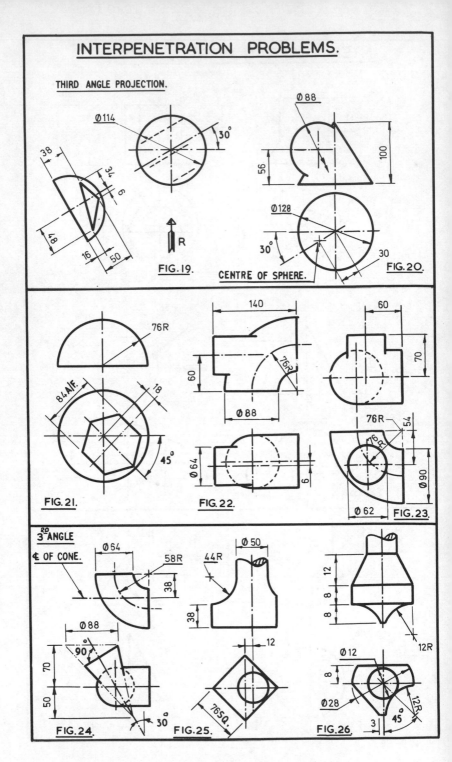

THIRD ANGLE PROJECTION.

Ø114
30°
38
34
6
48
16
50
FIG.19.

R

Ø88
56
100
Ø128
30°
30
CENTRE OF SPHERE.
FIG.20.

76R
84 A/F.
18
45°
FIG.21.

140
60
76R
Ø88
Ø64
6
FIG.22.

60
70
76R
54
76R
Ø90
Ø62
FIG.23.

3ᴿᴰ ANGLE
℄ OF CONE.
Ø64
58R
38
Ø88
90°
70
50
30°
FIG.24.

44R
Ø50
38
12
76 SQ.
FIG.25.

12
8
8
12R
Ø12
8
Ø28
12R
45
3
FIG.26.

66

20.   Two views of the interpenetration of a cone and sphere are shown in Figure 20. Complete these views with the interpenetration curves.

21.   Figure 14 shows the plan and incomplete elevation of a hemisphere pierced by a hexagonal hole 84mm across flats. Draw these views and complete the front elevation.

22.   Two views of an elbow piece with a branch cylinder are shown in Figure 22. Complete these views with the interpenetration curves.

23.   Construct the curve of interpenetration in the front elevation of the elbow and branch cylinder shown in Figure 23.

24.   Figure 24 shows incompletely a plan and front elevation of an elbow with an oblique conical branch, the views being in Third Angle projection. Using Third Angle projection construct the interpenetration curves for both views. Show the complete branch in the elevation.

25.   A plan and incomplete elevation of an eccentrically turned square bar are shown in Figure 25. Draw the given views and complete the elevation with the interpenetration curves.

26.   Figure 26 shows two views of a needle valve. The elevation shows the valve after being turned, and the plan shows it after being ground. Draw the given views and construct the interpenetration curves in the elevation produced by the grinding operation. Scale: Four times full size.

3

CONIC SECTIONS

Conic sections are produced when a plane intersects a right circular cone. They may be considered as loci, which was done in Chapter 4 of Volume 1, or, as here, they may be considered as curves of interpenetration. The surface of a cone is produced by the rotation of two straight lines which cross at some acute angle equal to half the apex angle of the cone. One line, which is shown vertical in Figure 1, is the axis; the other is the generator. Successive positions of the generator as it sweeps out the conic surface are called elements of the cone. The conic surface is considered to extend to infinity in both directions from the apex. Each half of the double cone is called a nappe.

Depending on the position of the cutting plane five sections are possible. These are illustrated in Figures 1 to 6.

(a) *Circle*. Produced when the plane is at right angles to the cone axis.

(b) *Ellipse*. Produced when the plane cuts all the elements but is not at right angles to the axis.

(c) *Parabola*. Produced by a plane parallel to one element of the cone.

(d) *Hyperbola*. Produced by a plane cutting both nappes of the cone.

(e) *Isosceles triangle*. Produced by a plane which cuts both nappes and passes through the apex of the cone.

THE ELLIPSE. Figure 7 shows a right circular cone cut by a plane XX. The plane cuts all the elements of the cone so the conic section is an ellipse. The ellipse appears in true size in an auxiliary view projected at right angles from XX.

To draw the ellipse cutting planes such as AA are used which are at right angles to the cone axis. These cutting planes produce circles as shown in the plan view. Where planes XX and AA intersect in the front view the widths across both planes are equal. This width W can be transferred from the plan view to the auxiliary view to plot two points on the ellipse. Additional cutting planes parallel to AA give more points on the ellipse.

CONIC SECTIONS

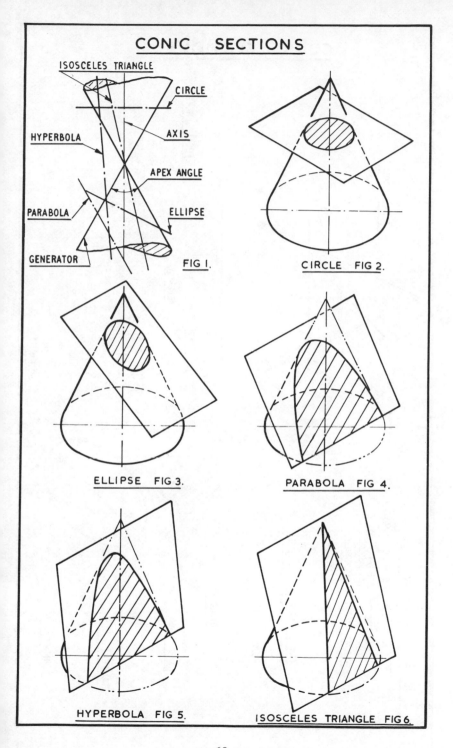

FIG 1.

CIRCLE FIG 2.

ELLIPSE FIG 3.

PARABOLA FIG 4.

HYPERBOLA FIG 5.

ISOSCELES TRIANGLE FIG 6.

69

CONIC SECTIONS

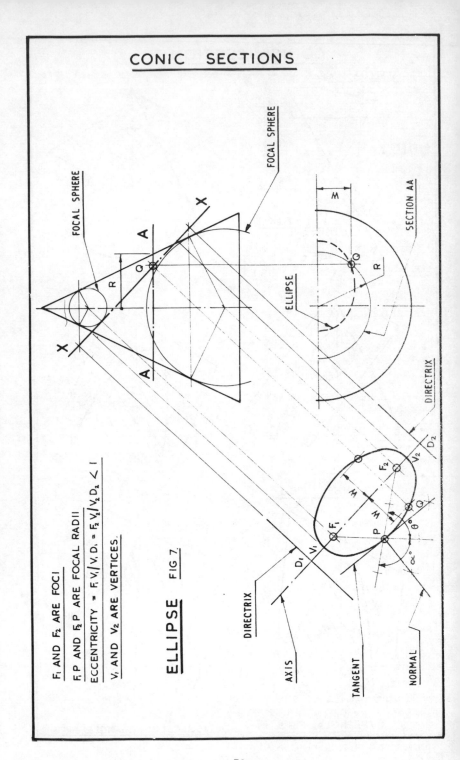

FOCAL SPHERE

FOCAL SPHERE

SECTION AA

ELLIPSE

DIRECTRIX

F₁ AND F₂ ARE FOCI

F₁P AND F₂P ARE FOCAL RADII

ECCENTRICITY = F_1V_1/V_1D_1 = F_2V_2/V_2D_2 < 1

V₁ AND V₂ ARE VERTICES.

ELLIPSE   FIG 7.

DIRECTRIX

AXIS

TANGENT

NORMAL

Note that the curve in the plan view through point Q is also an ellipse. Thus any view of plane XX, except an edge view, is an ellipse.

By using focal spheres the focal points F_1 and F_2 and the directrices may be established. The focal spheres are inscribed in the cone so that the conic surface and the cutting plane XX are tangential to them. The centres of the focal spheres projected onto the axis in the auxiliary view position the foci F_1 and F_2. The axis of the ellipse is the projection in the auxiliary view of the axis of the cone. The lines of intersection between XX and horizontal planes through the tangent circles of the focal spheres and cone give the directrices when projected into the auxiliary view.

To draw the tangent to the ellipse at any point P bisect the angle θ between the two focal radii F_1 P and F_2 P. To draw the normal at P bisect the angle α.

The ratio of the distances focus to vertex and vertex to directrix is called the eccentricity of the curve. For the ellipse the eccentricity is less than unity. The eccentricity is constant for any point on the curve.

THE PARABOLA. The cutting plane YY in Figure 8 is parallel to an element of the cone so the conic section is a parabola. It is shown in true shape in an auxiliary view projected at right angles from YY. The curve through point Q in the plan view is also a parabola, as is any view of YY, except an edge view.

As with the ellipse, cutting planes at right angles to the cone axis are used to draw the true shape view. The focus is the projection on the axis of the centre of the focal sphere which has the conic surface and YY tangential to it. The directrix is the line of intersection between YY and a horizontal plane through the tangent circle of the focal sphere and cone. The axis is the projection of the cone axis in the auxiliary view.

The tangent to the parabola at any point P is found by bisecting the angle θ between the focal radius FP and a diameter through P. The diameter is at right angles to the directrix. The normal at P bisects the angle α between the focal radius and the diameter.

For the parabola the eccentricity is unity and is the ratio FV to VD. It is constant for any point on the curve.

THE HYPERBOLA. The plane ZZ in Figure 9 cuts both nappes of the double cone and so produces a hyperbola. The plane is shown parallel to the cone axis but need not be, since any plane cutting both nappes without passing through the apex will produce a hyperbola.

Cutting planes such as AA, at right angles to the cone axis, are used as before to plot points on the true shape view of the hyperbola. The foci are the projections on the axis of the centres of the focal spheres. These spheres have the conic surface and ZZ tangential to them. The directrices

71

CONIC SECTIONS

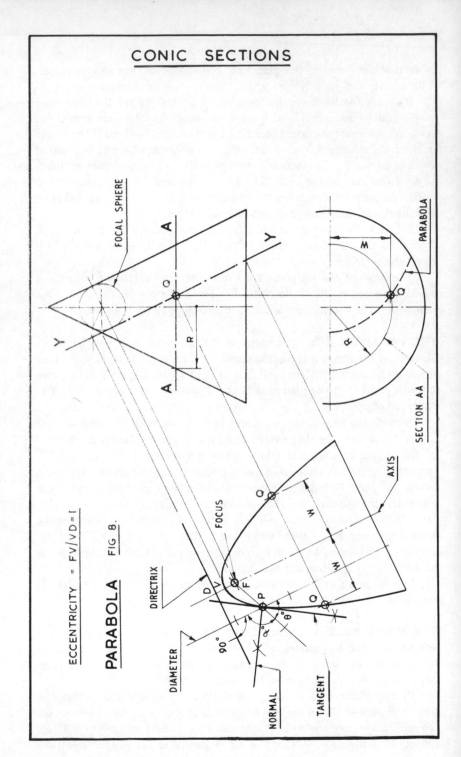

ECCENTRICITY = FV/VD = 1

PARABOLA   FIG 8.

FOCAL SPHERE

PARABOLA

SECTION AA

DIRECTRIX

FOCUS

AXIS

DIAMETER

90°

NORMAL

TANGENT

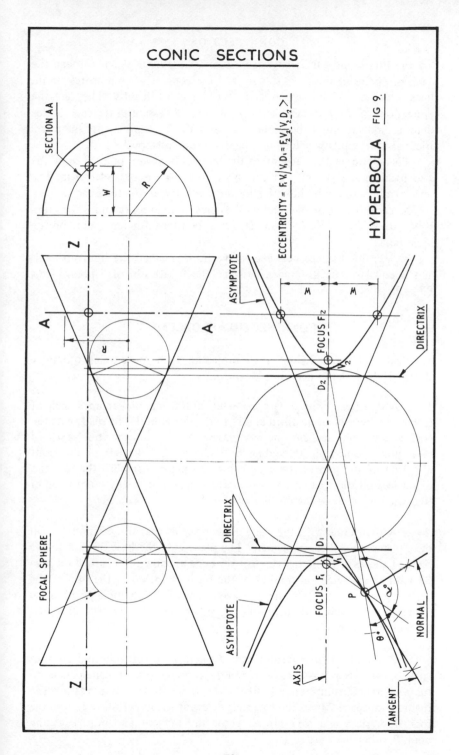

CONIC SECTIONS

SECTION AA

W

R

Z

A

A

R

Z

FOCAL SPHERE

DIRECTRIX

ASYMPTOTE

FOCUS F_1

V_1

D_1

AXIS

P

$\theta°$

$\alpha°$

NORMAL

TANGENT

ASYMPTOTE

FOCUS F_2

V_2

D_2

DIRECTRIX

M

M

ECCENTRICITY $= F_1 V_1 / V_1 D_1 = F_2 V_2 / V_2 D_2 > 1$

HYPERBOLA   FIG 9.

73

are the intersection lines between ZZ and horizontal planes through the tangent circles of the focal spheres and the cone. The asymptotes are the lines which would be tangential to the curves at infinity. They are the projections of the outer elements of the cone. To establish the asymptotes draw a circle through the vertices V_1 and V_2. This circle cuts the directrices at four points which lie on the asymptotes as shown.

To determine the tangent to the hyperbola at any point P draw the two focal radii F_1P and F_2P and bisect the angle θ between them. The normal at P is found by bisecting the angle α between the focal radii.

The eccentricity of the hyperbola is greater than unity and is the ratio F_1V_1 to V_1D_1 or F_2V_2 to V_2D_2. It is constant for any point on the hyperbola.

V_1V_2, the distance between the vertices, is called the transverse axis and is equal to the difference between the focal radii of a point. Thus $PF_2-PF_1=V_1V_2$.

CONIC SECTION PROBLEMS

Scale full size and First Angle projection to be used unless otherwise stated. Hidden detail need not be shown.

1.   A right cone with a base diameter of 100 mm and an apex angle of 60º is cut by a plane inclined at 45º to the horizontal. The plane cuts the cone axis 65 mm up from the base. Draw the views of the cone as shown in Figure 7 on Page 70, adding an end view on the left of the front elevation of the part of the cone below the plane. Establish the foci and directrices on the true shape view of the ellipse and at any point P, other than the vertex, draw the tangent and normal.

2.   A right cone with the same dimensions as that in Question 1 is cut by a plane parallel to an element. The plane cuts the base 32 mm to the right of the axis. Draw the views of the cone as shown in Figure 8 on page 72 with an end view on the left of the front elevation of the part of the cone below the plane. On the true shape view of the parabola position the focus and directrix. At any point P, other than the vertex, draw the tangent and normal.

3.   A double right cone has base diameters of 100 mm and an apex angle of 60º. Its axis is horizontal and the cone is cut by a plane parallel to the axis and 20 mm above it. Draw the views of the cone as shown in Figure 9 on page 73. In the true shape view of the hyperbola establish the foci, directrices and asymptotes. Draw the tangent and normal at any point P, other than the vertex.

CONIC SECTION PROBLEMS

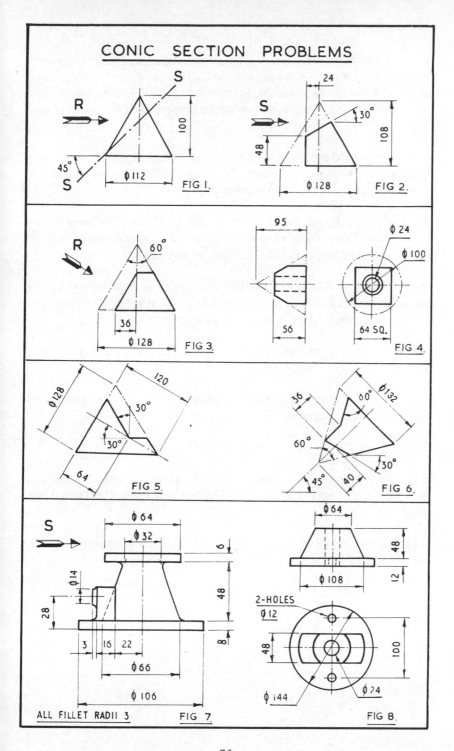

FIG 1.

FIG 2.

FIG 3.

FIG 4.

FIG 5.

FIG 6.

FIG 7

ALL FILLET RADII 3

FIG 8.

75

4.   A floodlight which projects a right circular conical beam is mounted on a pylon 7 metres above ground level. The axis of the beam makes an angle of 45° with the ground and the apex angle of the beam is 60°. Using a scale of 1 cm to ½ metre, determine the shape of the illuminated ground area. Use Third Angle projection.

5.   Draw the elevation of the right cone shown in Figure 1 and project a plan of the lower portion below the plane SS. Add an end view of the lower portion in the direction of arrow R.

6.   Figure 2 shows the elevation of part of a cone after being cut by two planes. Draw this elevation and project a plan and an end view in the direction of arrow S. Use Third Angle projection

7.   Copy the elevation of the part cone given in Figure 3 and draw a plan and auxiliary plan in the direction of arrow R to show the true view of the sloping face, which is parallel to an element.

8.   Draw the given views of the conical spacer shown in Figure 4 and complete the front elevation.

9.   Draw the elevation of the cone given in Figure 5 and project a plan. Use Third Angle projection.

10.   Copy the given elevation in Figure 6 and project a plan.

11.   The elevation of a bronze casting is shown in Figure 7. Draw this view and project an end view in the direction of arrow S. Use Third Angle projection.

12.   Draw the views of the cover given in Figure 8 and complete the elevation.

4

DEVELOPMENT

DEVELOPMENT is a term used in sheet metal work and means the unfolding or unrolling of a detail into a flat sheet called the pattern. There are three methods of pattern development, Parallel line, Radial line and Triangulation. Whilst most sheet metal details can be developed by triangulation it is simpler to use the method best suited to the component under consideration.

Objects such as spherical floats, which are composed of double curved surfaces, can only be developed by approximate methods, but the correct form of the object is obtained by stretching the material in the forming operation. The development of these objects is not dealt with here, since the approximate methods used depend to a large extent on the material to be worked.

Parallel Line Development

This method can only be used to develop objects having a constant cross-section for their full length, for example, prisms and cylinders. Parallel lines, parallel to the axis of the detail, are drawn on a view which shows them as their true lengths. These true lengths are projected into the pattern so that they remain true lengths. When the object is a prism, as in examples 1, 2 and 3, the corners of the detail will serve as surface lines. When the object is cylindrical, as in examples 4 to 7, surface lines are obtained by dividing the circumference into a number of equal parts, usually twelve for convenience. See the distances A in the solutions to examples 4 to 7. The length of the pattern, called the stretchout or girth, is the perimeter of the object measured in a plane at right angles to the axis.

Most pipe and duct work can be developed by the parallel line method, but in some cases interpenetration curves have to be obtained before the pattern can be laid out. See the solution to example 7.

Parallel Line Development Applied to Oblique Cylinders

Parallel line development can be used to develop oblique cylinders, but before considering this, the following definitions should be noted, in conjunction with Figures 1 and 2 on page 83.

DEVELOPMENT.

PRISMS.

EXAMPLE 1.

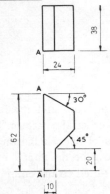

THIRD ANGLE PROJECTION.

DEVELOP FULL SIZE THE RECTANGULAR
TRUNK TRANSFORMER.
JOINT LINE TO BE AT A.A.

EXAMPLE 2.

46 A/F

THIRD ANGLE PROJECTION.

FULL HEXAGON
FOR THIS DEPTH.

30°

76

30°

DEVELOP THE PART HEXAGONAL
SHEET METAL DETAIL SHOWN.
SCALE FULL SIZE.
JOINT LINE TO BE TAKEN AT THE
SHORTEST EDGE.

EXAMPLE 3.

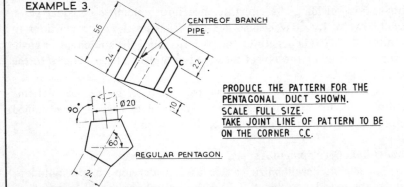

CENTRE OF BRANCH
PIPE.

PRODUCE THE PATTERN FOR THE
PENTAGONAL DUCT SHOWN.
SCALE FULL SIZE.
TAKE JOINT LINE OF PATTERN TO BE
ON THE CORNER C.C.

REGULAR PENTAGON.

DEVELOPMENT.

PRISMS.

EXAMPLE 1. SOLUTION.

STRETCHOUT.

FOLD LINES

RECTANGULAR PRISM.

EXAMPLE 2. SOLUTION.

FOLD LINES.

HEXAGONAL PRISM.

EXAMPLE 3. SOLUTION.

FOLD LINES.

DIA.

PENTAGONAL PRISM.

DEVELOPMENT

RIGHT CYLINDERS.

EXAMPLES 4 & 5.

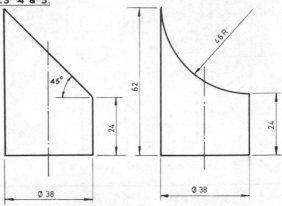

PRODUCE FULL SIZE COMPLETE PATTERNS FOR
THE PART CYLINDRICAL TUBES ILLUSTRATED ABOVE.
THE JOINT LINE IN EACH CASE TO BE TAKEN AT
THE ONE INCH LENGTH.

EXAMPLE 6.

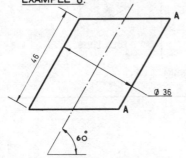

DEVELOP THE CYLINDER SHOWN
FULL SIZE.
JOINT LINE A.A.

EXAMPLE 7.

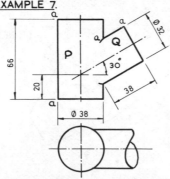

SEAM a a.

A CYLINDRICAL BRANCH CONNECTION
IS ILLUSTRATED IN THE ADJOINING
FIGURE. COMPLETE THE GIVEN
ELEVATION AND DRAW THE PATTERNS
FOR BRANCH PIPE "Q" AND MAIN PIPE "P"
FULL SIZE.

DEVELOPMENT.

RIGHT CYLINDERS.

EXAMPLE 4. SOLUTION.

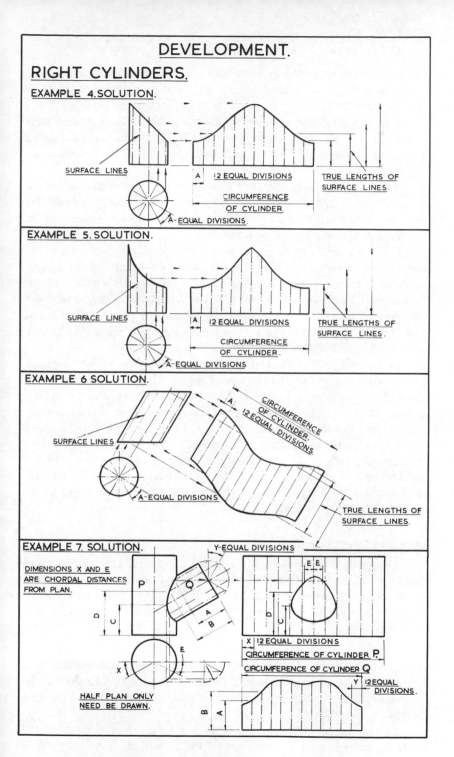

SURFACE LINES

A | 12 EQUAL DIVISIONS

CIRCUMFERENCE OF CYLINDER.

A-EQUAL DIVISIONS.

TRUE LENGTHS OF SURFACE LINES.

EXAMPLE 5. SOLUTION.

SURFACE LINES

A | 12 EQUAL DIVISIONS

CIRCUMFERENCE OF CYLINDER.

A-EQUAL DIVISIONS

TRUE LENGTHS OF SURFACE LINES.

EXAMPLE 6 SOLUTION.

SURFACE LINES

A-EQUAL DIVISIONS

A CIRCUMFERENCE OF CYLINDER. 12 EQUAL DIVISIONS.

TRUE LENGTHS OF SURFACE LINES.

EXAMPLE 7. SOLUTION.

Y-EQUAL DIVISIONS

DIMENSIONS X AND E ARE CHORDAL DISTANCES FROM PLAN.

P

Q

E E

D

C

A

B

D

U

HALF PLAN ONLY NEED BE DRAWN.

E

X

X | 12 EQUAL DIVISIONS

CIRCUMFERENCE OF CYLINDER P.

CIRCUMFERENCE OF CYLINDER Q

Y | 12 EQUAL DIVISIONS.

B

A

A right cylinder is one in which all sections at right angles to the axis are circular. Thus, when dimensioned, its diameter is indicated at right angles to the axis.

An oblique cylinder is one in which the axis is inclined at some angle to the plane of its circular base. Therefore, its cross-section at right angles to the axis is elliptical. When dimensioned, its diameter is shown at some angle to the axis.

It will be seen that oblique cylinders have a constant cross-section for their full length and, therefore, they can be developed by the parallel line method. However, a slight modification is necessary which will be apparent from the following explanation.

Referring to the solution to example 8, divide the circular cross-section into twelve equal parts and draw surface lines as for a right cylinder in the elevation. These surface lines will be true lengths and can be projected directly into the pattern. The stretchout of the pattern will not now be equal to the circumference of the circular section as it was with the right cylinder. The circumference now will equal the distance round the curved edge of the pattern.

Project the ends of the surface lines to the pattern, at right angles to the cylinder axis and fix the position of the joint line in the pattern. From the ends of the joint line strike arcs A equal to one-twelfth of the circumference of the circular base, to cut the projectors from the surface line nearest the joint line. This will fix two points on the edges of the pattern. From these points again strike arcs A to cut the projectors from the next surface line, and so on. This procedure ensures that the length of the curved edges of the pattern equals the circumference of the circular ends of the cylinder. It should be noted that the distances between surface lines on the pattern are not equal.

Radial Line Development

This method of development is used for right and oblique cones and employs radial surface lines drawn on the cone from the apex to the base. These radial lines are equally spaced by dividing the circular plan view of the cone into twelve equal parts. With pyramids the sloping edges are used as surface lines.

RIGHT CONES. The development of any right cone is a sector of a circle since the radial surface lines are all the same true length. The angle at the centre of the sector depends on the base radius of the cone and the slant height.

Let the radius of the base of the cone be r, the slant height of the cone R, and the angle at the centre of the pattern θ. Then the ratio of

DEVELOPMENT.

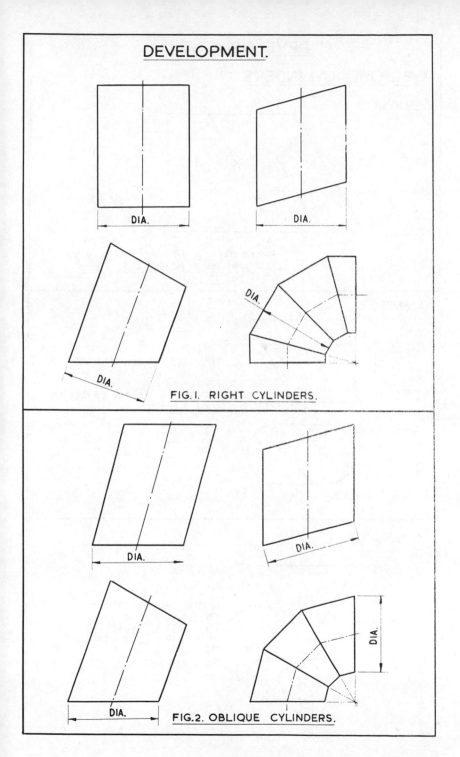

FIG. I. RIGHT CYLINDERS.

FIG. 2. OBLIQUE CYLINDERS.

DEVELOPMENT.

OBLIQUE CYLINDERS.

EXAMPLE 8.

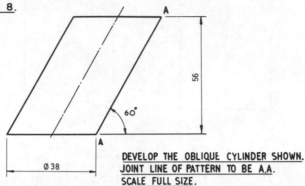

DEVELOP THE OBLIQUE CYLINDER SHOWN.
JOINT LINE OF PATTERN TO BE A.A.
SCALE FULL SIZE.

EXAMPLE 9.

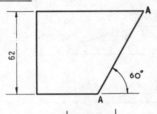

REPRODUCE THE TWO GIVEN VIEWS
OF A SHEET METAL HOPPER AND
DEVELOP HALF ITS PATTERN.
COMMENCE THE PATTERN ON EDGE A.A.
SCALE FULL SIZE.

EXAMPLE 10.

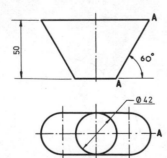

DEVELOP HALF THE PATTERN
FOR THE HOPPER SHOWN
THE COMPLETED PATTERN
TO BE SEAM WELDED ALONG
THE EDGE A.A.
SCALE FULL SIZE.

DEVELOPMENT.

OBLIQUE CYLINDERS.

EXAMPLE 8. SOLUTION.

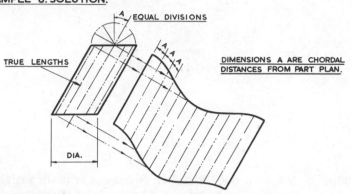

EQUAL DIVISIONS

TRUE LENGTHS

DIMENSIONS A ARE CHORDAL
DISTANCES FROM PART PLAN.

DIA.

EXAMPLE 9. SOLUTION.

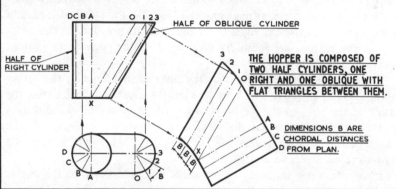

DCBA   O 1 2 3   HALF OF OBLIQUE CYLINDER

HALF OF
RIGHT CYLINDER

THE HOPPER IS COMPOSED OF
TWO HALF CYLINDERS, ONE
RIGHT AND ONE OBLIQUE WITH
FLAT TRIANGLES BETWEEN THEM.

DIMENSIONS B ARE
CHORDAL DISTANCES
FROM PLAN.

EXAMPLE 10. SOLUTION.

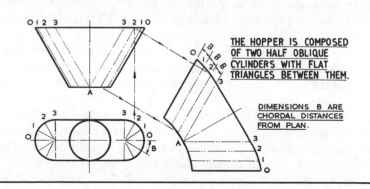

O 1 2 3   3 2 1 O

THE HOPPER IS COMPOSED
OF TWO HALF OBLIQUE
CYLINDERS WITH FLAT
TRIANGLES BETWEEN THEM.

DIMENSIONS B ARE
CHORDAL DISTANCES
FROM PLAN.

$\theta°$ to 360° equals the ratio of the curved length of the pattern, L, to the circumference of a circle of radius R. See the solution to example 11. The length L equals the circumference of the base of the cone.

$$\text{Thus} \qquad \frac{\theta°}{360°} = \frac{2\pi r}{2\pi R} = \frac{r}{R}$$

$$\text{And} \qquad \theta° = \frac{r}{R} \times 360°$$

When θ is known the pattern can be laid out as in the solution to example 11. The solution to example 12 shows that the pattern for a frustum of a cone is a sector with a smaller sector removed from it. When a cone is cut in other ways, as in examples 13 and 14, the radial surface lines are used to obtain the cut edges in the pattern. The positions of the radial lines on the pattern are found by dividing θ or the edge of the pattern into twelve equal parts. The student should realise that the only surface lines in the orthographic views of the cone which are true lengths are those which define the outside of the cone in the elevation. So, when using the other radial lines to obtain the cut edges of the pattern their ends are projected to the outside of the cone to obtain the true lengths. This is illustrated in the solutions to examples 13 and 14.

It is sometimes necessary to use radial lines additional to the twelve equally spaced ones, as in the solution to example 15. These additional lines are drawn as required in the elevation and the positions of their ends, A, B and C are found in the plan by projection. Points A, B and C are plotted on the pattern by using arcs 4-A, 3-C and 2-B transferred from the plan.

When developing a cone for which the vertical height is given in place of the slant height, it is more convenient, instead of calculating θ, to draw in the pattern the arc representing the base of the cone and to step off around it twelve chords each equal to the chord of one-twelfth of the base circumference of the cone. This method fixes the size of the pattern and the positions of the radial lines in one operation and avoids having to divide an unusual angle into twelve parts. The size of the pattern, however, is not quite as accurate as that obtained by using the angle θ, but this is offset by the convenience of the method. See dimensions A in the solutions to examples 11 and 12.

DEVELOPMENT.

RIGHT CONES.

<u>EXAMPLES 11. 12. & 13.</u>

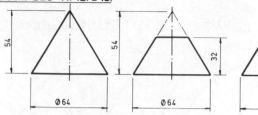

SCALE FULL SIZE.
PRODUCE COMPLETE PATTERNS FOR THE
CONE AND PART CONES SHOWN ABOVE.

<u>EXAMPLE.14.</u>

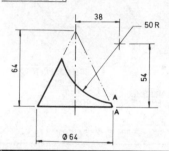

DEVELOP THE PART CONICAL
DETAIL SHOWN, FULL SIZE.
JOINT LINE OF PATTERN TO BE A.A.

<u>EXAMPLE 15.</u>

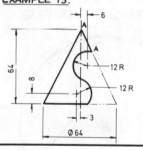

A SHEET METAL FITTING CONFORMING
TO PART OF A RIGHT CONE IS SHOWN
IN THE ADJACENT VIEW.
CONSTRUCT THE COMPLETE PATTERN
FOR THE DETAIL FULL SIZE.
SEAM TO BE AT A.A.

<u>EXAMPLE 16.</u>

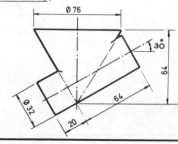

DETAILS OF A CONICAL HOPPER
ARE GIVEN. DEVELOP THE HOPPER
MAKING THE JOINT LINE ON THE
SHORTEST EDGE.
CONSTRUCT ALSO THE SHAPE OF
THE HOLE IN THE PATTERN OF
THE CYLINDRICAL PIPE PRIOR TO
BENDING. SCALE FULL SIZE.

DEVELOPMENT.

RIGHT CONES.

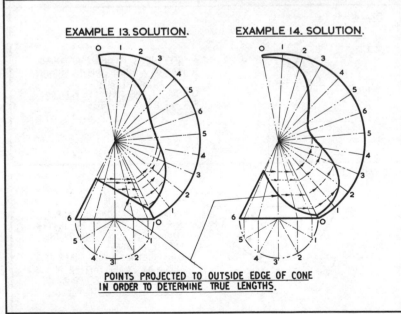

EXAMPLE 11. SOLUTION.

R

θ

L

DIMENSIONS A ARE
CHORDAL DISTANCES
FROM PLAN.

6 EQUAL
DIVISIONS

HALF PLAN VIEW
OF CONE

r

EXAMPLE 12. SOLUTION.

L

A

HALF PLAN VIEW
OF CONE.

r = RADIUS OF BASE OF CONE.
R = SLANT HEIGHT OF CONE
$\theta = \dfrac{r}{R} \times 360°$
L = CIRCUMFERENCE OF BASE OF CONE.

EXAMPLE 13. SOLUTION.

EXAMPLE 14. SOLUTION.

POINTS PROJECTED TO OUTSIDE EDGE OF CONE
IN ORDER TO DETERMINE TRUE LENGTHS.

88

DEVELOPMENT.

RIGHT CONES.

EXAMPLE 15. SOLUTION.

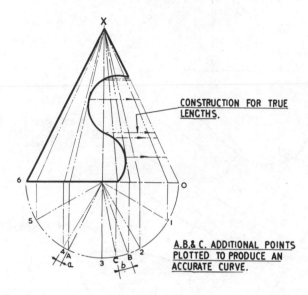

CONSTRUCTION FOR TRUE LENGTHS.

A.B.& C. ADDITIONAL POINTS PLOTTED TO PRODUCE AN ACCURATE CURVE.

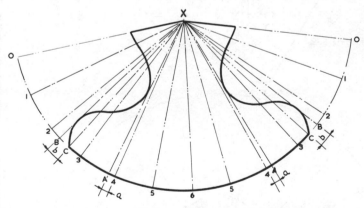

DIMENSIONS a AND b ARE CHORDAL DISTANCES FROM PLAN.

DEVELOPMENT.
RIGHT CONES.

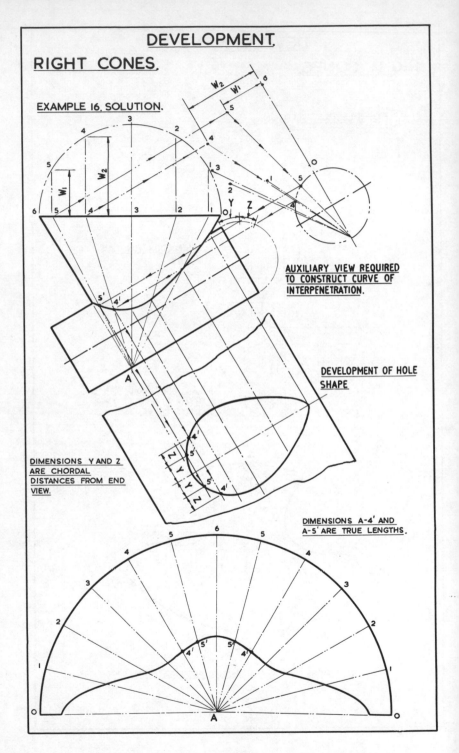

EXAMPLE 16. SOLUTION.

AUXILIARY VIEW REQUIRED
TO CONSTRUCT CURVE OF
INTERPENETRATION.

DEVELOPMENT OF HOLE
SHAPE

DIMENSIONS Y AND Z
ARE CHORDAL
DISTANCES FROM END
VIEW.

DIMENSIONS A-4' AND
A-5' ARE TRUE LENGTHS.

OBLIQUE CONES. An oblique cone has its axis at some angle to the plane of its circular base and its development is, therefore, different from a right cone. Referring to the solution to example 17, the plan view of the circular base is divided into twelve equal parts which are used to draw radial surface lines on the elevation and plan. As with a right cone, only the two outside surface lines A-6 and A-0, in the elevation are true lengths. The true lengths of the remainder are found by rotating their plans about the apex until they meet the vertical plane and joining these points to the apex in the elevation. The pattern is drawn by fixing the joint line A0 and from A striking an arc equal to the true length of surface line A-1 to cut an arc P, equal to one twelfth of the circumference of the base, struck from 0. This procedure is repeated for each surface line until the pattern is completed.

It will be realised that this method ensures that the length round the curved edge of the pattern equals the circumference of the circular base of the cone. Compare this with the development of oblique cylinders in examples 8, 9 and 10.

When an oblique cone is cut as in example 18, the method for obtaining the true lengths of parts of the surface lines is similar to that used for a right cone. The end of each part surface line in the elevation is projected parallel to the base of the cone to the *appropriate* true length line.

Additional surface lines may be employed where required exactly as for a right cone, such as lines A-X in the solution to example 19.

PYRAMIDS. The same general method of development which is used for cones can be applied to pyramids. Example 20 is a right pyramid and, therefore, all the sloping edges are the same true length. To find this true length, rotate the plan of a sloping edge such as OQ until it is parallel with the vertical plane. Project to A in the elevation and join to the apex O. OA is then the required true length. The true lengths of the part sloping edges are found by projecting their ends to C and B on OA. The base edges such as SR and ST are true lengths in the plan. The true length of the seam VP is on the edge of the pyramid in the elevation.

The pattern should be started by laying off the true length OP in a convenient position. Complete the first half side by drawing an arc PQ taken from the plan, to cut an arc OQ equal to the true length OA. This arc OQ may be extended round the pattern as all the sloping edges are the same length. Fix the points R, S and T on this arc by stepping round it the plan lengths QR, RS and ST. Join R, S and T to O and add the other half side OPT to give the pattern of the complete pyramid. To position the points W, X, Y and Z on the cut-out, mark off the true lengths OC and OB on the appropriate fold lines in the pattern.

A right triangular pyramid is shown in example 21. In this case the

DEVELOPMENT.

OBLIQUE CONES.

EXAMPLE 17.

DRAW THE PATTERN FOR THE GIVEN
OBLIQUE CONE   FULL SIZE.
JOINT LINE TO BE AT A.A.

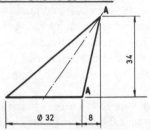

EXAMPLE 18.

PRODUCE THE SHAPE OF SHEET TIN PLATE
NECESSARY TO MAKE THE PART OBLIQUE CONE
SHOWN.   PLATE TO BE JOINED ALONG EDGE A.A.
SCALE FULL SIZE.

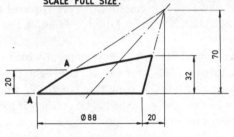

EXAMPLE 19.

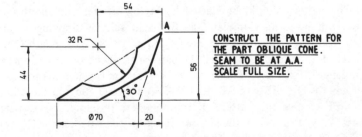

CONSTRUCT THE PATTERN FOR
THE PART OBLIQUE CONE.
SEAM TO BE AT A.A.
SCALE FULL SIZE.

DEVELOPMENT.

OBLIQUE CONES.

EXAMPLE 17. SOLUTION.

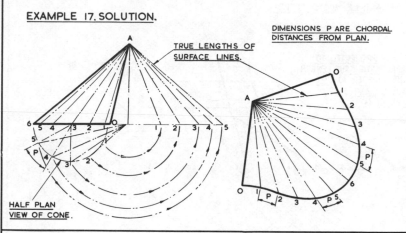

TRUE LENGTHS OF SURFACE LINES.

DIMENSIONS P ARE CHORDAL DISTANCES FROM PLAN.

HALF PLAN VIEW OF CONE.

EXAMPLE 18. SOLUTION.

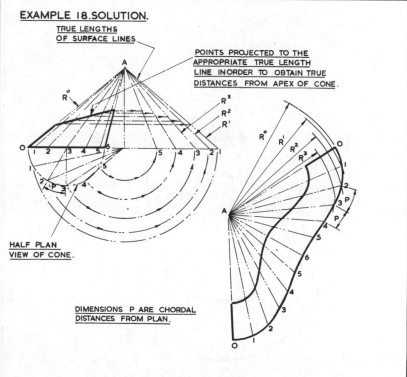

TRUE LENGTHS OF SURFACE LINES

POINTS PROJECTED TO THE APPROPRIATE TRUE LENGTH LINE IN ORDER TO OBTAIN TRUE DISTANCES FROM APEX OF CONE.

HALF PLAN VIEW OF CONE.

DIMENSIONS P ARE CHORDAL DISTANCES FROM PLAN.

93

DEVELOPMENT.

OBLIQUE CONES.

EXAMPLE 19 SOLUTION.

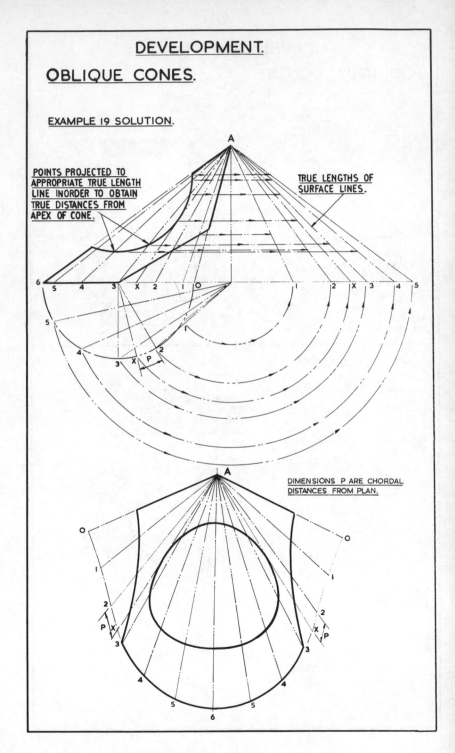

POINTS PROJECTED TO APPROPRIATE TRUE LENGTH LINE INORDER TO OBTAIN TRUE DISTANCES FROM APEX OF CONE.

TRUE LENGTHS OF SURFACE LINES.

DIMENSIONS P ARE CHORDAL DISTANCES FROM PLAN.

DEVELOPMENT.

PYRAMIDS.

EXAMPLE 20.

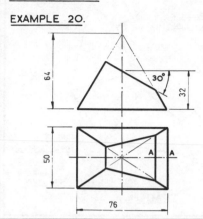

DEVELOP FULL SIZE THE PATTERN
FOR THE GIVEN RECTANGULAR
RIGHT PYRAMID. THE SEAM IS
TO BE THE LINE A.A.

EXAMPLE 21.

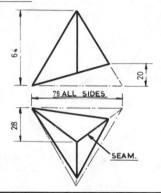

LAY OUT FULL SIZE THE PATTERN
FOR THE TRIANGULAR RIGHT PYRAMID
SHOWN. POSITION THE SEAM WHERE
SHOWN.

EXAMPLE 22

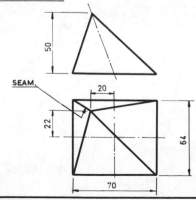

PRODUCE FULL SIZE THE
DEVELOPMENT OF THE GIVEN
RECTANGULAR OBLIQUE PYRAMID.
THE SEAM TO BE ON THE SHORTEST
SIDE AS SHOWN.

95

DEVELOPMENT.

PYRAMIDS.

EXAMPLE 20. SOLUTION.

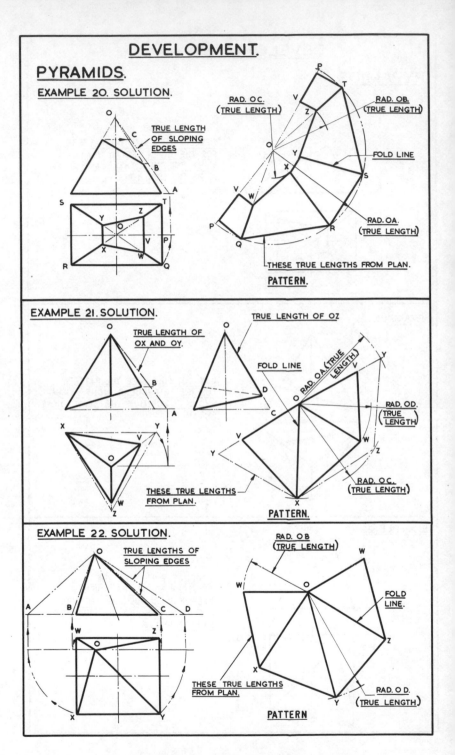

TRUE LENGTH OF SLOPING EDGES

RAD. OC. (TRUE LENGTH)

RAD. OB. (TRUE LENGTH)

FOLD LINE

RAD. OA. (TRUE LENGTH)

THESE TRUE LENGTHS FROM PLAN.

PATTERN.

EXAMPLE 21. SOLUTION.

TRUE LENGTH OF OX AND OY.

TRUE LENGTH OF OZ

FOLD LINE

RAD. OA (TRUE LENGTH)

RAD. OD. (TRUE LENGTH)

RAD. OC. (TRUE LENGTH)

THESE TRUE LENGTHS FROM PLAN.

PATTERN.

EXAMPLE 22. SOLUTION.

TRUE LENGTHS OF SLOPING EDGES

RAD. OB (TRUE LENGTH)

FOLD LINE.

THESE TRUE LENGTHS FROM PLAN.

RAD. O D. (TRUE LENGTH)

PATTERN

96

true length of the sloping side OZ differs from the true length of the other sides OX and OY. It may be found by projecting an end view, when OC will be the true length of OZ. This end view will also enable W to be positioned in the plan. The true length of OX and OY is found by rotating a plan length and projecting to the front elevation as before. The construction of the pattern is similar to that for example 20 and should be evident from the given solution.

Example 22 shows an oblique rectangular pyramid. Here the true lengths of the sloping edges are all different and each must be found by rotating the plan length and projecting to the elevation at A, B, C and D. OA, OB, OC and OD are then the true lengths of OX, OW, OZ and OY, respectively, and the pattern can be laid out as before.

Development By Triangulation

In this method of development the surface of the object is divided into a number of triangles. The true sizes of the triangles are found and they are drawn in order, side by side, to produce the pattern. It will be apparent that to find the true sizes of the triangles it is first necessary to find the true lengths of their sides. How this is done is shown in Figures 3 and 4 on page 98.

Figure 3 shows a rectangle to round transforming piece having the top and bottom edges on two parallel horizontal planes. This is the simplest case for a triangulation problem. Two surface lines AC and EF are shown in plan and elevation. Their true lengths are found by placing their plan lengths at right angles to their vertical heights. Then the hypotenuses of the right angled triangles so formed are the true lengths of the surface lines.

Since the top and bottom edges of the transformer are parallel to the horizontal plane, distances on these edges may be taken direct from the plan as in this view they are true lengths. Using these lengths and the true lengths of the surface lines found as above, the triangles into which the object is divided may be laid out in order and the pattern obtained.

When the object does not lie between two parallel planes as in Figure 4, the procedure is similar to that outlined above. Now, however, the distance O-1 on the top of the object is not a true length in either view. Its true length must be found as the true lengths of the surface lines were found before. Also care must be exercised in projecting vertical heights of surface lines from the elevation to the true length diagram as these vertical heights now vary. Reference to Figure 4 will make these points clear.

When dividing the surface of an object into triangles prior to developing it, care should be taken that all surface lines lie as far as possible on the surface of the object and are straight. For example, in Figure 4 a line from

DEVELOPMENT.

TRIANGULATION.

TRUE LENGTH CONSTRUCTIONS.

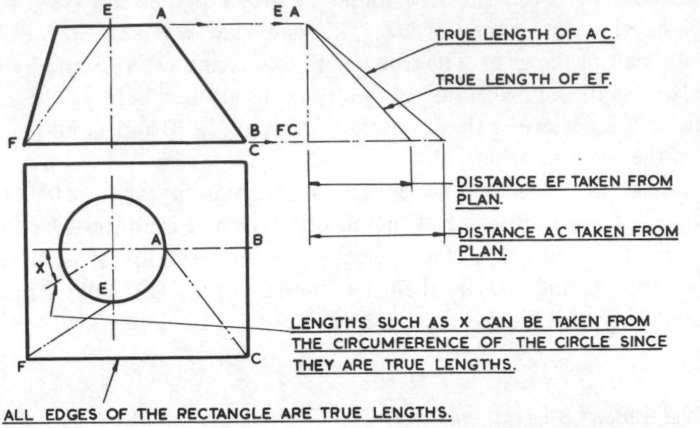

TRUE LENGTH OF A C.

TRUE LENGTH OF E F.

DISTANCE EF TAKEN FROM PLAN.

DISTANCE A C TAKEN FROM PLAN.

FIG. 3.

LENGTHS SUCH AS X CAN BE TAKEN FROM THE CIRCUMFERENCE OF THE CIRCLE SINCE THEY ARE TRUE LENGTHS.

ALL EDGES OF THE RECTANGLE ARE TRUE LENGTHS.

TRUE LENGTH O TO I.
TRUE LENGTH A TO I.
TRUE LENGTH B TO 2.
DISTANCE O TO I FROM PLAN.

DISTANCE A TO I FROM PLAN.

DISTANCE B TO 2 FROM PLAN.

EDGES FB AND ED ARE TRUE LENGTHS IN ELEVATION.
EDGES FE AND BD ARE TRUE LENGTHS IN PLAN.

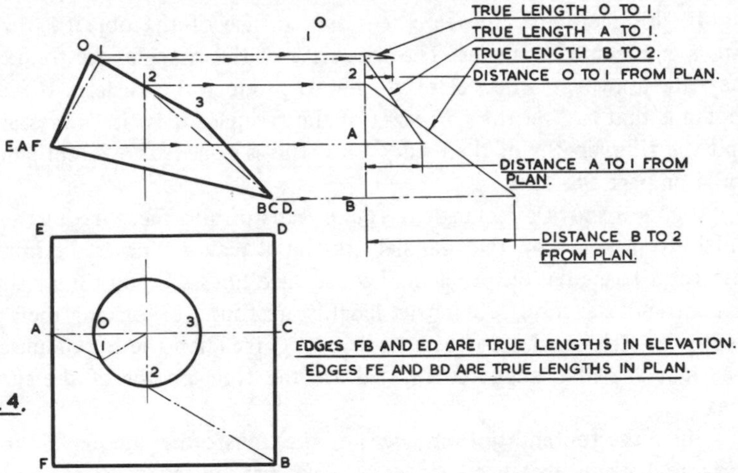

FIG. 4.

NOTE.

1. WHEN THE TOP AND BOTTOM EDGES OF A SHEET METAL DETAIL ARE PARALLEL TO THE H.P. THE LENGTHS OF THESE EDGES MAY BE TAKEN DIRECT FROM THE PLAN VIEW.

2. SHOULD THE EDGE BE CIRCULAR, CHORDAL DISTANCES MAY BE TAKEN AND TRANSFERRED TO THE PATTERN. WHILE SUCH LENGTHS ARE NOT THEORETICALLY ACCURATE THEY ARE SATISFACTORY FOR DEVELOPMENT WORK.

3. FOR ALL TRANSFORMER PIECES HAVING INCLINED TOP AND BOTTOM EDGES, TRUE LENGTH CONSTRUCTIONS MUST BE CARRIED OUT IF THESE EDGES ARE CURVED.

4. NEAT AND WELL DEFINED NOTATION SHOULD BE INTRODUCED TO ALL DEVELOPMENT DRAWINGS INORDER THAT THE CONSTRUCTION TECHNIQUE MAY BE PROGRESSIVE AND EASILY FOLLOWED

DEVELOPMENT.

TRIANGULATION.

EXAMPLE 23.

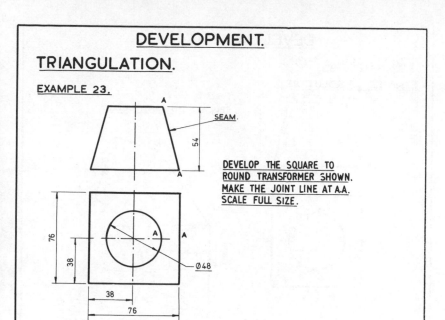

SEAM.

54

DEVELOP THE SQUARE TO
ROUND TRANSFORMER SHOWN.
MAKE THE JOINT LINE AT A.A.
SCALE FULL SIZE.

76

38

Ø48

38

76

EXAMPLE 24.

EXAMPLE 25.

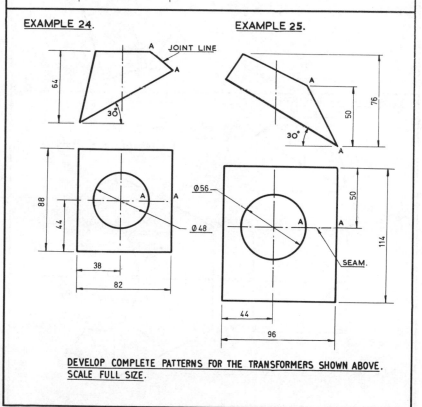

JOINT LINE

64

30°

88

44

38

82

Ø48

Ø56

30°

76

50

50

114

44

96

SEAM.

DEVELOP COMPLETE PATTERNS FOR THE TRANSFORMERS SHOWN ABOVE.
SCALE FULL SIZE.

DEVELOPMENT.

TRIANGULATION.

EXAMPLE 23. SOLUTION.

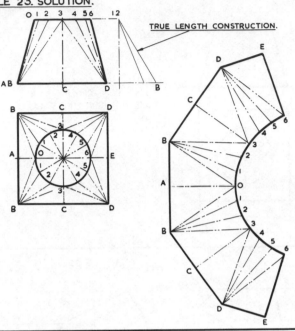

TRUE LENGTH CONSTRUCTION.

EXAMPLE 24 SOLUTION.

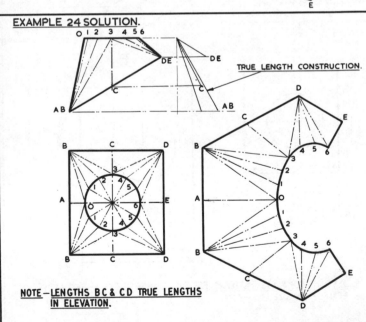

TRUE LENGTH CONSTRUCTION.

NOTE — LENGTHS BC & CD TRUE LENGTHS
IN ELEVATION.

DEVELOPMENT.

TRIANGULATION.

EXAMPLE 26

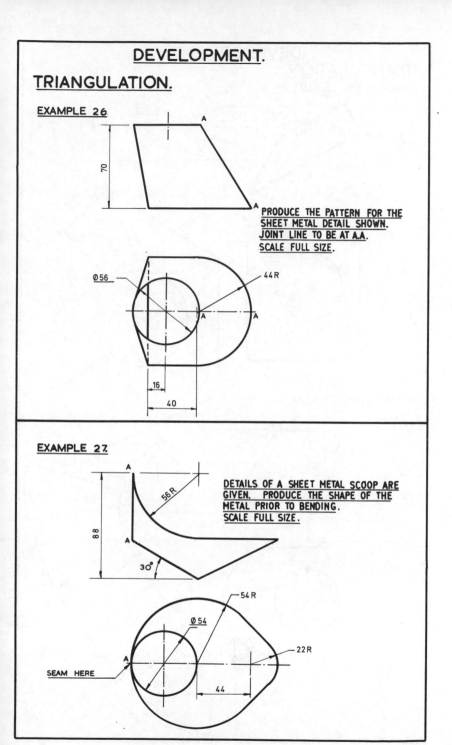

PRODUCE THE PATTERN FOR THE SHEET METAL DETAIL SHOWN. JOINT LINE TO BE AT A.A. SCALE FULL SIZE.

Ø56   44R

70   16   40

EXAMPLE 27

DETAILS OF A SHEET METAL SCOOP ARE GIVEN. PRODUCE THE SHAPE OF THE METAL PRIOR TO BENDING. SCALE FULL SIZE.

56R   88   30°

54R   Ø54   22R   44

SEAM HERE

DEVELOPMENT.

TRIANGULATION.

<u>EXAMPLE 25. SOLUTION.</u>

<u>EXAMPLE 26. SOLUTION.</u>

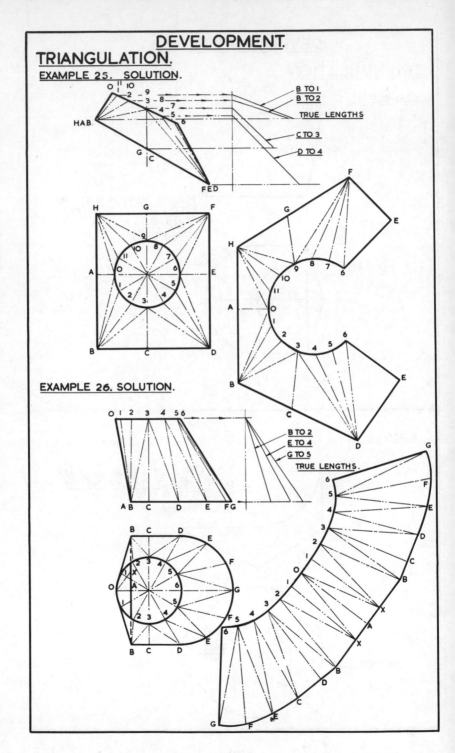

DEVELOPMENT.

TRIANGULATION.

EXAMPLE 27. SOLUTION.

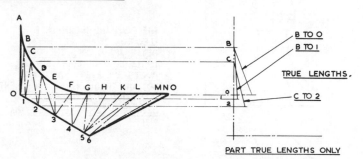

TRUE LENGTHS.

B TO O
B TO I
C TO 2

PART TRUE LENGTHS ONLY

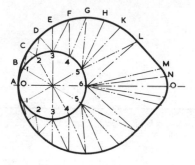

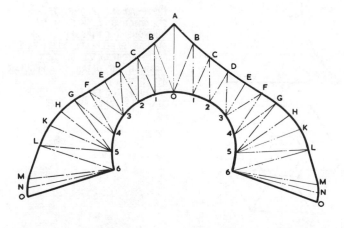

DEVELOPMENT.

PANELS.

EXAMPLE 28.

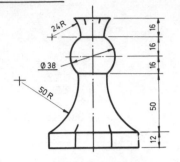

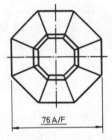

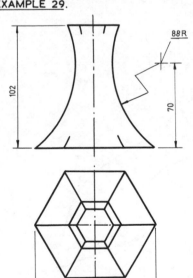

76 A/F

THE PLAN AND INCOMPLETE
ELEVATION OF A SHEET METAL
DETAIL ARE GIVEN. THE DETAIL
IS MADE UP OF EIGHT SIMILAR
PANELS AND EVERY HORIZONTAL
SECTION THROUGH THE COMPONENT
IS A REGULAR OCTAGON.
DEVELOP A COMPLETE PANEL FULL
SIZE.

EXAMPLE 29.

THE PLAN AND INCOMPLETE
ELEVATION OF A SHEET METAL
COMPONENT COMPOSED OF SIX
SIMILAR PANELS ARE ILLUSTRATED.
EVERY HORIZONTAL SECTION
THROUGH THE DETAIL IS A REGULAR
HEXAGON.
PRODUCE THE PATTERN FOR ONE
COMPLETE PANEL FULL SIZE.

102 A/C

DEVELOPMENT.

PANELS.

EXAMPLE 28. SOLUTION.

STRETCHOUT IS SUM OF LENGTHS SUCH AS A AND B FROM OUTSIDE PROFILE OF ELEVATION.

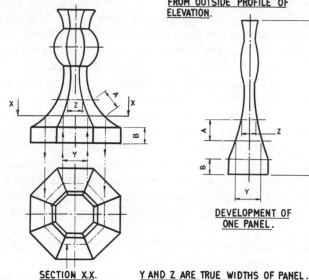

DEVELOPMENT OF ONE PANEL.

SECTION X.X.   Y AND Z ARE TRUE WIDTHS OF PANEL.

EXAMPLE 29, SOLUTION.

STRETCHOUT FROM END VIEW.

END VIEW TO OBTAIN STRETCHOUT OF PANEL.

DEVELOPMENT OF ONE PANEL

SECTION S.S.   V AND W ARE TRUE WIDTHS OF PANEL

1 to E could only lie on the surface of the transformer if it were curved. If it were straight it would only touch the surface at its ends.

Panel Development

Example 28 shows a sheet metal detail composed of eight similar panels. The development of one panel may be obtained as follows.

Draw an elevation and plan, positioning the detail so that the edges of one panel are parallel to the vertical plane. Obtain the profile of this panel in the elevation by taking a series of horizontal sections such as XX. Project the width Y of the panel at XX, back of the elevation from the plan. This width Ẏ will be a true length. The stretchout of the panel is found from the outside profile of the end view where it appears as a true length.

Start the pattern by drawing a centre line and mark off along it distances such as A and B from the outside profile of the elevation. These distances are those between successive horizontal sections. Through the points so obtained on the pattern centreline draw horizontals and mark off on them the appropriate widths, Y, Z, etc. Complete the pattern by lining in the profile.

Example 29 is similar to example 28 but now horizontal sections such as SS produce hexagons in the plan. The method is similar to that given above except that because the elevation does not show the true length of the panel centreline, an end view is necessary to obtain the stretchout of a panel. The end view is projected by transferring widths such as T from the sections in the plan.

DEVELOPMENT PROBLEMS

In the problems on pages 107 to 109 develop the details full size making no allowance for metal thickness or seams. Give full patterns in every case.

1–3. These are right prisms, open at each end.

4–6. These are right cylinders, open at each end. In Problems 4 and 6 develop the pipes marked A.

7, 8. These are combinations of right cylinders and prisms, open at each end.

9–11. These are oblique cylinders. In Problem 10, develop the gusset piece A and the two right cylinders. In Problem 11, develop cylinder A only.

12–19. These are right and oblique cones. In Problem 14 the 30mm

DEVELOPMENT PROBLEMS.

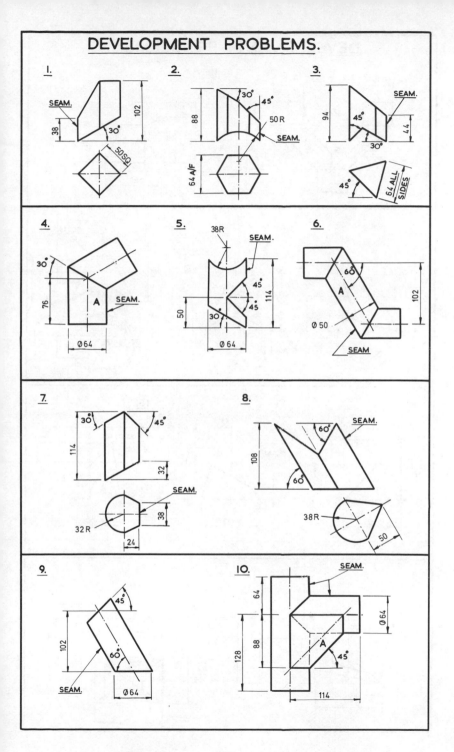

1.

SEAM.
38
102
30°
50 SQ.

2.

30°
45°
50 R
SEAM.
88
64 A/F

3.

SEAM.
94
45°
44
30°
45°
64 ALL SIDES

4.

30°
76
A
SEAM.
Ø 64

5.

38R
SEAM.
45°
114
50
45°
30°
Ø 64

6.

60°
A
102
Ø 50
SEAM

7.

30°
45°
114
32
SEAM.
38
32 R
24

8.

60°
SEAM.
108
60°
38R
50

9.

45°
102
60°
SEAM.
Ø 64

10.

SEAM.
64
Ø 64
128
88
A
45°
114

DEVELOPMENT PROBLEMS.

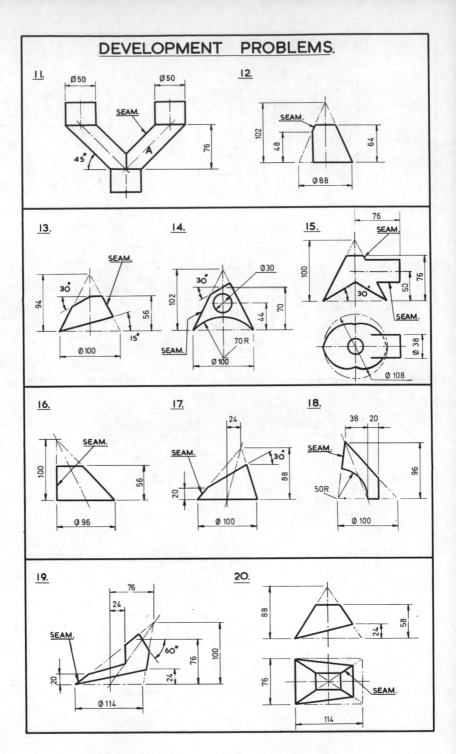

108

DEVELOPMENT PROBLEMS.

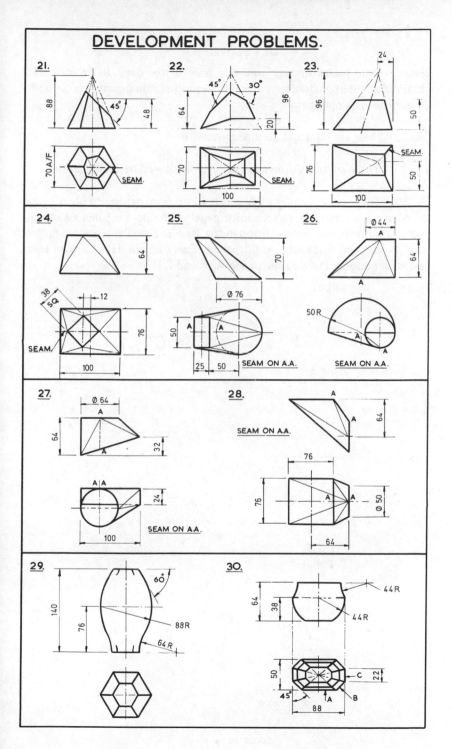

diameter hole passes through one side only of the cone. In Problem 15 obtain the interpenetration curve between the cylinder and cone and develop both components.

20–23 These are right and oblique pyramids.

24–28. These are transformer pieces to be developed by triangulation.

29, 30. These are examples of details built up from panels. Problem 29 is an exhaust flare made from six similar panels. Develop one panel assuming that every horizontal section through the flare is a regular hexagon. Problem 30 is a bowl made from eight panels. Every horizontal section in this case is an octagon. Develop the panels A, B and C.

5

CAMS

A CAM is a device having a profile or groove machined on it, which gives to a "follower" an irregular or special motion. The type of follower and the motion required of it decide the shape of the profile or groove.

Types of Cams

Cams fall into two main classes, radial, edge or plate cams and cylindrical cams. The follower with a radial cam reciprocates or oscillates in a plane perpendicular to the cam axis, whilst with a cylindrical cam the follower moves parallel to the cam axis.

Figure 1(a) shows the most elementary type of cam. A block with a sloping top face has a follower, which is a knife edged rod, resting on it. When the block is reciprocated on the horizontal plane, the follower is caused to reciprocate in its guide in the vertical plane. In Figure 1(b) the cam oscillates about a centre causing the follower to reciprocate up and down, whilst in Figure 1(c) the cam rotates, giving a reciprocating motion to the follower. These are all examples of edge cams.

A cylindrical cam is illustrated in Figure 2. Here a groove is cut in the surface of the cylinder, which reciprocates the follower as the cylinder oscillates. Sometimes a radial follower, oscillating about one end, is used. The cam may rotate instead of oscillate.

Instead of cutting a groove in a cylinder, the end may be machined to a special form when the cam is called an end cam. In this case thrust is only applied to the follower in one direction, whereas the groove applies it in both directions.

Types of Followers (Figure 3)

The simplest type of follower is one having a knife edge or point which works on the profile of the cam. It is not often used as it wears rapidly but it has the advantage that any form can be given to the cam profile.

With the roller follower the rate of wear is reduced, but the profile of the cam must not have any concave portions with a radius smaller than the roller radius.

The flat follower is sometimes used but here the cam profile must

CAMS.

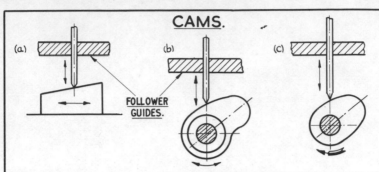

(a) (b) (c)

FOLLOWER GUIDES.

RADIAL OR DISC CAMS. IN WHICH THE WORKING SURFACE OF THE CAM IS SO
SHAPED THAT THE FOLLOWER RECIPROCATES OR
OSCILLATES IN A PLANE AT RIGHT ANGLES TO THE AXIS
OF THE CAM.

FIG.1.

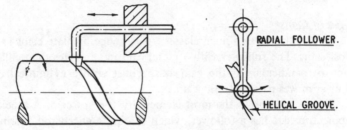

RADIAL FOLLOWER.

HELICAL GROOVE.

CYLINDRICAL CAMS. IN WHICH THE FOLLOWER RECIPROCATES OR OSCILLATES
IN A PLANE PARALLEL TO THE AXIS OF THE CAM.

FIG.2.

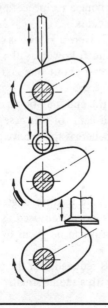

KNIFE EDGE FOLLOWER.
RARELY USED OWING TO RAPID RATE OF WEAR
NO LIMIT IMPOSED ON THE SHAPE OF THE
CAM.

ROLLER FOLLOWER.
PROVIDES A ROLLING MOTION BUT SIDE THRUST
EXISTS BETWEEN FOLLOWER AND ITS GUIDES.
ANY CONCAVE PORTION OF THE WORKING
SURFACE OF THE CAM MUST HAVE A RADIUS
GREATER THAN THE FOLLOWER RADIUS.

FLAT FOLLOWER,
THE ONLY THRUST ON THE GUIDE IS THAT DUE
TO FRICTION.
ALL WORKING SURFACES OF THE CAM MUST
BE CONVEX.

FIG 3

have no concave portions.

Followers to work with radial cams are generally spring loaded to keep them always in contact with the cam profile.

Types of Follower Motions

When studying the motions which are given to a follower by the profile of a radial cam, it is convenient to make use of a cam graph or displacement diagram in which the lift of the follower is plotted against the angular displacement of the cam. The complete 360° rotation of the cam is laid off in 15° steps along the horizontal axis, to a convenient scale, and the lift of the follower is shown on the vertical axis, full size.

There are three motions which may be given to the follower, uniform velocity, simple harmonic motion and uniform acceleration and retardation.

For the follower to have uniform velocity, it must move through equal increments of lift or fall as the cam turns through equal angles. Thus the graph is a straight line, as shown in Figure 4. It is usual in practice to smooth out the abrupt changes of direction at each end of the motion by radii. If this is not done large accelerations are given to the follower which tends to jump on the cam profile.

Simple harmonic motion when plotted on the cam graph is a sine curve and may be drawn as in Figure 5. A semi-circle is drawn on the rise or fall of the follower and divided into a number of equal parts. Six is a convenient number. The cam displacement is divided into the same number of equal parts and through these points verticals are erected. Horizontal lines drawn through the points on the semi-circle to cut these verticals give points on the graph.

Figure 6 shows the construction for a curve of uniform acceleration and retardation. In this case the curve is parabolic in form. The angular displacement of the cam and the lift of the follower are each divided into the same even number of equal divisions. During the first part of the motion the follower is accelerated at uniform rate; during the second part it is retarded. The construction, which is the circumscribing rectangle method of drawing a parabola, should be clear from the Figure.

In the worked examples which follow it has been assumed that the follower is the part which is to be given the special motion by the cam. This is not always the case. A third part of the mechanism may require the special motion, the follower being only an intermediary between this part and the cam. If this is so, the motion required by the third part should be plotted on the line along which it moves and transferred to the cam profile through the follower. Problems 10 and 16 on pages 127 and 131 are illustrations of this point.

113

CAMS.

MOTIONS IMPARTED TO FOLLOWERS.

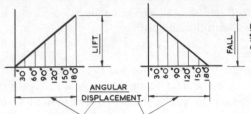

FOR UNIFORM VELOCITY THE SLOPE OF THE DISPLACEMENT CURVE MUST BE CONSTANT.

LIFT

FALL

ANGULAR DISPLACEMENT.

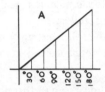 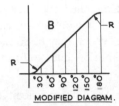

A

B

MODIFIED DIAGRAM.

R

R

CONDITIONS SUCH AS THOSE SHOWN AT "A" ARE IMPRACTICABLE AND IT IS NECESSARY TO MODIFY THE MOTION SO THAT THE ACCELERATION AND THE RETARDATION ARE REDUCED TO FINITE PROPORTIONS. SEE DIAGRAM "B".

CONSTRUCTION FOR UNIFORM VELOCITY.　　FIG. 4.

EQUAL INCREMENTS OF LIFT OR FALL ARE SET AGAINST EQUAL INCREMENTS OF ANGULAR DISPLACEMENT.

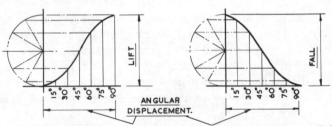

LIFT

FALL

ANGULAR DISPLACEMENT.

CONSTRUCTION FOR SIMPLE HARMONIC MOTION.　FIG. 5.

DRAW SEMI-CIRCLE ITS DIAMETER BEING THE STROKE OF THE FOLLOWER. DIVIDE SEMI-CIRCLE INTO A CONVENIENT NUMBER OF EQUAL PARTS. THE ANGLE THROUGH WHICH THE CAM ROTATES DURING THE FOLLOWER MOVEMENT IS DIVIDED INTO THE SAME NUMBER OF DIVISIONS.

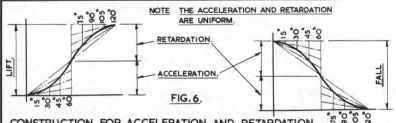

NOTE　THE ACCELERATION AND RETARDATION ARE UNIFORM.

RETARDATION.

ACCELERATION.

LIFT

FALL

FIG. 6.

CONSTRUCTION FOR ACCELERATION AND RETARDATION.

ANGLE THROUGH WHICH CAM ROTATES DIVIDED INTO AN EVEN NUMBER OF DIVISIONS. FOR HALF THESE DIVISIONS FOLLOWER IS ACCELERATED. DURING THE SECOND HALF FOLLOWER IS RETARDED.

CAMS

To Construct a Plate Cam Profile

The method for drawing the profile of a plate cam to operate a point or knife edged follower is shown on page 116. The same general method is used for all plate cams but it is varied by the type of follower and its position relative to the cam axis.

First position the cam centre and the nearest approach of the follower to it. From this point lay off the maximum lift of the follower. Draw circles through these two points about the cam centre and divide them into 15° divisions. Construct the cam graph, positioning the angular displacement axis on a level with the lowest position of the follower. Now imagine the cam to be held stationary and the follower to be moved round it. To obtain the same motion as with the cam rotating, the follower must be moved in the opposite direction to the cam rotation. When the follower has moved through 15° its height will be given by the point on the cam graph at the 15° station. Project this point to the line of action of the follower, which in this case is the vertical centreline of the cam, and swing it about the cam centre with compasses to cut the 15° line on the cam. Succeeding points are obtained in the same way. Where the follower remains at the same height, or 'dwells', the radius of the cam is constant. When points on all the 15° radial lines have been plotted, a smooth curve drawn through them will be the cam profile. Complete the cam by an arrow showing the direction of rotation.

In the worked examples 15° angular displacement divisions have been used. Cases may arise in which other divisions would be necessary.

The construction of a radial cam to work with a flat follower is shown on page 117. As before, points on the profile of the cam are positioned on the radial displacement lines by projection from the cam graph. These points lie on the face of the flat follower. Lines representing the follower face are drawn through them at right angles to the angular displacement lines. The cam profile must be tangential to these lines.

It should be noticed that the point of contact between the cam profile and the follower face is in most cases a considerable distance from the angular displacement line. This point must be borne in mind when deciding the size of the follower face.

The example on page 118 is a plate cam which gives motion to a roller follower. In this case points projected from the cam graph to the radial displacement lines on the cam are positions of the centre of the follower roller. The roller must be drawn at each of these positions, the cam profile being tangential to the rollers.

Note, that in examples involving roller followers the angular displacement axis of the cam graph is positioned on a level with the start position of the roller centre. This ensures that lift points on the cam graph can be projected directly to the cam.

CAMS.

PLATE CAM DESIGNED TO IMPART MOTION TO KNIFE EDGE FOLLOWER.

CAM DATA.
0°–180° LIFT 24mm WITH SIMPLE HARMONIC MOTION.
180°–240° REST INTERVAL
240°–360° FALL 24mm WITH ACCELERATION AND RETARDATION. (UNIFORM)

ROTATION OF CAM ANTI-CLOCKWISE.
LEAST THICKNESS OF METAL ROUND CAM CENTRE 38mm
DIA. OF CAM SHAFT 24mm

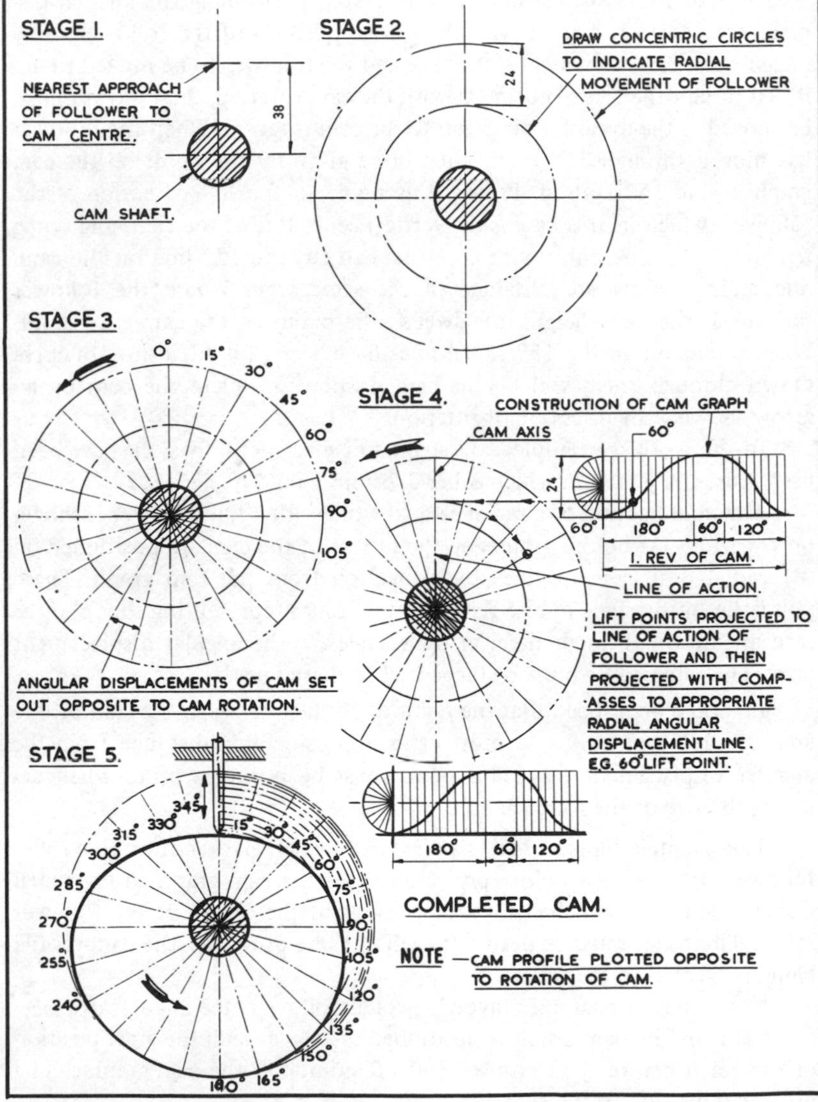

STAGE 1.

NEAREST APPROACH
OF FOLLOWER TO
CAM CENTRE.

38

CAM SHAFT.

STAGE 2.

24

DRAW CONCENTRIC CIRCLES
TO INDICATE RADIAL
MOVEMENT OF FOLLOWER

STAGE 3.

0° 15° 30° 45° 60° 75° 90° 105°

ANGULAR DISPLACEMENTS OF CAM SET
OUT OPPOSITE TO CAM ROTATION.

STAGE 4.

CAM AXIS

CONSTRUCTION OF CAM GRAPH

60°

24

60° 180° 60° 120°

1. REV OF CAM.

LINE OF ACTION.

LIFT POINTS PROJECTED TO
LINE OF ACTION OF
FOLLOWER AND THEN
PROJECTED WITH COMP-
ASSES TO APPROPRIATE
RADIAL ANGULAR
DISPLACEMENT LINE.
E.G. 60° LIFT POINT.

STAGE 5.

345° 330° 315° 300° 285° 270° 255° 240°
15° 30° 45° 60° 75° 90° 105° 120° 135° 150°
180° 165°

180° 60° 120°

COMPLETED CAM.

NOTE — CAM PROFILE PLOTTED OPPOSITE
TO ROTATION OF CAM.

CAMS.

PLATE CAM DESIGNED TO IMPART MOTION TO A FLAT FOLLOWER.

CAM DATA.
0° - 120° LIFT 32mm WITH UNIFORM VELOCITY
120° - 180° DWELL INTERVAL.
180° - 360° FALL 32mm WITH SIMPLE HARMONIC MOTION.
CAM ROTATION ANTI-CLOCKWISE. CAM SHAFT DIA. 24mm
NEAREST APPROACH OF FOLLOWER TO CAM CENTRE 32mm

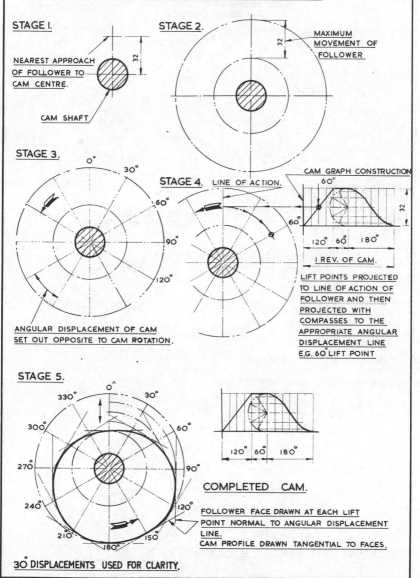

STAGE 1.

NEAREST APPROACH OF FOLLOWER TO CAM CENTRE.

CAM SHAFT

STAGE 2.

MAXIMUM MOVEMENT OF FOLLOWER

STAGE 3.

ANGULAR DISPLACEMENT OF CAM SET OUT OPPOSITE TO CAM ROTATION.

STAGE 4. LINE OF ACTION.

CAM GRAPH CONSTRUCTION

I REV. OF CAM.

LIFT POINTS PROJECTED TO LINE OF ACTION OF FOLLOWER AND THEN PROJECTED WITH COMPASSES TO THE APPROPRIATE ANGULAR DISPLACEMENT LINE E.G. 60° LIFT POINT

STAGE 5.

COMPLETED CAM.

FOLLOWER FACE DRAWN AT EACH LIFT POINT NORMAL TO ANGULAR DISPLACEMENT LINE.
CAM PROFILE DRAWN TANGENTIAL TO FACES.

30° DISPLACEMENTS USED FOR CLARITY.

CAMS.

PLATE CAM DESIGNED TO IMPART MOTION TO A ROLLER FOLLOWER

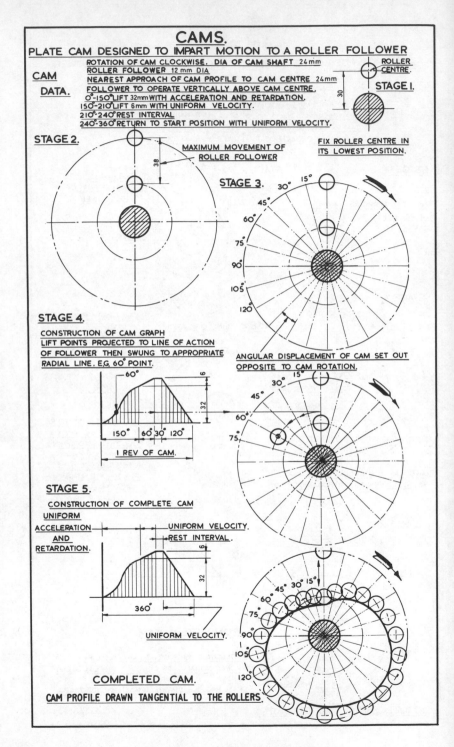

CAM DATA.

ROTATION OF CAM CLOCKWISE. DIA OF CAM SHAFT 24mm
ROLLER FOLLOWER 12 mm DIA
NEAREST APPROACH OF CAM PROFILE TO CAM CENTRE 24mm
FOLLOWER TO OPERATE VERTICALLY ABOVE CAM CENTRE.
0°-150° LIFT 32mm WITH ACCELERATION AND RETARDATION.
150°-210° LIFT 6mm WITH UNIFORM VELOCITY.
210°-240° REST INTERVAL
240°-360° RETURN TO START POSITION WITH UNIFORM VELOCITY.

ROLLER CENTRE.
STAGE I.

STAGE 2.

MAXIMUM MOVEMENT OF ROLLER FOLLOWER

FIX ROLLER CENTRE IN ITS LOWEST POSITION.

STAGE 3.

15° 30° 45° 60° 75° 90° 105° 120°

STAGE 4.

CONSTRUCTION OF CAM GRAPH
LIFT POINTS PROJECTED TO LINE OF ACTION
OF FOLLOWER THEN SWUNG TO APPROPRIATE
RADIAL LINE. E.G. 60° POINT.

ANGULAR DISPLACEMENT OF CAM SET OUT
OPPOSITE TO CAM ROTATION.

60°

6
32

150° 60° 30° 120°

I REV OF CAM.

15° 30° 45° 60° 75°

STAGE 5.

CONSTRUCTION OF COMPLETE CAM

UNIFORM
ACCELERATION
AND
RETARDATION.

UNIFORM VELOCITY.

REST INTERVAL.

6
32

360°

UNIFORM VELOCITY.

15° 30° 45° 60° 75° 90° 105° 120°

COMPLETED CAM.

CAM PROFILE DRAWN TANGENTIAL TO THE ROLLERS.

CAMS.

DESIGN OF CAM TO IMPART MOTION TO AN OFFSET ROLLER FOLLOWER.

CAM DATA.

ROTATION OF CAM CLOCKWISE.
DIA. OF CAMSHAFT 24mm
NEAREST APPROACH OF ROLLER CENTRE TO CAM CENTRE 38mm
LINE OF ACTION OF FOLLOWER OFFSET 20mm TO RIGHT OF CAM ℄
ROLLER FOLLOWER Ø 20
0°-105° LIFT 24mm WITH UNIFORM VELOCITY.
105°-150° REST INTERVAL.
150°-240° LIFT 12mm WITH SIMPLE HARMONIC MOTION.
240°-360° RETURN TO START POSITION WITH ACCELERATION AND RETARDATION.

STAGE 1.

FIX ROLLER CENTRE IN LOWEST POSITION.

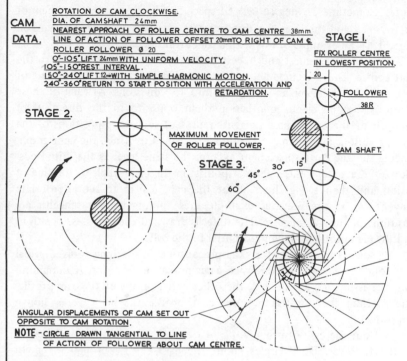

FOLLOWER
38R
CAM SHAFT.

STAGE 2.

MAXIMUM MOVEMENT OF ROLLER FOLLOWER.

STAGE 3.

ANGULAR DISPLACEMENTS OF CAM SET OUT OPPOSITE TO CAM ROTATION.

NOTE - CIRCLE DRAWN TANGENTIAL TO LINE OF ACTION OF FOLLOWER ABOUT CAM CENTRE.

STAGE 4. CONSTRUCTION OF CAM GRAPH
LIFT POINTS PROJECTED TO LINE OF ACTION OF FOLLOWER AND THEN SWUNG TO THE APPROPRIATE TANGENT E.G. 210° POINT.

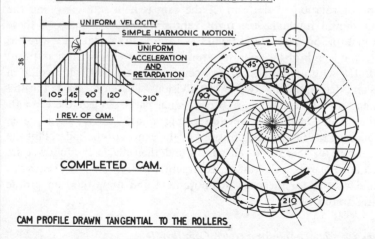

UNIFORM VELOCITY
SIMPLE HARMONIC MOTION.
UNIFORM ACCELERATION AND RETARDATION
36
105° 45° 90° 120° 210°
1 REV. OF CAM.

COMPLETED CAM.

CAM PROFILE DRAWN TANGENTIAL TO THE ROLLERS.

The previous examples of cam design have all had in-line followers, that is, the line of action of the follower has been vertically above the cam centre. Sometimes, owing to lack of space for the mechanism, this cannot be arranged and the line of action must be offset to one side. The cam on page 119 is an example of this with a roller follower.

First fix the highest and lowest positions of the roller relative to the cam centre. Draw a circle about the cam centre tangential to the line of action of the follower and divide it into 15° divisions. At each of these divisions draw tangents, numbering them opposite to the direction of rotation of the cam. These tangents represent successive positions of the line of action, as it is moved round the cam. Construct the cam graph, placing the angular displacement axis on the same level as the initial position of the roller centre. Project points on the cam graph to the line of action and then swing them about the cam centre to the appropriate tangent. As in the previous example these points on the tangents are positions of the roller centre. The roller is drawn at each of these positions and the cam profile is drawn tangential to the rollers.

In some applications, for example, automatic machine tools, a radial arm follower is more suitable than a reciprocating follower. A radial arm follower is pivoted at one end, the other end working on the cam profile. The method for constructing the cam profile in this case is shown opposite.

Set out the cam centre, pivot centre and extreme positions of the end of the follower. Draw circles about the cam centre through the pivot centre and ends of the follower. Divide the circle through the pivot into 15° divisions, starting from the pivot, and number them opposite to the direction of rotation of the cam. If the cam is held stationary and the follower moved round it, the pivot centre will move to each of these points in turn. So, with these points as centres draw arcs with a radius equal to the length of the follower arm. The follower is to move outward through 45° with uniform angular velocity during the first half revolution of the cam, that is, the first twelve 15° divisions. Therefore, divide the 45° movement of the follower into twelve equal parts. Project these points from the lift line of the follower to the appropriate arcs R_1, R_2, R_3, etc., thus obtaining the first twelve positions of the centre of the roller. Plot the roller centres for the 30° dwell period and then divide the follower arc into ten equal parts for the return movement. Position the roller centres in the same way as for the outward movement and draw the cam profile tangential to the rollers.

To Draw the Cam Graph for a Given Cam Profile

This is the reverse of the examples given previously. The example shown on page 122 illustrates the method and is for an offset roller follower.

CAMS.

PLATE CAM DESIGNED TO IMPART MOTION TO A RADIAL ARM ROLLER ENDED FOLLOWER.

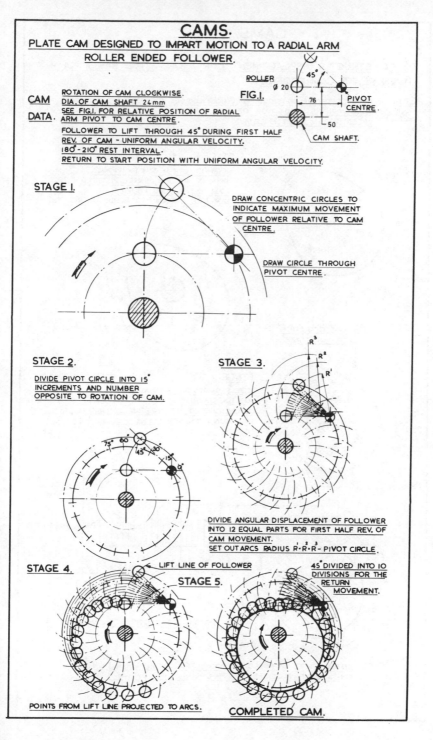

FIG.I.

ROLLER Ø 20   45°   PIVOT CENTRE.
76   50   PIVOT CENTRE.
CAM SHAFT.

CAM DATA.
ROTATION OF CAM CLOCKWISE.
DIA. OF CAM SHAFT 24mm
SEE FIG.I. FOR RELATIVE POSITION OF RADIAL ARM PIVOT TO CAM CENTRE.
FOLLOWER TO LIFT THROUGH 45° DURING FIRST HALF REV. OF CAM - UNIFORM ANGULAR VELOCITY.
180° - 210° REST INTERVAL.
RETURN TO START POSITION WITH UNIFORM ANGULAR VELOCITY.

STAGE I.

DRAW CONCENTRIC CIRCLES TO INDICATE MAXIMUM MOVEMENT OF FOLLOWER RELATIVE TO CAM CENTRE.

DRAW CIRCLE THROUGH PIVOT CENTRE.

STAGE 2.

DIVIDE PIVOT CIRCLE INTO 15° INCREMENTS AND NUMBER OPPOSITE TO ROTATION OF CAM.

STAGE 3.

DIVIDE ANGULAR DISPLACEMENT OF FOLLOWER INTO 12 EQUAL PARTS FOR FIRST HALF REV. OF CAM MOVEMENT.
SET OUT ARCS RADIUS $R^1 \cdot R^2 \cdot R^3$ - PIVOT CIRCLE.

STAGE 4.

LIFT LINE OF FOLLOWER

POINTS FROM LIFT LINE PROJECTED TO ARCS.

STAGE 5.

45° DIVIDED INTO 10 DIVISIONS FOR THE RETURN MOVEMENT.

COMPLETED CAM.

CAMS.

TO CONSTRUCT A DISPLACEMENT CURVE ON A TIME BASIS FOR A GIVEN PLATE CAM PROFILE.

CAM DATA. PROFILE SHOWN IN FIG I. FOLLOWER OFFSET 24mm TO LEFT OF CAM SHAFT CENTRE. ROTATION OF CAM CLOCKWISE. SPEED OF CAM SHAFT 15 R.P.M.

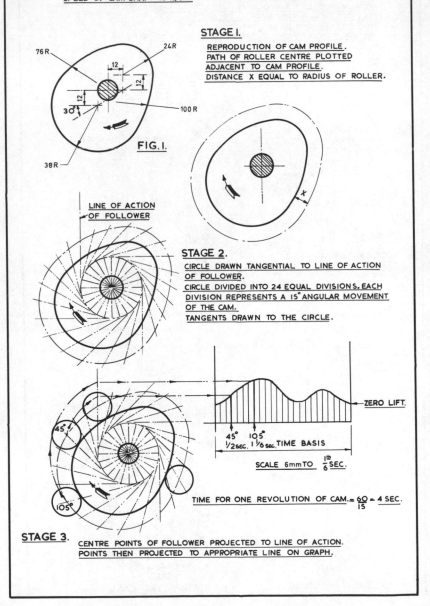

STAGE I.
REPRODUCTION OF CAM PROFILE.
PATH OF ROLLER CENTRE PLOTTED
ADJACENT TO CAM PROFILE.
DISTANCE X EQUAL TO RADIUS OF ROLLER.

FIG. I.

STAGE 2.
CIRCLE DRAWN TANGENTIAL TO LINE OF ACTION
OF FOLLOWER.
CIRCLE DIVIDED INTO 24 EQUAL DIVISIONS. EACH
DIVISION REPRESENTS A 15° ANGULAR MOVEMENT
OF THE CAM.
TANGENTS DRAWN TO THE CIRCLE.

LINE OF ACTION OF FOLLOWER

ZERO LIFT.

45°   105° TIME BASIS
½SEC. 1⅙SEC.

SCALE 6mm TO $\frac{1^{th}}{6}$ SEC.

TIME FOR ONE REVOLUTION OF CAM. $= \frac{60}{15} = 4$ SEC.

STAGE 3.
CENTRE POINTS OF FOLLOWER PROJECTED TO LINE OF ACTION.
POINTS THEN PROJECTED TO APPROPRIATE LINE ON GRAPH.

122

The method for in-line followers of other types can easily be determined by the student.

Start by drawing the cam profile and plot round it a parallel curve representing the path of the roller centre. Position the line of action of the follower and draw a circle tangential to it using the cam centre as centre. Divide this circle into 15° divisions and draw tangents at each, numbering them opposite to the rotation of the cam. Where these tangents cut the curve drawn parallel to the cam profile, are positions of the roller centre. Swing these points round the cam centre to the line of action of the follower and project them into the cam graph to the appropriate displacement line.

The cam graph may have a time basis as shown, instead of an angular displacement basis. To determine the time basis calculate the time taken by the cam to make one revolution and divide it by twenty-four. This gives the time for the cam to turn through 15°, enabling the graph to be related to the roller centre positions on the cam.

Cylindrical Cams

The drawing of a cylindrical cam, illustrated on page 124, requires a development of the cam surface. From this development a template is made which is used in the manufacture of the cam.

Start by drawing an elevation and end view of the cam blank, dividing both into a number of equal parts. Twelve have been used in the illustration for clarity but the motion of the follower may require 15° divisions or others. From the elevation project the development of the cam surface, dividing it into the same number of equal parts as the elevation and end view. Lay off on the development the extreme positions of the follower and between these points plot the motion of the centre of the follower roller in the same way that motions are plotted on a plate cam graph. Draw the roller at each point where the curve crosses an angular displacement line, and draw the profile of the roller groove tangential to these circles. The elevation can then be completed by projection from the development.

It is usual to use a roller follower to work with a cylindrical cam but the roller must be conical or it will slip on the groove profile. This happens because points on the outside of the cam move faster than points at the bottom of the groove. For simplicity a cylindrical roller has been assumed for the cam in the worked example and in the problems which follow.

CAM PROBLEMS

1. A plate cam rotating in a clockwise direction is to give an in-line point follower the following motion.

0°−120° Lift 32 mm with uniform velocity.

120°−180° Dwell.

180°−360° Fall 32 mm with simple harmonic motion.

CAMS.

DESIGN OF A CYLINDRICAL CAM.

CAM DATA.
0° – 180° FOLLOWER MOVES 64mm TO RIGHT WITH SIMPLE HARMONIC MOTION
180° – 240° FOLLOWER DWELLS.
240° – 360° FOLLOWER RETURNS TO START POSITION WITH SIMPLE HARMONIC MOTION. CAM DIA. 64mm CAM LENGTH 88mm CAM ROTATION CLOCKWISE.
ROLLER DIA. 10mm GROOVE DEPTH 6mm

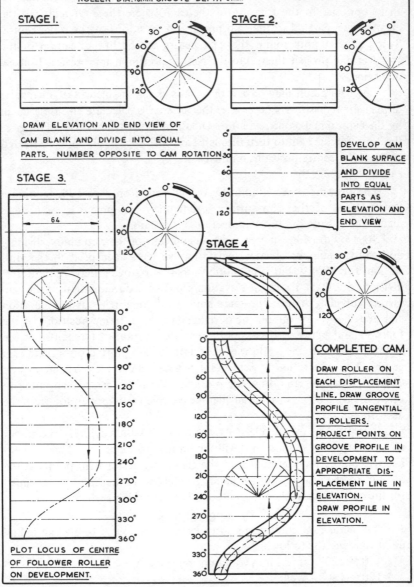

STAGE I.

STAGE 2.

DRAW ELEVATION AND END VIEW OF CAM BLANK AND DIVIDE INTO EQUAL PARTS. NUMBER OPPOSITE TO CAM ROTATION

DEVELOP CAM BLANK SURFACE AND DIVIDE INTO EQUAL PARTS AS ELEVATION AND END VIEW

STAGE 3.

64

STAGE 4

COMPLETED CAM.

DRAW ROLLER ON EACH DISPLACEMENT LINE. DRAW GROOVE PROFILE TANGENTIAL TO ROLLERS. PROJECT POINTS ON GROOVE PROFILE IN DEVELOPMENT TO APPROPRIATE DIS-PLACEMENT LINE IN ELEVATION. DRAW PROFILE IN ELEVATION.

PLOT LOCUS OF CENTRE OF FOLLOWER ROLLER ON DEVELOPMENT.

Draw full size the cam profile if the minimum cam radius is 38 mm and the cam shaft diameter is 24 mm.

2. Draw full size the profile of a radial cam to operate an in-line knife edge follower, the follower motion being
    0°– 60° Dwell
    60°–180° Lift 38 mm with uniform acceleration and retardation.
    180°–240° Dwell.
    240°–360° Fall 38 mm with simple harmonic motion.
The cam rotates anti-clockwise, the least thickness of metal round the cam centre is 32 mm and the cam shaft diameter is 22 mm.

3. An in-line flat follower is to be given the motion described below by a plate cam rotating anti-clockwise. The nearest approach of the follower to the cam centre is to be 38 mm and the cam shaft diameter is to be 24 mm. Set out full size the profile of the cam.
    0°–150° Lift 44 mm with uniform acceleration and retardation.
    150°–210° Dwell.
    210°–270° Fall 20 mm with uniform velocity.
    270°–360° Fall 24 mm with simple harmonic motion.

4. Lay out full size the profile of a radial cam to give an in-line roller follower, 16 mm diameter, the following motion
    0°–90° Dwell.
    90°–180° Lift 38 mm with simple harmonic motion.
    180°–270° Dwell.
    270°–360° Fall 38 mm with uniform velocity.
Cam rotation clockwise, minimum cam radius 56 mm, cam shaft diameter 24 mm.

5. A plate cam rotating anti-clockwise at 10 r.p.m. is to give an in-line roller follower the following motion in one revolution.
    Lift 38 mm with simple harmonic motion in 1.5 seconds
    Dwell for 1 second.
    Fall 20 mm with uniform velocity in 1.25 seconds.
    Fall 18 mm with simple harmonic motion in 1.5 seconds.
    Dwell for the remainder of the revolution.
Draw full size the cam profile making the minimum distance from the cam centre to the roller centre 50 mm, the roller diameter 20 mm and the cam shaft diameter 32 mm. Use a scale of 20 mm to 1 second on the displacement axis of the cam graph.

6. An off-set roller follower, 20 mm diameter, is to be given the motion

set out below by a plate cam rotating clockwise. Construct full size the profile of the cam.

Lift 38 mm with uniform velocity in 120° of cam rotation.

Dwell for 60° of cam rotation.

Fall 38 mm with simple harmonic motion in 90° of cam rotation.

Dwell for the remainder of the revolution.

The line of action of the follower is off-set 32 mm to the left of the vertical centreline of the cam. The minimum distance from the cam centre to the roller centre is 56 mm. The cam shaft diameter is 24 mm.

7.   Draw full size the profile of a plate cam rotating clockwise which gives a 18 mm off-set roller follower the following motion.

0°−120° Lift 24 mm with uniform acceleration and retardation.

120°−180° Dwell.

180°−240° Lift 12 mm with uniform velocity.

240°−360° Fall 36 mm with simple harmonic motion.

The minimum distance from cam centre to roller centre is 50 mm, the cam shaft diameter is 20 mm and the line of action of the follower is off-set 24 mm to the right of the vertical centreline of the cam.

8.   A radial cam rotating anti-clockwise is to operate an off-set flat follower giving it the following motion.

0°−180° Lift 36 mm with uniform acceleration and retardation.

180°−270° Dwell.

270°−360° Fall 36 mm with simple harmonic motion.

Construct the cam profile full size if the follower is off-set 22 mm to the right of the vertical centreline of the cam. The nearest approach of the follower to the horizontal centreline of the cam is 40 mm and the cam shaft diameter is 32 mm.

9.   Figure 1 on page 128 shows a radial arm roller follower which is to be operated by a plate cam rotating clockwise. The motion given to the follower is to be

Dwell for first 45° of cam rotation.

Move outward through 30° with uniform angular velocity during the next 90° of cam rotation.

Dwell for next 45° of cam rotation.

Move inward through 15° with uniform angular velocity during the next 60° of cam rotation.

Dwell for next 60° of cam rotation.

Move inward through 15° with uniform angular velocity during the remainder of the revolution of the cam.

Construct the cam profile full size.

10. The guide block in the mechanism shown in Figure 2 on page 128 is reciprocated along the line AB by a plate cam rotating clockwise. The plate cam operates a radial arm roller follower which is linked to the guide block as shown. The block is to move 54 mm to the left with simple harmonic motion while the cam rotates through 90°. It is then to remain stationary for 180° of cam rotation, returning to its starting position with simple harmonic motion during the final 90° rotation of the cam. If the starting position is as shown in the Figure, construct full size the cam profile.

11. Figure 3 on page 128 shows the profile of a plate cam to operate an in-line roller follower. If the cam rotates clockwise determine the displacement curve for the follower on an angular basis using a scale of 6 mm to 15°. Assume the position of the cam in the Figure to be its starting position.

12. A plate cam to operate an off-set 24 mm diameter roller follower is shown in Figure 4 on page 128. If the line of action of the follower is 24 mm to the right of the vertical centreline of the cam, draw the cam displacement curve on a time basis when the cam makes 62.5 r.p.m. 15° angular divisions of cam rotation must be considered and a scale of 6 mm to $\frac{1}{25}$ of a second must be used when plotting the displacement curve. The cam rotates anti-clockwise.

13. The displacement curve for a radial cam to rotate clockwise at 40 r.p.m. is shown incompletely in Figure 5 on page 129. Complete the graph to the given scale and construct the cam profile full size if the roller follower is 20 mm diameter with the line of action off-set 32 mm to the left of the cam centre. The nearest approach of the roller centre to the cam centre is to be 40 mm and the cam shaft diameter is to be 25 mm.

14. Figure 6 on page 129 shows a blank for a cylindrical cam. Complete the given view full size, adding a development, if the follower moves 76 mm to the right with uniform velocity during one-third of a revolution of the cam, dwells for the next sixth of a revolution, and returns to the start position with simple harmonic motion during the remainder of the revolution. The cam rotates clockwise when viewed from the left of the given view.

15. The cylindrical cam shown in Figure 7 on page 129 is to move the follower 64 mm to the left with simple harmonic motion during the first half revolution of the cam, and return it to the start position with uniform velocity during the second half revolution. Draw the cam full size, with a

CAM PROBLEMS.

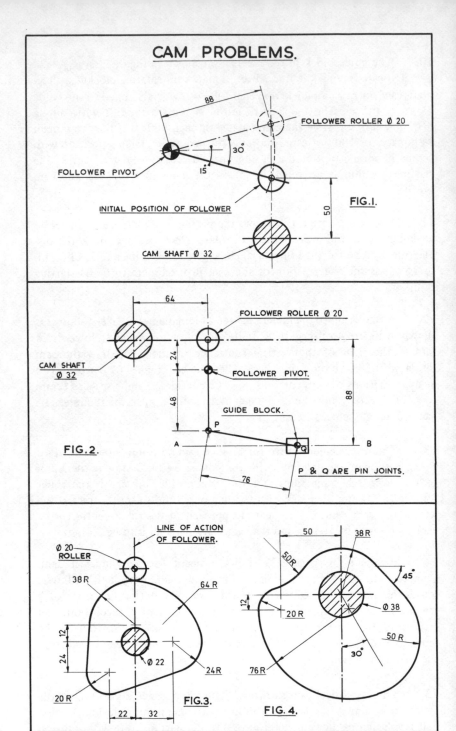

FOLLOWER ROLLER Ø 20

88

30°

FOLLOWER PIVOT

15°

INITIAL POSITION OF FOLLOWER

50

FIG.1.

CAM SHAFT Ø 32

64

FOLLOWER ROLLER Ø 20

CAM SHAFT
Ø 32

24

FOLLOWER PIVOT.

48

88

GUIDE BLOCK.

FIG.2.

P

A

Q

B

76

P & Q ARE PIN JOINTS.

LINE OF ACTION
OF FOLLOWER.

Ø 20
ROLLER

38 R

64 R

12

24

Ø 22

24R

20 R

22 32

FIG.3.

50

38 R

50 R

45°

12

20 R

Ø 38

50 R

76 R

30°

FIG. 4.

128

CAM PROBLEMS.

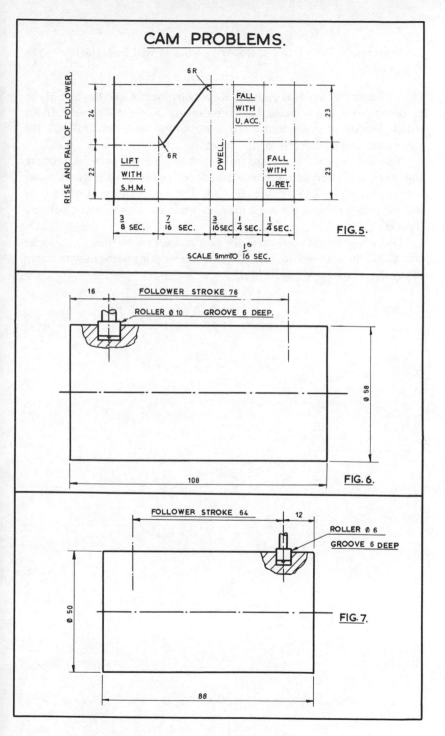

RISE AND FALL OF FOLLOWER.

6 R

24

22

6 R

LIFT
WITH
S.H.M.

DWELL.

FALL
WITH
U. ACC.

FALL
WITH
U. RET.

23

23

$\frac{3}{8}$ SEC. $\frac{7}{16}$ SEC. $\frac{3}{16}$ SEC $\frac{1}{4}$ SEC. $\frac{1}{4}$ SEC.

FIG. 5.

SCALE 5mm TO $\frac{1}{16}$ SEC.

---

16   FOLLOWER STROKE 76

ROLLER Ø 10   GROOVE 6 DEEP.

Ø 58

108

FIG. 6.

FOLLOWER STROKE 64   12

ROLLER Ø 6
GROOVE 6 DEEP

Ø 50

FIG. 7.

88

129

development, if the rotation is clockwise when viewed from the left of the given view.

16.   Figures 8 and 8(a) opposite show two blocks A and B which are to be reciprocated by an oscillating plate cam and a system of levers. If the initial position of the system is as shown in Figure 8, draw full size the cam profile from the following information.

Block A is to move 48 mm to the left with simple harmonic motion, and block B is to move 64 mm to the left with uniform velocity while the cam rotates anti-clockwise through 120°. The blocks are to return to their starting positions with the same motions while the cam rotates clockwise through 120°.

The non-working portions of the cam profile may be shown as circular arcs about the cam centre, blending into the working portions with 6 mm fillet radii, as shown in Figure 8(a).

CAM PROBLEMS

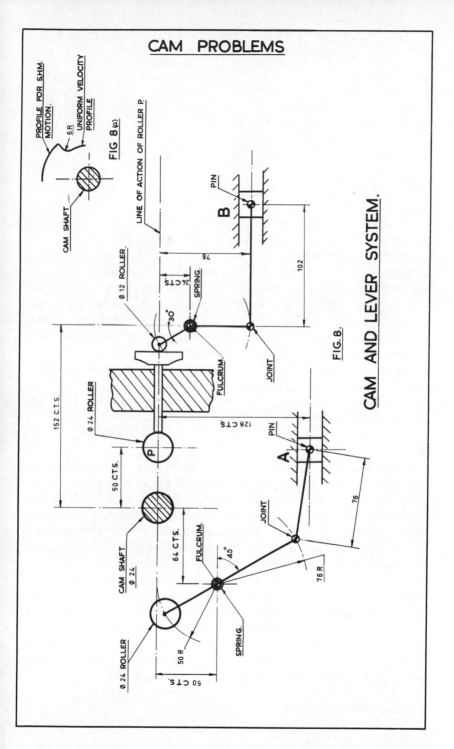

FIG 8 (a)

PROFILE FOR S.H.M. MOTION.
6 R
UNIFORM VELOCITY PROFILE

CAM SHAFT

LINE OF ACTION OF ROLLER P.

FIG. 8.

CAM AND LEVER SYSTEM.

131

6

INVOLUTE GEARS

Spur Gears

Imagine two cylinders in contact at a common point on their circumferences. If one cylinder is turned on its axis the other will be turned by the friction between the cylinders at the point of contact. The driven cylinder will rotate in the opposite direction to the driving cylinder and the ratio of the angular velocities will equal the inverse ratio of the diameters. It is obvious that very little power can be transmitted by this system before the cylinders slip on each other. To avoid this slipping, slots are cut in the cylinders with projections added between them. These slots and projections form teeth and the cylinders become spur gears. To keep the ratio of the angular velocities constant the teeth must have profiles of either cycloidal or involute form. The involute form is much commoner than the cycloidal, mainly because it is easier to manufacture. Only involute gears will be considered here.

Involute Construction

Figure 1 shows the method for constructing an involute to a circle. The involute is generated by rolling a straight line round the circle, when points on the line will trace out involutes. Draw the circle, which is called the base circle, and divide its circumference into a number of equal parts. Through the points so obtained on the circumference draw tangents. Mark off on these tangents the lengths of corresponding arcs on the base circle. The ends of the tangents will then be points on the involute.

Figure 2 shows the effect on the involute of varying the base circle diameter. If it is increased the involute becomes straighter, until when the base circle diameter is infinitely large the involute is a straight line. Thus an involute rack, which may be thought of as a gear with an infinitely large base circle diameter, has straight sided teeth. This property of an involute rack is made use of in the cutting of involute spur gear teeth on hobbing machines, the Sunderland gear planer and the Maag grinder.

Involute Spur Gear Terms

The names of the various parts and dimensions of spur gears and their teeth are illustrated in Figures 3, 4 and 5.

INVOLUTE GEARS.

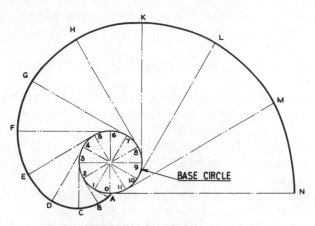

BASE CIRCLE

TANGENT LENGTH 1. A. = LENGTH O.1.
TANGENT LENGTH 2 B = LENGTH O.2.   FIG.1.
TANGENT LENGTH 3 C = LENGTH O.3.

CONSTRUCTION OF TRUE INVOLUTE.

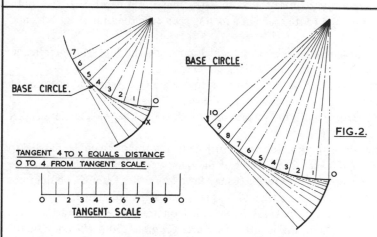

BASE CIRCLE.

BASE CIRCLE.

FIG.2.

TANGENT 4 TO X EQUALS DISTANCE
O TO 4 FROM TANGENT SCALE.

TANGENT SCALE

VARIATION IN INVOLUTE PROFILE AS A RESULT OF CHANGING
BASE CIRCLE DIAMETER.

NOTE.— WHEN THE BASE CIRCLE DIAMETER IS INCREASED TO INFINITY
THE INVOLUTE BECOMES A STRAIGHT LINE. THUS THE INVOLUTE
RACK HAS STRAIGHT SIDED TEETH.

The *pitch circle* is the circle representing the original cylinder which transmitted motion by friction, and its diameter the *pitch circle diameter.*

The *centre distance* of a pair of meshing spur gears is the sum of their pitch circle radii. One of the advantages of the involute system is that small variations in the centre distance do not affect the correct working of the gears.

The *pitch point* is the point of contact between the pitch circles of two gears in mesh.

The *line of action.* Contact between the teeth of meshing gears takes place along a line tangential to the two base circles. This line passes through the pitch point and is called the *line of action.*

The *pressure angle.* The angle between the line of action and the common tangent to the pitch circles at the pitch point is the *pressure angle* or *angle of obliquity.*

The *addendum* is the radial height of a tooth above the pitch circle.

The *dedendum* is the radial depth below the pitch circle.

The *clearance* is the difference between the addendum and the dedendum.

The *whole depth* of a tooth is the sum of the addendum and dedendum.

The *working depth* of a tooth is the maximum depth that the tooth extends into the tooth space of a mating gear. It is the sum of the addenda of the gears.

The *addendum circle* is that which contains the tops of the teeth and its diameter is the *outside* or *blank diameter.*

The *dedendum* or *root circle* is that which contains the bottoms of the tooth spaces and its diameter is the *root diameter.*

The *tooth face* is the surface of a tooth above the pitch circle, parallel to the axis of the gear.

The *tooth flank* is the tooth surface below the pitch circle, parallel to the axis of the gear. If any part of the flank extends inside the base circle it cannot have involute form. It may have any other form which does not interfere with mating teeth, and is usually a straight radial line.

Circular tooth thickness is measured on the tooth around the pitch circle, that is, it is the length of an arc. *Chordal tooth thickness* is the chord of this arc.

The *pitch* of gear teeth may be expressed in any of the following ways:

Diametral pitch is the number of teeth per inch of pitch circle diameter. This is a ratio.

Circular pitch is the distance from a point on one tooth to the corresponding point on the next tooth, measured round the pitch circle.

Module pitch is the reciprocal of diametral pitch.

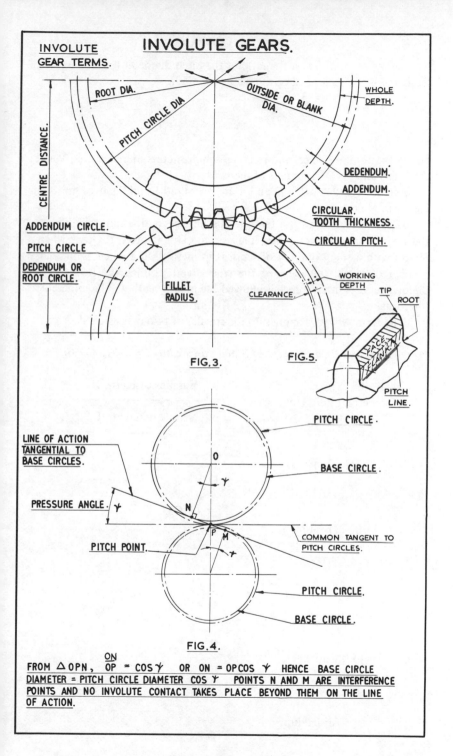

INVOLUTE GEARS.

INVOLUTE GEAR TERMS.

ROOT DIA.

OUTSIDE OR BLANK DIA.

WHOLE DEPTH.

PITCH CIRCLE DIA.

CENTRE DISTANCE.

ADDENDUM CIRCLE.

PITCH CIRCLE

DEDENDUM OR ROOT CIRCLE.

FILLET RADIUS.

CLEARANCE.

DEDENDUM.

ADDENDUM.

CIRCULAR. TOOTH THICKNESS.

CIRCULAR PITCH.

WORKING DEPTH

TIP

ROOT

FACE FLANK

PITCH LINE.

FIG. 3.

FIG. 5.

LINE OF ACTION TANGENTIAL TO BASE CIRCLES.

PRESSURE ANGLE. γ

PITCH POINT.

PITCH CIRCLE.

BASE CIRCLE.

COMMON TANGENT TO PITCH CIRCLES.

PITCH CIRCLE.

BASE CIRCLE.

FIG. 4.

FROM $\triangle$ OPN, $\dfrac{ON}{OP} = \cos\gamma$ OR ON = OP COS γ HENCE BASE CIRCLE DIAMETER = PITCH CIRCLE DIAMETER COS γ POINTS N AND M ARE INTERFERENCE POINTS AND NO INVOLUTE CONTACT TAKES PLACE BEYOND THEM ON THE LINE OF ACTION.

British Module 'm' is the ratio of the pitch diameter to the number of teeth and is the reciprocal of the diametral pitch.

$$m = \frac{D}{T} = \frac{d}{t}$$

where D and d are wheel and pinion pitch diameters in inches, and T and t are wheel and pinion numbers of teeth.

Metric Module: when D and d are measured in millimetres 'm' is the metric module.

If contact between the teeth of meshing gears does not take place on the line of action *interference* may occur. This is often the case when a pinion with a small number of teeth is in mesh with a wheel with a large number of teeth, the faces of the wheel teeth fouling the flanks of the pinion teeth. If interference is allowed the pinion teeth will be undercut at the roots.

The term *pinion* is applied to the smaller of two mating gears.

Proportions and Relationships of Standard Involute Spur Gear Teeth

$$\text{Diametral pitch, D.P.} = \frac{\text{number of teeth, T}}{\text{pitch circle diameter, P.C.D.}}$$

$$\text{Hence P.C.D.} = \frac{T}{D.P.}$$

$$\text{Circular pitch, p} = \frac{\pi \times P.C.D.}{T.}$$

$$\text{or, p} = \frac{\pi}{D.P.}$$

$$\text{Circular tooth thickness} = \frac{p}{2}$$

$$\text{Addendum} = \frac{1}{D.P.}$$

$$\text{Clearance} = \frac{p}{20} \text{ or } \frac{.157}{D.P.}$$

$$\text{Dedendum} = \text{Addendum} + \text{clearance.}$$

Pressure angle, ψ = 14½° or 20°. It is usually made 20° as this value reduces the possibility of interference. It also gives the tooth a wider root.

Base circle diameter, B.C.D. = P.C.D. cos ψ. (Refer to Figure 4 page 135). Involute gears will work correctly together if they have the same pressure angle and diametral pitch.

Approximate Constructions for the Involute Tooth Profile

It is usual to represent the involute curves on the teeth by circular arcs, since to draw them accurately would take too long. Three such approximate methods are shown in the following pages. The first two methods differ only at one point, depending on the number of teeth on the gear. First draw the pitch circle, diameter D, and a tangent to it to fix the pitch point. On the pitch circle radius draw a semi circle radius $\frac{D}{4}$ to cut at P an arc radius $\frac{D}{8}$ drawn with the pitch point as centre. Through P draw a circle about the gear centre. On this circle lie the centres of the profile arcs of the teeth. Draw the addendum and dedendum circles and from the pitch point mark off tooth widths $\frac{P}{2}$ around the pitch circle. From these points draw arcs radius $\frac{D}{8}$ to cut the circle for the centres of the profile arcs. For a gear of 30 teeth and over draw the profile arcs radius $\frac{D}{8}$ with these points as centres from the addendum circle to the dedendum circle. Complete the teeth with fillet radii equal to one-seventh of the widest tooth space. For a gear with less than 30 teeth draw the profile arcs as above and draw radial lines tangential to them before adding the fillet radii. This avoids having teeth which appear to be excessively undercut.

The third method can be used for a gear having any number of teeth and makes use of the base circle. This construction is more suitable for 20° pressure angle teeth than the previous methods as it produces teeth which have wider roots. Draw the pitch, addendum and dedendum circles and the base circle tangential to the line of action. On a convenient radial line fix a point A on the addendum circle and a point E on the base circle. Divide AE into three equal parts and through B, the division nearest A, draw a tangent to the base circle at D. Divide BD into four equal parts and through F, the division nearest D, draw a circle. The centres for the profile arcs lie on this circle and F is the centre for the profile arc passing through B. From C, the intersection of this profile arc and the pitch circle, mark

INVOLUTE GEARS.

CONSTRUCTION OF GEAR TEETH SUITABLE FOR GEARS OF 30 TEETH AND OVER. PRESSURE ANGLE 14½°

GEAR DATA   PRESSURE ANGLE 14½° D.P.2 NUMBER OF TEETH 30

CALCULATED DATA.

$$\text{PITCH CIRCLE DIAMETER} = D = \frac{T}{DP} = \frac{30}{2} = 15''$$

$$\text{ADDENDUM} = \frac{1}{DP} = \frac{1}{2} = \cdot5''$$

$$\text{CIRCULAR PITCH} \quad T = \frac{\pi D}{DP} = \frac{\pi}{2} = \frac{3\cdot142}{2} = 1\cdot571''$$

$$\text{CLEARANCE} = \frac{P}{20} = \frac{1\cdot571}{20} = \cdot07855''$$

$$\text{DEDENDUM} = \text{ADDENDUM} + \text{CLEARANCE}$$
$$= \cdot5 + \cdot07855 = \cdot57855''$$

$$\text{TOOTH THICKNESS} = \frac{P}{2} = \cdot7855''$$

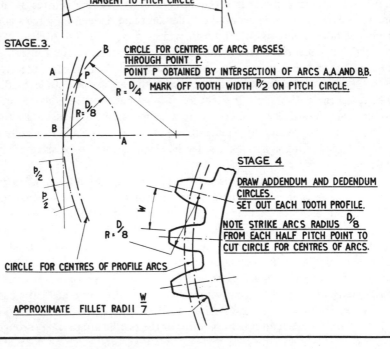

STAGE I.

STAGE 2.

PITCH CIRCLE

$R = \frac{D}{2}$

$R = \frac{D}{4}$

B

B

TANGENT TO PITCH CIRCLE

STAGE.3.

B   CIRCLE FOR CENTRES OF ARCS PASSES THROUGH POINT P.
POINT P OBTAINED BY INTERSECTION OF ARCS A.A AND B.B.
$R = \frac{D}{4}$ MARK OFF TOOTH WIDTH $\frac{P}{2}$ ON PITCH CIRCLE.

A
P
$R = \frac{D}{8}$
B
A

$\frac{P}{2}$
$\frac{P}{2}$
$R = \frac{D}{8}$

CIRCLE FOR CENTRES OF PROFILE ARCS

APPROXIMATE FILLET RADII $\frac{W}{7}$

STAGE 4

DRAW ADDENDUM AND DEDENDUM CIRCLES.
SET OUT EACH TOOTH PROFILE.

NOTE STRIKE ARCS RADIUS $\frac{D}{8}$ FROM EACH HALF PITCH POINT TO CUT CIRCLE FOR CENTRES OF ARCS.

W

138

INVOLUTE GEARS.

CONSTRUCTION OF GEAR TEETH SUITABLE FOR GEARS WITH LESS THAN 30 TEETH. PRESSURE ANGLE $14\frac{1}{2}°$

GEAR DATA. PRESSURE ANGLE $14\frac{1}{2}°$ D.P. 3. NUMBER OF TEETH 12.

CALCULATED DATA.

$$\text{PITCH CIRCLE DIAMETER} = D = \frac{T}{D.P.} = \frac{12}{3} = 4''$$

$$\text{ADDENDUM} = \frac{1}{D.P.} = \frac{1}{3} = \cdot3333''$$

$$\text{CIRCULAR PITCH} = \frac{\pi D}{T} = \frac{\pi}{D.P.} = \frac{3\cdot142}{3} = 1\cdot047''$$

$$\text{CLEARANCE} = \frac{P}{20} = \frac{1\cdot047}{20} = \cdot05235''$$

$$\text{DEDENDUM} = \text{ADDENDUM} + \text{CLEARANCE}$$
$$\cdot3333 + \cdot05235 = \cdot3856''$$

$$\text{TOOTH THICKNESS} = \frac{P}{2} = \cdot5235''$$

STAGE 1. DRAW PITCH CIRCLE AND TANGENT TO PITCH CIRCLE.

$R = \dfrac{D}{2}$

STAGE 2. CONSTRUCT ARCS A.A. AND B.B. TO MEET AT POINT P.

$R = \dfrac{D}{8}$ $R = \dfrac{D}{4}$

STAGE 3. DRAW CIRCLE FOR CENTRES OF PROFILE ARCS THROUGH POINT P.

CIRCLE FOR CENTRES OF ARCS.

STAGE 4. DRAW ADDENDUM AND DEDENDUM CIRCLES.

$R = \dfrac{D}{8}$ $R = \dfrac{D}{4}$

MARK HALF PITCH WIDTHS $\dfrac{P}{2}$ ALONG THE PITCH CIRCLE.

DEDENDUM CIRCLE.

ADDENDUM CIRCLE.

STAGE 5.

SET OUT ARCS RADIUS $\dfrac{D}{8}$ FROM EACH HALF PITCH POINT TO CUT CIRCLE FOR CENTRES OF ARCS.

DRAW THE CURVE PROFILE FOR EACH TOOTH.

DRAW TANGENTS TO THE ARCS FROM THE CENTRE OF THE GEAR.

NOTE PORTION OF TOOTH PROFILE CONFORMS TO A RADIAL LINE SEE LINES F AND G.

FILLET RADII AS FOR PREVIOUS CONSTRUCTION.

$R = \dfrac{D}{8}$

INVOLUTE GEARS.

CONSTRUCTION OF GEAR TEETH USING BASE CIRCLE AS A BASIS OF
CONSTRUCTION.

GEAR DATA. PRESSURE ANGLE 20° D.P. 2·5 NUMBER OF TEETH 25.

CALCULATED DATA.

PITCH CIRCLE DIAMETER = D = $\dfrac{T}{DP} = \dfrac{25}{2·5} = 10''$

ADDENDUM = $\dfrac{1}{DP} = \dfrac{2}{5} = ·4''$

CIRCULAR PITCH = $\dfrac{\pi D}{T} = \dfrac{\pi}{D.P.} = \dfrac{3·142}{2·5} = 1·257$

CLEARANCE = $\dfrac{P}{20} = \dfrac{1·257}{20} = ·0628''$

DEDENDUM = ADDENDUM + CLEARANCE

$= ·4 + ·0628 = ·4628''$

TOOTH THICKNESS = $\dfrac{P}{2} = ·628''$

STAGE 1.
DRAW TANGENT TO THE
PITCH CIRCLE.

PRESSURE ANGLE

STAGE 2.
DRAW BASE CIRCLE
TANGENTIAL TO LINE OF
ACTION.

PITCH CIRCLE.

LINE OF ACTION.

BASE CIRCLE.

STAGE 3. DRAW ADDENDUM AND DEDENDUM CIRCLES.

NOTE   POINT A ON ADDENDUM CIRCLE.
POINT E ON BASE CIRCLE.

DIVIDE A E SUCH THAT $\dfrac{AB}{BE} = \dfrac{1}{2}$

DRAW LINE B D TANGENTIAL TO BASE CIRCLE

DIVIDE BD SUCH THAT $\dfrac{FD}{BF} = \dfrac{1}{3}$

F IS THE CENTRE OF A PROFILE ARC PASSING THROUGH B.

FILLET RADIUS $\dfrac{W}{7}$

DEDENDUM CIRCLE

FROM POINT C MARK OFF HALF PITCH LENGTHS
ON THE PITCH CIRCLE.
CONSTRUCT A CIRCLE TO PASS THROUGH POINT F
TO PROVIDE CIRCLE FOR CENTRES OF ARCS.
CONSTRUCT ARC CENTRES BY STRIKING RADIUS
F B FROM HALF PITCH POINTS.

ADDENDUM CIRCLE

BASE CIRCLE

140

off tooth thicknesses round the circle. Draw profile arcs radius FB through these points, centred on the circle through F. The fillet radius at the roots of the teeth is again one-seventh of the widest tooth space.

On a working drawing of a spur gear it is usually unnecessary to show more than two or three teeth. The working drawing consists generally of two views, a circular view on which the addendum, dedendum and pitch circles are drawn in chain dot lines and a sectional view taken through the centreline of the gear. On the sectional view the hatching does not cross the teeth. The data relating to the teeth are generally shown in tabular form on the drawing.

Involute Racks

As explained previously, involute racks have straight sided teeth. The sides of the teeth are normal to the line of action, therefore, they are inclined to the vertical at the pressure angle.

To draw a standard involute rack approximately, first set out the pitch line and the addendum and dedendum lines, as shown on page 142. Step off on the pitch line the circular thickness $\frac{P}{2}$ of the teeth of the mating gear. Through these points draw the tooth faces at the pressure angle and complete the teeth with the tips and roots. The fillet radii are 0.1 of the circular pitch.

In practice rack teeth are relieved slightly at the tips but the amount is so small that for drawing purposes it can be ignored.

Bevel Gears

This type of gearing is used to transmit power between shafts in the same plane whose axes would intersect if produced. The angle between the shafts is usually a right angle, but it may have any value up to 180°.

When the transmission of motion by spur gears was considered, the starting point was two cylinders in contact at a point on their circumferences. With bevel gears the starting point is two cones in contact along a pair of generators, the apices of the cones being coincident, as shown in Figure 1. These cones are the pitch cones of the gears. If they roll on each other without slipping the velocity ratio is the inverse ratio of the diameters of their bases. These diameters are the pitch circle diameters.

The teeth on a bevel wheel lie on the curved surface of a second cone having the same base as the pitch cone and with its generators at right angles to the generators of the pitch cone. This cone is the back cone of the gear.

If the curved surface of the back cone is viewed normally the teeth have the same profiles as the teeth on a spur gear. The addendum and dedendum have the same proportions as spur gear teeth but are measured above and below the pitch circle, parallel to the back cone generator. Pressure angles for bevel gears are usually 14½° or 20° as for spur gears.

INVOLUTE RACKS.

RACK DATA. PRESSURE ANGLE 20°. D.P. 2. RACK TO MESH WITH 30 TOOTH GEAR

CALCULATED DATA.

PITCH OF RACK TEETH $= \dfrac{\pi}{2} = \dfrac{3.142}{2}$ 1·571″

ADDENDUM $= \dfrac{1}{D.P.} = \dfrac{1}{2} = \cdot 5''$

CLEARANCE $= \dfrac{P}{20} = \dfrac{1.571}{20} = \cdot 0785''$

DEDENDUM = ADDENDUM + CLEARANCE

$= \quad \cdot 5 \quad + \quad \cdot 0785 = \cdot 5785$

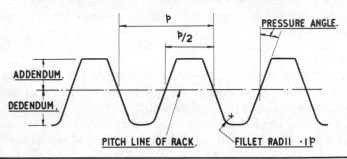

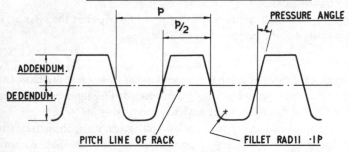

PITCH LINE OF RACK.   FILLET RADII ·1P

RACK DATA. PRESSURE ANGLE 14 ½° D.P. 2. RACK TO MESH WITH 30 TOOTH GEAR.

CALCULATED DATA AS IN THE PREVIOUS EXAMPLE.

PITCH LINE OF RACK   FILLET RADII ·1P

NOTE — THE PITCH LINE OF RACK TEETH SHOULD BE TANGENTIAL
TO THE PITCH CIRCLE OF THE GEAR WHEN PRODUCING
DRAWINGS OF GEARS AND RACKS IN MESH,

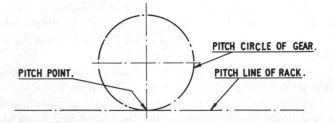

PITCH CIRCLE OF GEAR.

PITCH POINT.   PITCH LINE OF RACK.

142

Bevel Gear Terms

In addition to those terms used for spur gears the following are also used and are illustrated in Figure 1.

The *pitch cone angle* is the angle between the axis of the gear and the pitch cone generator. When the pitch cone angle is 45° the gear is a mitre gear.

The *cutting angle* or *root cone angle* is the angle between the gear axis and the root cone generator.

The *face angle* is the angle between a line at right angles to the axis and the top surfaces of the teeth.

The *edge angle* is the angle between a line at right angles to the axis and the generator of the back cone.

The *addendum angle* is the angle between the pitch cone generator and the top surfaces of the teeth.

The *dedendum angle* is the angle between the pitch cone generator and the bottoms of tooth spaces.

The *width* of the tooth face is the width measured parallel to the pitch cone generator.

The *angular addendum* is the addendum measured on a line at right angles to the gear axis.

The *outside diameter* is the diameter of the gear at the tops of the teeth.

The *vertex distance* is the height of a cone with the outside diameter as base.

Approximate Construction for Involute Bevel Gear Teeth

This is shown opposite and is due to Tredgold. First draw the gear centreline with the pitch circle diameter crossing it at right angles. On the pitch circle diameter lay out the pitch cone, using the pitch cone angle. Draw the back cone with the generators at right angles to the pitch cone generators. On the back cone set out the addendum and dedendum and join these points to the vertex. Mark off the face width of the teeth on the pitch cone and complete the sectional view of the tooth. Draw lines across the view at right angles to the axis through the tip and root points and points on the pitch cone at each end of the teeth. Now develop the back cone by swinging arcs about O from the addendum, dedendum and pitch points on the back cone. These arcs fix the addendum, dedendum and pitch circles of the developed teeth. Using the same construction as for a spur gear, lay out on these circles the profiles of one or two teeth. In the end view set out the centrelines of the teeth and draw six circles representing the addendum, dedendum and pitch circles at each end of the teeth. Fix three points on the profiles of teeth at the large end by transferring the widths X, Y and Z from the developed view of the teeth. The view may now be completed by filling in the teeth profiles with a french curve

BEVEL GEARS.

TERMS USED IN BEVEL GEARING.

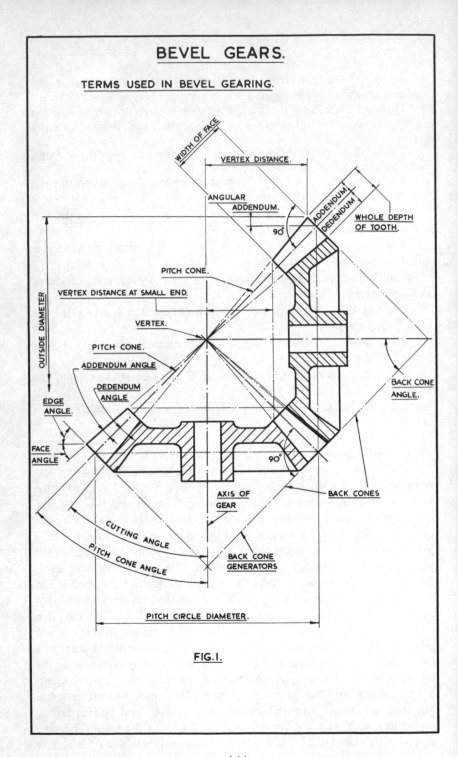

FIG.1.

BEVEL GEARS.

APPROXIMATE CONSTRUCTION OF BEVEL GEAR TEETH.

GEAR DATA.

NUMBER OF TEETH 15.
PITCH CONE ANGLE 45°
PITCH CIRCLE DIA. 4″
PRESSURE ANGLE 14½°

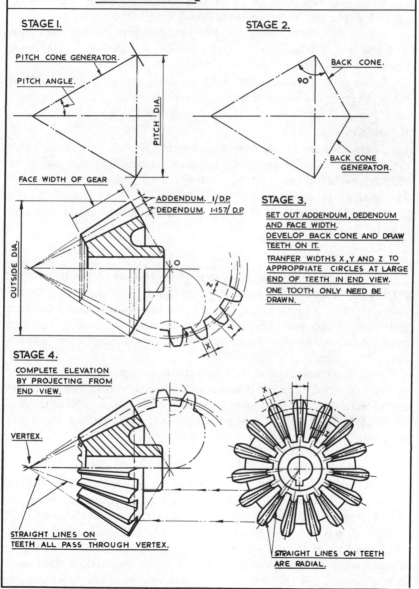

STAGE I.

PITCH CONE GENERATOR.

PITCH ANGLE.

PITCH DIA.

FACE WIDTH OF GEAR

OUTSIDE DIA.

ADDENDUM. 1/D.P.
DEDENDUM. 1·157/ D.P.

STAGE 2.

BACK CONE.

90°

BACK CONE
GENERATOR.

STAGE 3.

SET OUT ADDENDUM, DEDENDUM
AND FACE WIDTH.
DEVELOP BACK CONE AND DRAW
TEETH ON IT.
TRANFER WIDTHS X, Y AND Z TO
APPROPRIATE CIRCLES AT LARGE
END OF TEETH IN END VIEW.
ONE TOOTH ONLY NEED BE
DRAWN.

STAGE 4.

COMPLETE ELEVATION
BY PROJECTING FROM
END VIEW.

VERTEX.

STRAIGHT LINES ON
TEETH ALL PASS THROUGH VERTEX.

STRAIGHT LINES ON TEETH
ARE RADIAL.

or with circular arcs. All straight lines on the teeth are radial and this enables three points on the profile of the teeth at the small end to be fixed. The elevation can be completed by projection from the end view. All straight lines on the teeth in this view pass through the vertex if produced.

It will be seen from the illustration that when the back cone is developed a spur gear is formed with a pitch circle diameter equal to twice the length of the back cone generator. This spur gear is called the virtual spur gear and it is used in the manufacturing calculations for the bevel wheel.

Other types of gears which are in common use are briefly described below. Detailed discussion of them is outside the scope of this book.

Hypoid Gears

These gears are similar to bevel gears but the basic surfaces on which the teeth are cut are hyperboloids instead of cones. A hyperboloid is the solid of revolution generated by rotating a hyperbola about its directrix. The teeth of hypoid gears are helical and the axes of the shafts do not intersect when produced. Hypoid gears are commonly used in the rear axles of cars.

Helical Gears

These are a development of spur gears. Instead of the teeth being parallel to the axis of the gear they lie on helices. This means that contact between teeth in mesh takes place along a diagonal line across the faces and flanks of the teeth. Thus one pair of meshing teeth remain in contact until the following pair engage, and so the load on the teeth is distributed over a larger area.

With single helical gears the helical tooth form produces an end thrust on the shaft which must be absorbed with a thrust bearing. The end thrust is avoided if double helical gears are used. These have one half of the face width of the gear with a right hand helix and the other half with a left hand helix.

Worms and Worm Wheels

These connect shafts at right angles which lie in different planes. The worm is essentially a screw, which may be double or triple threaded, which engages with teeth cut on the worm wheel. The worm originally was cylindrical, but now it is frequently waisted to give greater contact with the worm wheel. Such worms are known as globoidal, encircling or Hindley worms. With parallel worms the teeth are straight sided on a section through the axis, and have the same proportions as standard involute rack teeth.

INVOLUTE GEARS

Note (Both Imperial and S.1. Units are used in these problems).

1. Lay out twice full size five teeth of a spur gear with 35 teeth of involute form, 5 D.P. and 14½° pressure angle. Use the approximate construction shown on page 138. Give a table showing the number of teeth, D.P., pressure angle, pitch circle diameter, circular pitch, addendum and dedendum.

2. Draw twice full size five teeth of a 15 tooth involute spur gear, 3 D.P. and 14½° pressure angle, using the approximate construction on page 139. Show in tabular form the important dimensions of the gear.

3. A 16 tooth pinion metric module 10 has a 20° pressure angle. Using the approximate construction shown on page 141 set out twice full size five teeth on the pinion. Add a table showing the important gear dimensions.

4. Make a dimensioned working drawing of a 18 tooth pinion, 3 D.P., 14½° pressure angle using the following information.
    Face width 1½ inches, central web ½ inch thick, boss length 2 inches, boss diameter 1¾ inches, boss drilled 1¼ inches diameter, inside rim diameter 4½ inches, four equi-spaced lightening holes $\frac{7}{8}$ inch diameter, through the web on a $3\frac{1}{8}$. inch diameter pitch circle. Fillet radii $\frac{1}{8}$ inch.
    Draw full size in First Angle projection a front elevation showing three teeth drawn by an approximate method, and a sectional end view. In the end view the boss is positioned symmetrically about the centreline. Show a table giving the gear data.

5. Draw full size in First Angle projection a dimensioned front elevation and sectional end view of a 30 tooth spur gear, metric module 6.5, 20° pressure angle. Show three teeth on the front elevation drawn approximately and a table of the gear data. The face width of the gear is 25mm, rim diameter 158mm, boss diameter 34mm, drilled 24mm diameter, boss length 50mm. The boss is supported by four straight spokes of elliptical cross section, the minor diameter being constant at 10mm and the major diameter tapering from 24mm at the boss to 22mm at the rim. Fillet radii 5mm. The boss is symmetrical about the centreline in the end view. Show a revolved section of one spoke on the elevation.

6. Draw full size one view of a pair of involute spur gears in mesh showing five teeth on each gear. The gears have 32 teeth and 24 teeth of 4 D.P., and 14½° pressure angle.

147

The 32 tooth gear has a rim diameter of 6¾ inches, boss diameter of 1⅞ inches and a shaft diameter of 1⅛ inches. There are six lightening holes 1⅜ inches diameter on a pitch circle of 4¼ inches diameter.

On the 24 tooth gear the rim diameter is 4¾ inches, the boss diameter 1⅜ inches, the shaft diameter ⅞ inch and there are three 1¼ inch diameter lightening holes on a pitch circle diameter of 3 inches.

Show the gear data in tabular form.

7. A 12 inch pitch circle diameter involute spur gear is to mesh with a pinion with an 8 inch pitch circle diameter. If the gears have a pressure angle of 20° and a D.P. of 3, draw full size four teeth on each gear in mesh at the pitch point. Give a table of gear data.

8. The centre distance of an involute spur gear and pinion is 7 inches and the speed reduction is 2½ to 1. Assuming the D.P. to be 2½ and the pressure angle 20° calculate the following:

    (a) The pitch circle diameters of gear and pinion.
    (b) The base circle diameters of gear and pinion.
    (c) The number of teeth on gear and pinion.
    (d) The circular pitch of the teeth.
    (e) The addendum.
    (f) The dedendum.

9. A pinion with 20 teeth is to mesh with a rack whose teeth have a pressure angle of 20° and an addendum of 0.250 inch. The travel of the rack is to be 5 inches. Draw twice full size all the teeth on the rack and five teeth on the pinion. Show the rack and pinion in mesh and tabulate their data.

10. A machine work table is driven by an involute rack whose teeth have a pitch of 1.5708 inches and a pressure angle of 14½°. The rack is operated by a pinion and intermediate wheel, the gear train giving a speed reduction of 3 to 1. The pitch circle diameter of the pinion is 6 inches. Draw full size the intermediate gear and rack in mesh showing five teeth on each. Tabulate the data for the two gears and the rack.

11. A pair of bevel gears is to connect 1½ inch diameter shafts having an included angle of 90°. The velocity ratio of the driver shaft to the driven shaft is to be 3 to 2, the D.P. of the teeth 2·5 and the face width 2¼ inches. The pinion is to have 16 teeth. Draw full size a half sectional elevation and half end view of each gear, similar to the views shown on

page 145. All other dimensions necessary to complete these views are to be supplied by the student.

12.   A reduction gear in the form of a pair of bevel gears connects 1¼ inch diameter shafts having an included angle of 90°. The pinion, which is the driver, revolves at 120 r.p.m. and has a 4 inch pitch circle diameter, a face width of ⅞ inch and a D.P. of 2·5. The bevel wheel is to revolve at 75 r.p.m. Draw the following views of the assembly full size.

(a)   A front elevation similar to that shown on page 144, the wheels being shown in half section with the pinion axis vertical.
(b)   An outside plan view of the pinion only.
(c)   An outside end view on the right of the front elevation showing the wheel only. Dimensions for the hubs etc., are to be supplied by the student.

VECTOR GEOMETRY

MANY problems in engineering involve quantities such as (a) displacement—change of position, (b) velocity—rate of change of displacement with respect to time, (c) force—the action of one body on another.

These quantities have magnitude, direction and line of action and may be represented on a drawing by a line, drawn to scale and drawn in the stated direction with an arrow indicating the sense of the line. This line is called a *vector*.

Typical vector lines are illustrated in Figure 1. ab represents a vector 3½ units long directed in an upward direction to the right at 45° to the horizontal and cd represents a vector 5 units long directed horizontally from left to right.

Addition of Vector Quantities

When adding vector quantities we have to take into account not only their numerical value but also their direction. To add two or more vectors proceed as follows. Draw the first vector in the direction of its arrow, continue the second one on the end of the first, the third on the end of the second, and so on. The sum of the vectors is the vector joining the beginning of the first to the end of the last in the series. The final diagram will be a closed polygon.

Figure 2 (A) shows four vector quantities A, B, C and D. To determine the sum of these quantities proceed by drawing ab equal and parallel to vector A; on the end b draw bc equal and parallel to vector B; on the end c draw cd equal and parallel to vector C and from d draw de equal and parallel to vector D. The sum of A, B, C and D is the vector ae, and its direction is indicated by the arrow. See Figure 2 (B).

Subtraction of Vector Quantities

Again considering the vector quantities in Figure 2 (A). If we wish to subtract the vector C from the sum of the vectors A, B and D then we may add −C to A+B+D. A minus vector is a positive one with the direction of its arrow reversed.

Solving the problem in the same order as before we now have A+B+(−C) +D (See Figure 3).

VECTOR GEOMETRY

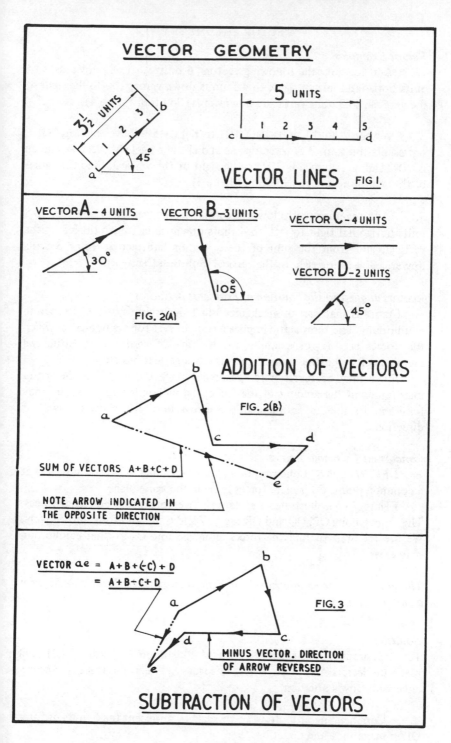

VECTOR LINES FIG I.

VECTOR **A** – 4 UNITS

VECTOR **B** – 3 UNITS

VECTOR **C** – 4 UNITS

VECTOR **D** – 2 UNITS

FIG. 2(A)

ADDITION OF VECTORS

FIG. 2(B)

SUM OF VECTORS A+B+C+D

NOTE ARROW INDICATED IN
THE OPPOSITE DIRECTION

VECTOR ae = A+B+(-C) + D
       = A+B–C+D

FIG. 3

MINUS VECTOR. DIRECTION
OF ARROW REVERSED

SUBTRACTION OF VECTORS

151

Vector Examples

1.   Add together the following vectors; 6 units vertically upwards, to 4 units horizontal left to right, to 4.5 units downwards, 10° to the right of the vertical, to 3 units vertically downwards (Solution Figure 4).

2.   A vector ab 15 units long, left to right, 45° above the horizontal, represents the sum of two vectors, ac and cb. The angle between ac and cb is 30°, and ac is upwards 30° to the right of the vertical. Find the values of the vectors ac and cb (Solution Figure 5).

3.   Add together the following vectors; 4 units vertically upwards, to 5 units horizontal right to left, to 4 units downwards 15° to the left of the vertical, and from the sum of these vectors subtract a vector 3 units upwards 30° to the right of the vertical (Solution Figure 6).

Vectors applied to the Solution of Problems in Statics

Statics is that part of mechanics which deals with systems of forces in equilibrium. The term static implies a state of rest for the bodies on which the forces act, as for example, in the case of roof trusses, structural members of supporting frames, columns, bridge sections etc.

Force may be represented vectorially since the length of the vector may represent the amount of the force, the inclination of the vector may represent its line of action and the arrow head will show its sense or direction.

Concurrent Co-planar Forces

DEFINITIONS: Concurrent—forces whose lines of action intersect at a common point. Co-planar—forces lying in the same plane.

Figure 7 (A), illustrates a system of five concurrent co-planar forces. The forces along OP, OQ and OR are 5, 7 and 6 units of force respectively. We are required to find the forces along OS and OT so that equilibrium may exist.

The condition for equilibrium is that the vectors when drawn should form a closed polygon.

Solution

1.   Reproduce the space diagram as illustrated in Figure 7 (B), and place the letters ABCD and E in the spaces between the forces in accordance with Bow's notation.

2.   Commencing at a, draw ab to scale to represent the 5 units of force OP in magnitude and direction.

VECTOR GEOMETRY

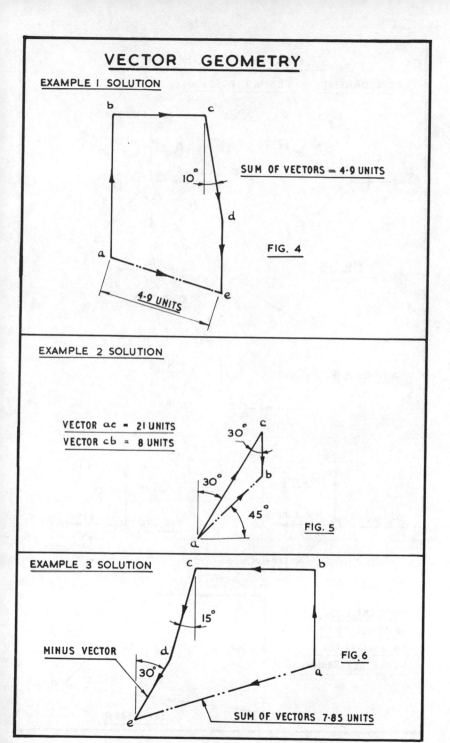

EXAMPLE 1 SOLUTION

SUM OF VECTORS = 4·9 UNITS

10°

FIG. 4

4·9 UNITS

EXAMPLE 2 SOLUTION

VECTOR ac = 21 UNITS
VECTOR cb = 8 UNITS

30°

30°

45°

FIG. 5

EXAMPLE 3 SOLUTION

15°

MINUS VECTOR

30°

FIG. 6

SUM OF VECTORS 7·85 UNITS

153

VECTOR GEOMETRY

CONCURRENT CO PLANAR FORCES

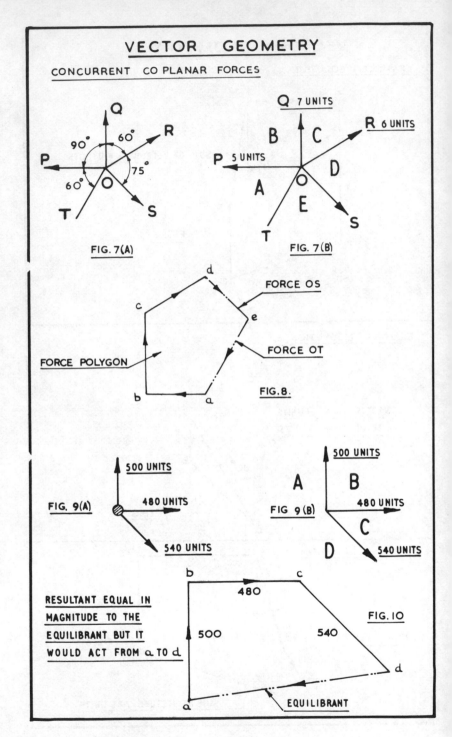

FIG. 7(A)

FIG. 7(B)

FORCE OS

FORCE OT

FORCE POLYGON

FIG. 8.

FIG. 9(A)   500 UNITS   480 UNITS   540 UNITS

FIG 9(B)   A   B   500 UNITS   480 UNITS   C   D   540 UNITS

RESULTANT EQUAL IN MAGNITUDE TO THE EQUILIBRANT BUT IT WOULD ACT FROM a TO d

480   500   540   FIG. 10

EQUILIBRANT

3.   From b draw bc to represent the 7 units of force OQ in magnitude and direction.

4.   From c draw cd to represent the 6 units of force OR in magnitude and direction.

5.   Through d draw a line parallel to the force OS, the length of this line will be unknown since the magnitude of the force OS is unknown.

6.   Through a draw a line parallel to the force OT so that this line intersects the line drawn through d (stage 5) in point e.

7.   The vectors de and ea represent in magnitude and direction the forces OS and OT.

Note that the arrows must follow through in direction in the force polygon as shown in Figure 8.

To Determine the Equilibrant and Resultant of a System of Concurrent Co-planar Forces.

Three electric wires attached to the top of a pole are illustrated in Figure 9 (A). The wires have the following pulls and directions;
(a)   500 units of force due north, (b) 480 units of force due east,
(c)   540 units of force south-east. Determine the equilibrant of this system of forces.

Solution

1.   Produce a space diagram as illustrated in Figure 9 (B) and place the letters A, B, C and D between the forces.

2.   Commencing at a, draw ab to scale to represent the 500 unit force in magnitude and direction.

3.   From b draw bc to represent the 480 unit force in magnitude and direction.

4.   From c draw cd to represent the 540 unit force in magnitude and direction.

5.   The line joining d to a will represent the equilibrant in magnitude and direction, see Figure 10.

Note that the polygon closes and the equilibrant acts from d to a, the arrow following in the same direction as those on other vector quantities. The magnitude of the resultant of this system of forces would have the

155

same value as the equilibrant but its sense would be opposite to the equilibrant, that is, it would act from a to d.

To Determine the Resultant of a System of Non-Concurrent Co-Planar Forces.

Definition of 'non-concurrent'—forces whose lines of action do not intersect at a common point.

Figure 11 illustrates a system of three forces A, B and C which are all acting in one plane but which do not pass through the same point. Let the values of A, B and C be 8, 6 and 4 units of force respectively. The magnitude and direction of the resultant can be determined by the usual method of drawing the force polygon, Figure 12 (A). This however will not give the complete answer to the problem since we do not know the position in which the resultant acts. Its line of action must still be determined.

In order to determine the line of action of the resultant it is necessary to draw another diagram which is known as the *Link* or *Funicular Polygon.*

The construction of the *link polygon* is carried out as follows:

1.   Draw the force polygon, pqrs, in the usual way, and obtain the magnitude and direction of the resultant as represented by the vector ps.

2.   Choose any point O either inside or outside the force polygon, and join O to each corner of the force polygon. Figure 12 (B).

3.   Referring to Figure 13, from any point 1 in the line of action of force A, draw a line in space P parallel to the line op.

4.   From the point 1, draw the line 1 to 2 in space Q parallel to oq and cutting the line of action of force B in point 2. It may be necessary to produce the line of action of force B to get the necessary intersection.

5.   From point 2, draw the line 2 to 3 in space R parallel to line or and cutting the line of action of force C in point 3. Again the line of action of force C may have to be produced in order to obtain the intersection point.

6.   From point 3, draw the line 3 to 4 in the space S parallel to the line os which will intersect the line parallel to op, drawn through point 1, in 4.

7.   The resultant of the forces will pass through point 4. Through 4 draw a line parallel to ps to represent the resultant force R.

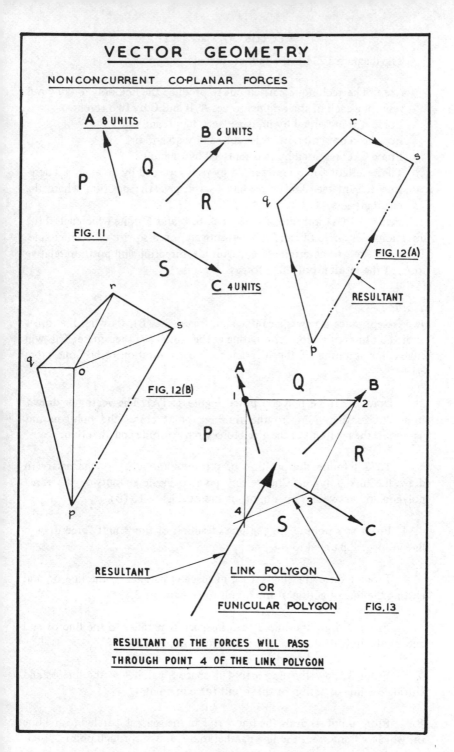

VECTOR GEOMETRY

NONCONCURRENT CO-PLANAR FORCES

A 8 UNITS

B 6 UNITS

P

Q

R

FIG. 11

S

C 4 UNITS

FIG. 12 (A)

RESULTANT

FIG. 12 (B)

A

Q

B

P

R

S

C

RESULTANT

LINK POLYGON
OR
FUNICULAR POLYGON

FIG. 13

RESULTANT OF THE FORCES WILL PASS
THROUGH POINT 4 OF THE LINK POLYGON

157

The diagram 1234 is the link or funicular polygon.

Note: The technique carried out to produce the link polygon involves replacing each of the original forces A, B and C by two forces.
Force A represented by pq is replaced by po and oq.
Force B represented by qr is replaced by qo and or.
Force C represented by rs is replaced by ro and os.
The resultant force represented by ps is replaced by po and os. Therefore the intersection of po and os will give the position where the resultant acts.

Figure 14 (A) indicates forces of 8, 6, 4 and 5 units which act in the directions CA, DB, BC and AB respectively, on a square of 50 mm side. The problem is to determine the magnitude, direction and position relative to A, of the resultant of these forces.

Solution

1.   Reproduce a new space diagram, Figure 14 (B), showing the forces with their lines of action terminating at the corners of the square. This will enable the lettering of the diagram for Bow's notation to be done more easily.

2.   Draw the force polygon pqrst, Figure 15 (A). The vector pt drawn from the starting point to the finishing point closes the polygon and represents the resultant of the given forces in magnitude and direction.

3.   To determine the position of the resultant it is now necessary to draw the link polygon. Choose any point o inside or outside the force polygon and draw lines op, oq, or, os and ot. Figure 15 (B).

4.   From any point 1 on the line of action of the 8 unit force draw a line in space P parallel to the line op.

5.   From 1 draw the line 1 to 2 in space Q parallel to the line oq and cutting the line of action of the 6 unit force in point 2.

6.   From 2 draw the line 2 to 3 in space R parallel to the line or and cutting the line of action of the 5 unit force in point 3.

7.   From 3 draw the line 3 to 4 in space S parallel to the line os and cutting the line of action of the 4 unit force in point 4.

8.   From point 4, draw the line 4 to 5 in the space T parallel to the line ot, which will intersect the line parallel to op, drawn through point 1, in 5.

VECTOR GEOMETRY

NONCONCURRENT COPLANAR FORCES

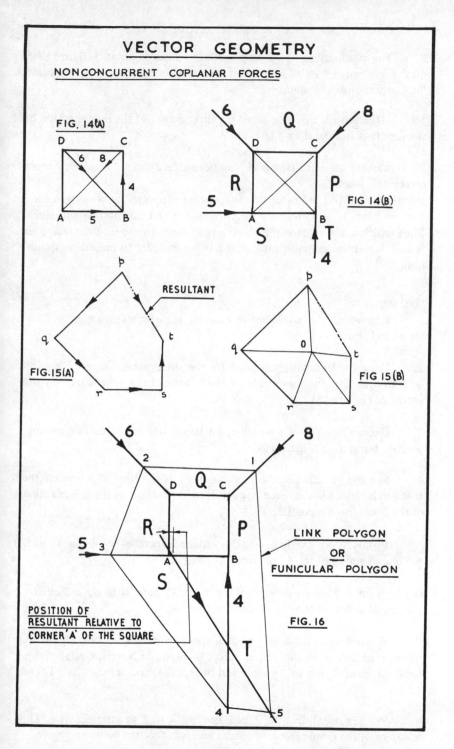

FIG. 14(A)

FIG 14(B)

RESULTANT

FIG. 15(A)

FIG 15(B)

LINK POLYGON
OR
FUNICULAR POLYGON

POSITION OF
RESULTANT RELATIVE TO
CORNER 'A' OF THE SQUARE

FIG. 16

9. The resultant of the forces will pass through point 5. Through 5 draw a line parallel to pt to represent the resultant force. Figure 16 shows the complete link polygon.

10. Measure the distance from the intersection of the line of action of the resultant and the square to point A.

To Determine the Resultant and Reactions of a Parallel System of Forces acting on a Beam

Figure 17 (A) indicates a loaded beam supported at its extremities. The problem is to determine the magnitude and position of the single force which could replace the three given forces, and to find the reactions R and R_1 at the extreme ends of the beam in order to maintain equilibrium.

Solution

1. Reproduce the given space diagram with Bow's notation as illustrated in Figure 17 (B).

2. Draw the force diagram abcd for the three parallel forces. This will be a straight line, the magnitude of the resultant being represented by the vector ad (Figure 18).

3. Choose any point o which must be outside the force diagram and join ao, bo, and do (Figure 19).

4. See Figure 20. Choose any point 1 on the line of action of the reaction R, draw a line in space A, parallel to oa, and cutting the line of action of the 2 unit force in point 2.

5. From 2 draw the line 2 to 3 in space B, parallel to ob and cutting the line of action of the 6 unit force in point 3.

6. From 3 draw the line 3 to 4 in space C, parallel to oc and cutting the line of action of the 4 unit force in point 4.

7. From 4 draw the line 4 to 5 in space D, parallel to od and cutting the line of action of the reaction R_1, in point 5. Note the relationship between space A and oa, space B and ob, space C and oc, and space D and od.

8. Produce the line 1 to 2 and the line 4 to 5 to intersect in 6. The resultant of the given system of forces will pass through point 6.

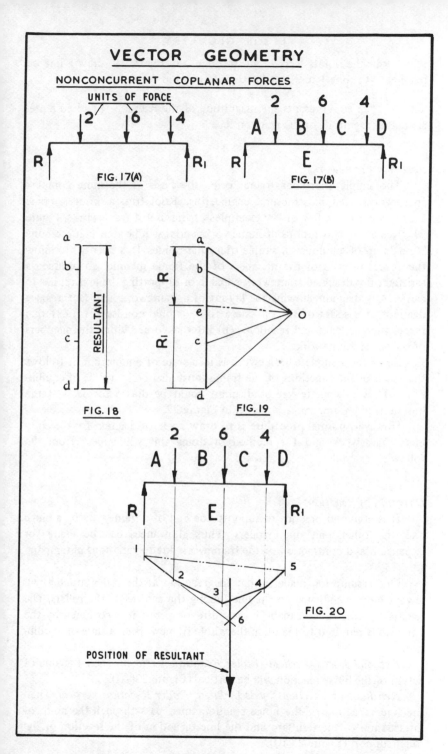

VECTOR GEOMETRY

NONCONCURRENT COPLANAR FORCES

UNITS OF FORCE

FIG. 17(A)

FIG. 17(B)

FIG. 18

FIG. 19

FIG. 20

POSITION OF RESULTANT

9.   Join the points 1 to 5, and through o in Figure 19, draw a line oe parallel to the line 1 to 5, cutting the vector ad in e.

10.   Then ae represents the magnitude of the reaction R and ed represents the magnitude of the reaction R_1.

Forces in Frameworks

The simple triangular frame forms the basis of the more complex frameworks used in structural engineering. Roof trusses, bridges, crane supports are but a few of the examples of the use of frameworks. Figure 21 gives a few illustrations of frameworks and it will be seen that each one is made up of a number of simple triangular frames. It is essential to know the forces in each of the members of the frame in order to produce a satisfactorily designed framework capable of supporting the loads it has to carry. Any diagram showing the layout of a framework is in fact a space diagram of a series of forces. These forces would consist of (a) external forces such as loads and reactions, (b) internal forces within the members of the actual framework.

Since the complete framework is in a state of equilibrium it follows that each of the junctions of the frame must also be in a state of equilibrium. Thus a separate vector diagram could be drawn for each of the junctions of a framework, as shown in Figure 22.

However, normal procedure is to draw a vector diagram for the complete framework and the method of doing this will appear from the following examples.

Direction of Reactions

It is common practice to support one end of a framework by a hinge and the other end upon rollers. Thus allowances can be made for expansion and contraction of the framework due to variations in temperature.

One assumption made is that the reaction at the roller support will always be perpendicular to the line joining the centres of the rollers. The reaction at the hinge can be in any direction, but it is governed by the conditions required to maintain the whole framework in a state of equilibrium.

External Loads Vertical—Roller Reaction Vertical. Then the line of action of the hinge reaction will be vertical (Figure 23(A)).

Resultant of External Loads Inclined, Roller Reaction Vertical. Then the line of action of the hinge reaction must pass through the point of intersection of the resultant and the line of action of the reaction of the roller support (Figure 23(B)).

VECTOR GEOMETRY

FORCES IN FRAMEWORKS

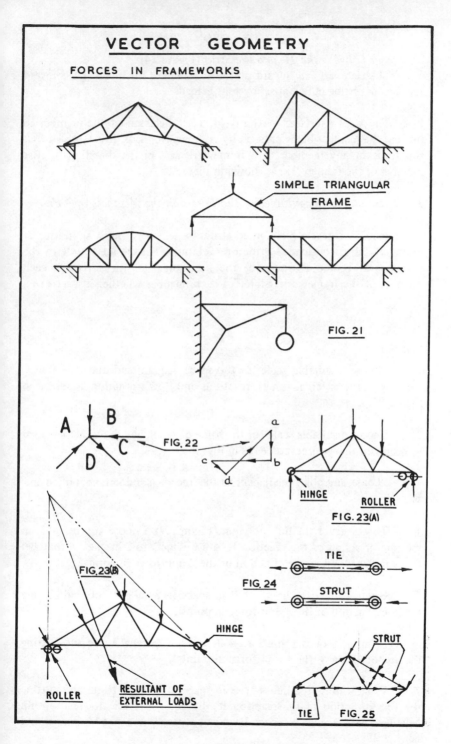

SIMPLE TRIANGULAR FRAME

FIG. 21

FIG. 22

HINGE ROLLER

FIG. 23(A)

FIG. 23(B)

HINGE

ROLLER

RESULTANT OF EXTERNAL LOADS

TIE

STRUT

FIG. 24

STRUT

TIE FIG. 25

163

Difference between the Tie and the Strut (Figure 24)

1. The tie exerts an inward pull at each end of the member to prevent the member being pulled apart by tensile loads.

2. The strut exerts an outward force at each end of the member to prevent the member being crushed by compressive loads. It is assumed that the force in any member of a framework acts in the direction of that member of the framework, as shown in Figure 25.

To Determine the Magnitudes of the Forces in the Members of a Framework

Figure 26 shows a pin jointed structure which is simply supported at R and R_1. For the loaded structure determine (a) the magnitude of the reactions at R and R_1 and (b) the magnitudes of the forces in each member of the framework. State for each member whether it is a tie or a strut.

Solution

1. Choose a suitable scale for the space diagram and draw the frame work with the external forces, reactions and Bow's notation as shown in Figure 27.

2. Choose a suitable scale for the force diagram, and draw the line abcd to represent the external forces as in Figure 28.

3. Choose any point o adjacent to the line abcd and join ao, bo, co and do.

4. To construct the link polygon (Figure 29). Choose any point 1 on the line of action of the reaction R, draw a line 1 to 2 in space A, parallel to oa and cutting the line of action of the 2 unit force in point 2.

5. From 2 draw the line 2 to 3 in space B, parallel to ob and cutting the line of action of the 3 unit force in point 3.

6. From 3 draw the line 3 to 4 in space C, parallel to oc and cutting the line of action of the 1 unit force in point 4.

7. From 4 draw the line 4 to 5 in space D, parallel to od and cutting the line of action of the reaction R_1 in point 5. Note the relationship between space A and oa, space B and ob, space C and oc and space D and od.

VECTOR GEOMETRY

FORCES IN FRAMEWORKS

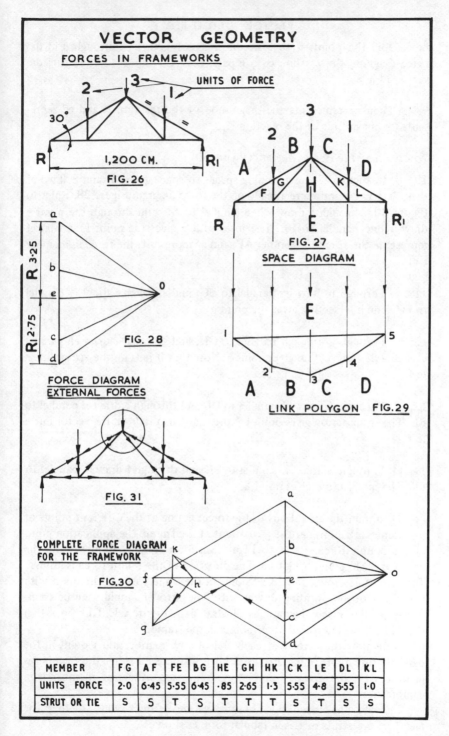

FIG. 26

1,200 CM.

30°

R   R₁

UNITS OF FORCE

FIG. 27
SPACE DIAGRAM

FORCE DIAGRAM
EXTERNAL FORCES

FIG. 28

LINK POLYGON   FIG.29

FIG. 31

COMPLETE FORCE DIAGRAM
FOR THE FRAMEWORK

FIG.30

MEMBER	FG	AF	FE	BG	HE	GH	HK	CK	LE	DL	KL
UNITS FORCE	2·0	6·45	5·55	6·45	·85	2·65	1·3	5·55	4·8	5·55	1·0
STRUT OR TIE	S	S	T	S	T	T	T	S	T	S	S

165

8.   Join the points 1 to 5 of the link polygon, and through o in the force diagram, draw a line o to e parallel to the line 1 to 5, cutting the vector ad in e.

9.   Then ae represents the magnitude of the reaction R and ed represents the magnitude of the reaction R_1.

To Complete the Force Diagram (Figure 30)

10.   In Figure 27 the adjoining spaces to space A are F and E. Two of these letters, A and E are already on the force diagram Figure 28. Refer to Figure 30. Through a draw a line parallel to AF and through the point e draw a line parallel to FE. The intersection gives the point f, so that af represents the force in member AF, and ef represents the force in member EF.

11.   Through b draw bg parallel to BG, and through f draw fg parallel to FG. The intersection gives the point g.

12.   Through g draw gh parallel to GH, and through e draw eh parallel to EH. The intersection gives point h. Note that h falls on the vector line e to f.

13.   Through d draw dl parallel to DL and through e draw el parallel to EL. The intersection gives point l. Note that l also falls on the vector line e to f.

14.   Through c draw ck parallel to CK and through l draw lk parallel to LK. The intersection gives point k.

To obtain the directions of the forces acting at the different points of the framework, consider the peak point of the frame, the application point of the 3 unit force. Refer to Figure 30. Starting at b, follow round the points c, k, h, g and back to b. The direction of the 3 unit force is known. The arrows as shown should all point in the same forward direction with the arrow on bc pointing downwards. The arrows should then be transferred to the space diagram as illustrated in Figure 31. This operation should be repeated for all other points in the frame.

Note that the arrows at each end of any member must point in the opposite direction. If the arrows point towards each other the member is in tension; if the arrows point away from each other the member is in compression.

Indicate the magnitude of the various forces and whether the members are struts or ties in tabular form as shown.

166

Figure 32A shows a pin jointed structure loaded at the point S and hinged at point P. The structure is maintained in equilibrium with SP horizontal by the pull in the horizontal chain TR. Determine the pull in the chain and the force in each member of the structure, stating whether it is a tie or a strut.

Solution

1.   Choose a suitable scale for the space diagram and draw the structure with the external forces and Bow's notation (Figure 32 (B)).

2.   Since for equilibrium all three external forces, 2 units of force, reaction at P and the pull in the chain must pass through one point, the direction of CA can be determined. Produce the line of action of the 2 unit force, until it meets the line of action of the chain in point I (Figure 33). The line of action of CA must also pass through this point, so draw the reaction at P to pass through the point I.

3.   Choose a suitable scale for the force diagram (Figure 34). Draw bc to represent the 2 unit force. Draw ca parallel to the reaction at P and draw ba parallel to IR, intersecting ca at a. Then ca represents the reaction at P and ab represents the pull in the chain.

4.   Through b draw be parallel to BE, through a draw ae parallel to AE. The intersection gives point e.

5.   Through e draw ed parallel to ED, and through a draw ad parallel to AD. The intersection gives point d.
       Note that the line cd should be parallel to DC.

6.   Measure the lengths of the lines in the force diagram and hence obtain the magnitudes of the forces in the members of the frame.

7.   The directions of the forces acting in the members are obtained as in the previous example (See Figure 35). Tabulate the forces in the members as shown.

A pin jointed structure is shown in Figure 36. Determine the magnitudes and directions of the reactions when the structure is carrying the loading shown. Determine also the forces in the members, distinquishing between tension and compression.

Solution

1.   Choose a suitable scale for the space diagram and draw the framework with the external forces, reactions and Bow's notation as shown in Figure 38. Note that the 2 and 3 units of force have been replaced by a

VECTOR GEOMETRY

FORCES IN FRAMEWORKS

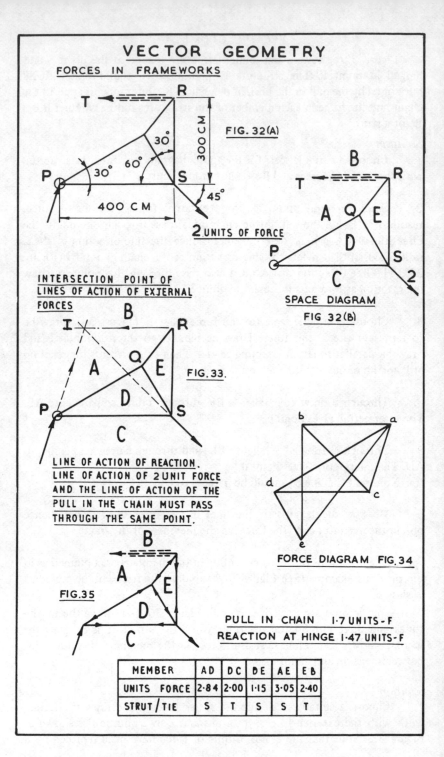

FIG. 32(A)

300 CM

400 C M

30°

30°   60°

45°

2 UNITS OF FORCE

T

R

P

S

INTERSECTION POINT OF
LINES OF ACTION OF EXTERNAL
FORCES

FIG. 33.

LINE OF ACTION OF REACTION.
LINE OF ACTION OF 2 UNIT FORCE
AND THE LINE OF ACTION OF THE
PULL IN THE CHAIN MUST PASS
THROUGH THE SAME POINT.

SPACE DIAGRAM
FIG 32(B)

FORCE DIAGRAM FIG. 34

FIG.35

PULL IN CHAIN 1·7 UNITS - F
REACTION AT HINGE 1·47 UNITS - F

MEMBER	AD	DC	DE	AE	EB
UNITS FORCE	2·84	2·00	1·15	3·05	2·40
STRUT / TIE	S	T	S	S	T

168

single inclined force acting at P. Figure 37 shows the construction for determining the value of this single force.

2.   Choose a suitable scale for the force diagram and draw the lines ab and bc to represent the external forces. The line ac will be the resultant of the external forces (Figure 39).

3.   Choose any point o adjacent to ab and bc and join ao, bo and co (Figure 39).

4.   To construct the link polygon (Figure 38). Choose any point 1 on the line of action of the inclined force and draw a line through this point in space A, parallel to ao.

5.   From point 1 draw a line in space B, parallel to ob, to cut the line of action of the 9 unit force in point 2.

6.   Through point 2 draw a line in space C parallel to oc, to cut the line through 1 in point 3.

7.   The resultant of all the external forces will have its line of action passing through this point 3.

8.   Since the line of action of each reaction and the line of action of the resultant of the external forces must pass through the same point to maintain equilibrium, draw a line through 3, parallel to ac, to meet the vertical line of the right hand reaction, in point X.

9.   Join X to T (Figure 38) to give the line of action of the reaction R.

10.   Referring to Figure 39. Draw a line ad, parallel to the line of action of the reaction R. Then ad represents the magnitude of the reaction R and dc represents the magnitude of the reaction R_1.

11.   Repeat as in the previous example to complete the force polygon (Figure 40).

To Determine the Centre of Gravity of a Given System of Masses

Figure 41 shows four masses, 4, 2, 8 and 1 unit of mass, having fixed relative positions. It is required to determine the centre of gravity of this system.

VECTOR GEOMETRY

FORCES IN FRAMEWORKS

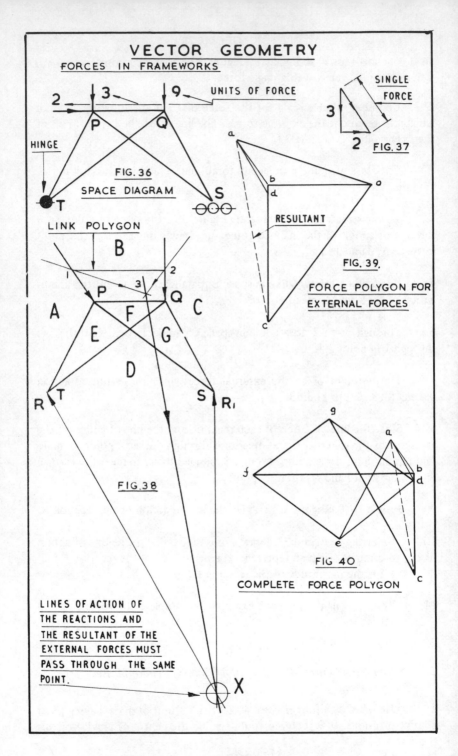

UNITS OF FORCE

SINGLE FORCE

FIG. 37

HINGE

FIG. 36

SPACE DIAGRAM

LINK POLYGON

RESULTANT

FIG. 39.

FORCE POLYGON FOR EXTERNAL FORCES

FIG. 38

FIG 40

COMPLETE FORCE POLYGON

LINES OF ACTION OF THE REACTIONS AND THE RESULTANT OF THE EXTERNAL FORCES MUST PASS THROUGH THE SAME POINT.

170

Solution

1.   The weights of the masses could be considered to be acting along the lines PQ, QR, RS and ST. Draw the force diagram pqrst, Figure 42, so that the vectors pq, qr, rs and st represent the 8, 1, 2 and 4 units of mass respectively.

2.   Choose any point 0 away from the vector line p to t and connect po, qo, ro, so and ot.

3.   The link polygon (Figure 43) can now be constructed in the usual way, and the resultant of the four masses can be seen to act through point N.

4.   The mass system can now be turned through any angle, for convenience one of 90°. The weights of the masses now act along the lines AB, BC, CD and DE.

5.   Construct another force diagram as shown in Figure 44. The second resultant can be seen to act through point M of the link polygon (Figure 45).

6.   The intersection of the two lines of action of the resultants, will give point G, the position of the centre of gravity of the system of masses.

Figure 46 shows a plane figure and it is required to find the centre of area of this figure.

Solution

1.   Divide the figure into three rectangles, A, B and C, as shown in Figure 47.

2.   Draw the force diagram pqrs such that the vector lengths pq, qr, and rs are given magnitudes proportional to the areas of the rectangles C, B and A respectively (Figure 48).

3.   The link polygon (Figure 49) will give the position of the resultant, point N.

4.   Complete the construction by drawing a second force diagram Figure 50, and a second link polygon Figure 51, and thus obtain a second resultant acting through point M.

VECTOR GEOMETRY

TO DETERMINE THE CENTRE OF GRAVITY OF A GIVEN
SYSTEM OF MASSES.

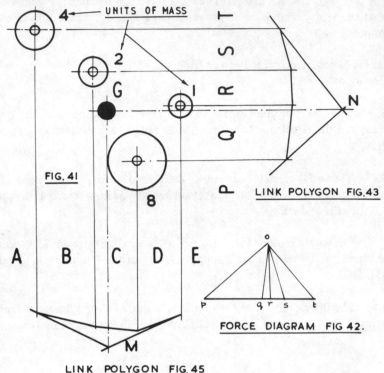

4 ← UNITS OF MASS

2

G

1

8

FIG. 41

A   B   C   D   E

LINK POLYGON FIG. 43

P   Q   R   S   T   N

LINK POLYGON FIG. 45.

M

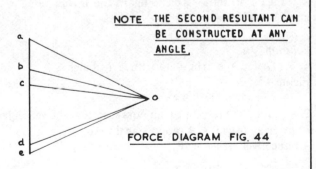

FORCE DIAGRAM FIG 42.

o

p   q r s   t

NOTE THE SECOND RESULTANT CAN
BE CONSTRUCTED AT ANY
ANGLE.

a
b
c

o

d
e

FORCE DIAGRAM FIG. 44

RESULTANTS OF MASSES ACT THROUGH POINTS M AND N

172

VECTOR GEOMETRY

TO DETERMINE THE CENTRE OF AREA OF A GIVEN
SYSTEM OF MASSES.

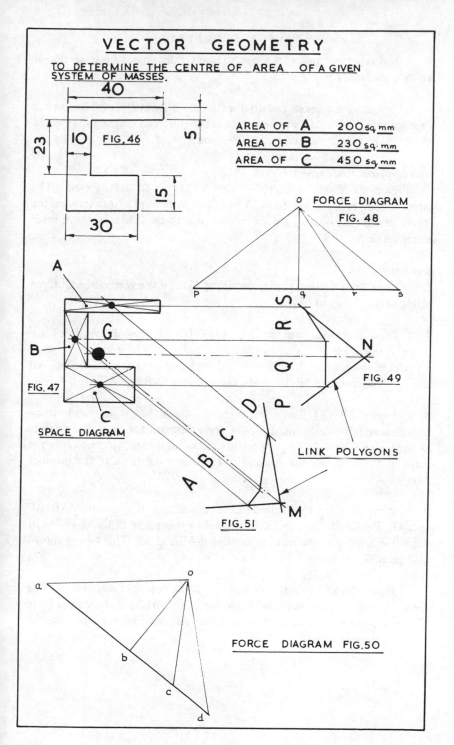

FIG. 46

AREA OF **A**   200 sq. mm
AREA OF **B**   230 sq. mm
AREA OF **C**   450 sq. mm

O   FORCE DIAGRAM
FIG. 48

FIG. 47

SPACE DIAGRAM

FIG. 49

LINK POLYGONS

FIG. 51

FORCE DIAGRAM FIG. 50

5.   The centre of area of the section is at G, the point of intersection of the two resultants.

The vectors are taken in two directions; horizontally, and inclined at approximately 45°. 45° was chosen to avoid the small diagram that would result if the vectors were taken at 90° to each other.

Non co-planar Concurrent Forces.
    Figure 52 shows a pictorial view of a tripod arrangement. The members AB and AC are equal in length. It is required to determine the forces in each member of the framework due to the load of a 4 unit force acting vertically at A.

Solution
1.   Consider a vertical plane containing AD and the vertical 4 unit force acting at A (Figure 53 (A)).

2.   Draw the space diagram (Figure 53 (B)) showing the vertical loading, the back leg AD and another member AE. The latter member is introduced to provide equilibrium and replaces the two shorter legs AB and AC. The member AE lies in the same plane as AB and AC.

3.   Figure 53 (B) illustrates three co-planar forces in equilibrium. Choose a suitable scale and draw the force diagram for these three forces as shown in Figure 54; pq represents the vertical load, qr represents the force in the new member AE and rp represents the force in the member AD.

4.   Now consider the inclined plane containing the members AB, AC and AE; Figure 55. A view taken normal to this plane in the direction of the arrow S will give the true inclination of AB and AC. This view is shown in Figure 56.

5.   Figure 56 again illustrates three co-planar forces in equilibrium. The force diagram wxy representing these forces vectorially is shown in Figure 57; xy represents the force in the member AE, yw and wx represent the forces in the members AC and AB.

VECTOR GEOMETRY.

CONCURRENT NONCOPLANAR FORCES

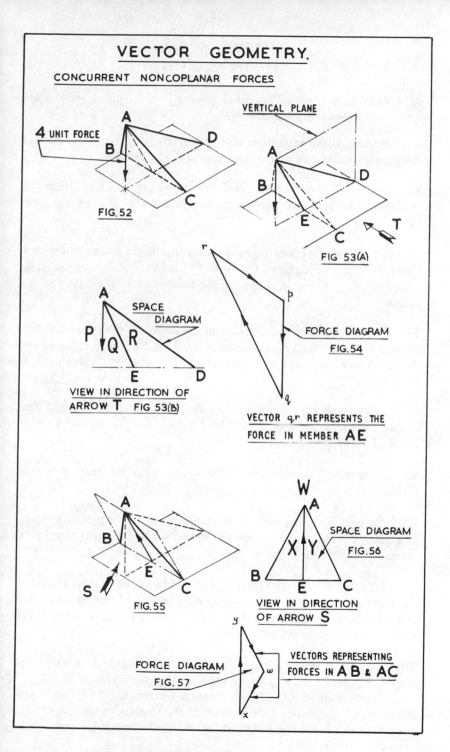

FIG. 52

4 UNIT FORCE

VERTICAL PLANE

FIG 53(A)

A

SPACE DIAGRAM

P Q R

VIEW IN DIRECTION OF ARROW T FIG 53(B)

FORCE DIAGRAM FIG.54

VECTOR qr REPRESENTS THE FORCE IN MEMBER AE

FIG.55

S

W

SPACE DIAGRAM FIG.56

X Y

VIEW IN DIRECTION OF ARROW S

FORCE DIAGRAM FIG. 57

VECTORS REPRESENTING FORCES IN AB & AC

175

VECTOR PROBLEMS

1.   Determine the resultant force for the given co-planar, concurrent force system shown in Figure 1.

2.   Determine the magnitude and the direction of the equilibrant for the given co-planar, concurrent force system shown in Figure 2.

3.   Figure 3 shows the directions of four concurrent forces referred to axes OX and OY. Determine the equilibrant and give its sense and inclination to OX.

4.   Three forces are located by means of the square shown in Figure 4. Determine the equilibrant of this system of forces, and the perpendicular distance from the line of action of the equilibrant to the centre of the square.

5.   Forces of 8, 6, 4 and 5 kilogrammes act in the directions CA, DB, BC and AB respectively, of a square A B C D of 50 mm side. Determine the magnitude, direction and position relative to B of the resultant of these forces.

6.   Figure 5 shows a pin jointed square frame with loads acting at each corner. Determine the magnitude, direction and position relative to A of the resultant of these forces.

7.   Determine the reactions at the supports for the beam shown in Figure 6.

8.   Determine the reactions at the supports for the loaded beam shown in Figure 7. Note that the beam carries two loads and is acted on by an upward force of 4 Kg.

9.   The beam shown in Figure 8 is hinged to a fixed support at the left hand end and is supported at a point 3 units of length from the right hand end, so as to be in the horizontal position. Determine the reactions at the supports for the given system of loading.

10.   Figure 9 shows a pin jointed structure loaded at point Q and hinged at point P. The structure is maintained with PQ vertical by the pull in the vertical chain RT. QR is horizontal. Determine (a) the pull in the chain; (b) the magnitude and direction of the reaction at the hinge P; (c) the forces in the members PQ and SR. State whether each member is in tension or compression.

VECTOR PROBLEMS

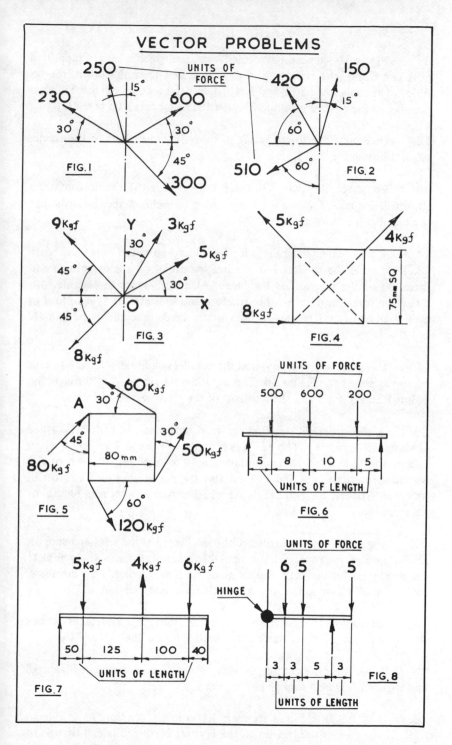

FIG. 1

FIG. 2

FIG. 3

FIG. 4

FIG. 5

FIG. 6

FIG. 7

FIG. 8

11.   Figure 10 shows a pin jointed structure which is simply supported at A and B. For the system of loading illustrated determine (a) the magnitudes of the reactions at A and B; (b) the magnitude of the force in each member of the structure stating whether the member is a tie or a strut.

12.   Determine the forces acting in the various members of the framework shown in Figure 11.

13.   Construct the complete force polygon for the simple roof truss shown in Figure 12. State the force acting in each member and whether the member is a tie or a strut.

14.   A pin jointed structure is loaded and supported as shown in Figure 13. Determine the tension T in the bracing cable and the magnitude and direction of the reaction at the hinge. All members are of equal length. Draw the force diagram for the structure and indicate the type of load in each member. State the magnitudes of the loads in members HJ and JK only.

15.   Using the link polygon, find the parallel equilibrants for the system of forces shown in Figure 14. The equilibrants are to pass through the points P and Q. Find also the resultant of the given system of forces.

16.   A roof truss with a 10 metre span and a rise of 4 metres, is loaded as shown in Figure 15. The end X is hinged and the end Y merely rests on a support. Determine the magnitude and the direction of each of the resultant reactions at X and Y. Find also the magnitudes of the forces in members GH, HI, KL and LG. State whether the member is in tension or compression.

17.   Figure 16 shows a loaded roof truss hinged at the left hand support and supported on rollers at the right hand support. Draw the complete force diagram for the truss and tabulate the forces acting in the members, indicating which are in tension and which are in compression.

18.   Determine the centre of gravity of the given system of masses shown in Figure 17. State its position relative to the lines AB and CD.

19.   Determine the centres of area of the figures shown in Figure 18 and Figure 19. Dimensions given are in mm.

20.   Two legs of a tripod are each 400 cm long, the third leg is 396 cm long. If the feet of the legs lie on the corners of an equilateral triangle of

VECTOR PROBLEMS

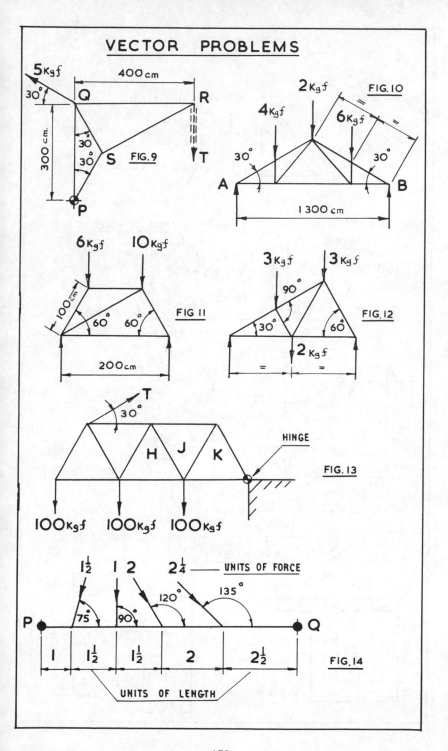

179

VECTOR PROBLEMS

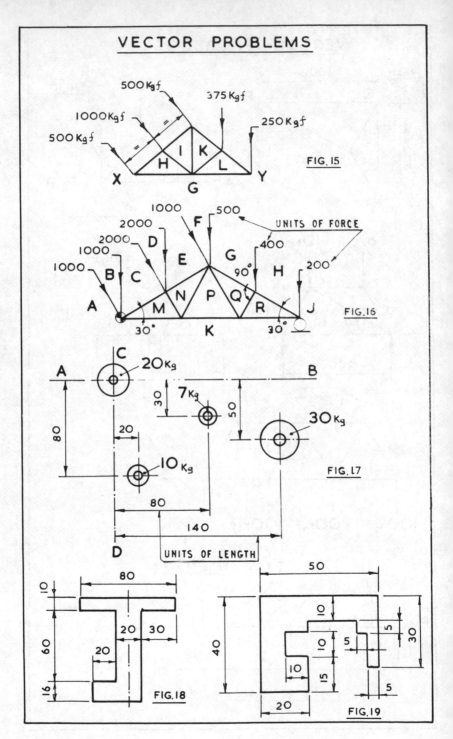

180

side 300 cm, lying in a horizontal plane, find the force in each leg when a weight of 2000 kilogrammes is suspended from the apex of the tripod.

21.   In a tripod the length of each of the legs OA, OB and OC is 6 metres. The lines joining their feet are AB = 4 metres, BC = 3.5 metres, and AC = 3 metres. If a load of 5000 kilogrammes is suspended from the apex O, determine the force in each leg of the tripod.

8

TRACES

Traces of Lines

FIGURE 1 on page 183 shows the principal planes of projection in the first quadrant. Figure 2 shows the same planes with a line AB positioned between them. The line is projected on to each plane giving the elevation A^1B^1 on the vertical plane and the plan A^2B^2 on the horizontal plane. In Figure 3 the line is produced to pierce the vertical and horizontal planes. The point where the line, produced if necessary, pierces the vertical plane is the vertical trace of the line. The point where the line, produced if necessary, pierces the horizontal plane is called the horizontal trace of the line. The abbreviations VT and HT are commonly used. It can be seen from Figure 3 that the VT of AB lies on the elevation produced and similarly that the HT of AB lies on the plan produced.

Figure 4 shows the plan and elevation of AB drawn in orthographic projection and illustrates how the traces of a line are found. To find the vertical trace, produce the plan to meet XY. Relative to the plan, XY represents the vertical plane. The intersection of the plan and XY is therefore the vertical trace of the line in plan. Project this intersection into the elevation to cut the elevation of the line, or the elevation produced. This is the vertical trace of AB. The horizontal trace is found in a similar way. Produce the elevation to meet XY. Relative to the elevation, XY represents the horizontal plane, so the intersection of the elevation with XY is the horizontal trace in the elevation. Project this intersection into the plan to cut the plan of the line, produced if necessary. This is the horizontal trace of AB. A comparison of Figures 3 and 4 will make the method clear.

In general, the vertical trace of a line appears above the XY line and the horizontal trace below it. However, it is possible to position the line relative to the principal planes so that both traces appear above, or both traces appear below, the XY line. This is illustrated in Figures 5 to 8.

Figure 5 shows pictorially a line AB whose horizontal trace lies in the second quadrant. When the principal planes are rabatted and orthographic views of this line are drawn as in Figure 6, the horizontal trace will lie above XY with the vertical trace.

In Figure 7 the vertical trace of AB lies in the fourth quadrant. Therefore, after rabatting the principal planes, the orthographic views shown in Figure 8 will have the vertical trace below XY with the horizontal trace.

TRACES

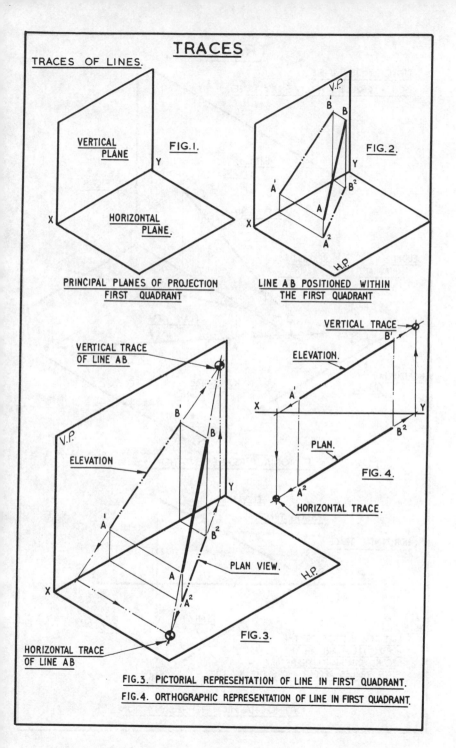

TRACES OF LINES.

VERTICAL PLANE   FIG. 1.

Y

X   HORIZONTAL PLANE.

PRINCIPAL PLANES OF PROJECTION
FIRST QUADRANT

V.P.

B'   B

FIG. 2.

A'   Y   B²

X   A

A²   H.P.

LINE A B POSITIONED WITHIN
THE FIRST QUADRANT

VERTICAL TRACE
OF LINE AB

V.P.

B'   B

ELEVATION

Y

A'   B²

X   A   A²

PLAN VIEW.   H.P.

FIG. 3.

HORIZONTAL TRACE
OF LINE AB

VERTICAL TRACE

B'

ELEVATION.

A'

X   Y   B²

PLAN.   FIG. 4.

A²

HORIZONTAL TRACE.

FIG. 3. PICTORIAL REPRESENTATION OF LINE IN FIRST QUADRANT.
FIG. 4. ORTHOGRAPHIC REPRESENTATION OF LINE IN FIRST QUADRANT.

183

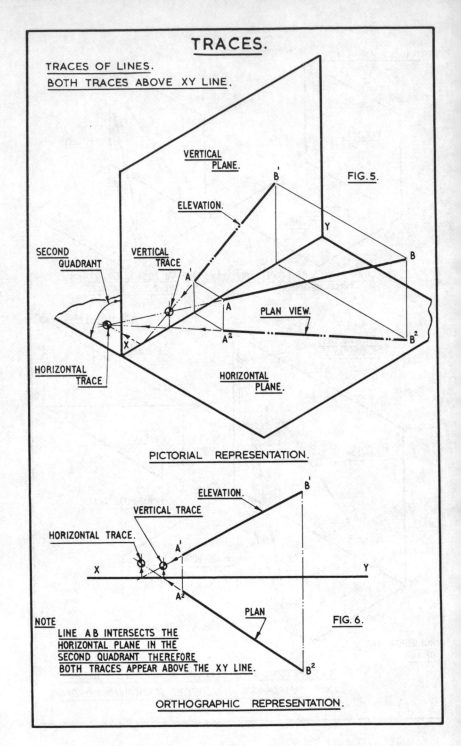

TRACES.

TRACES OF LINES.
BOTH TRACES ABOVE XY LINE.

FIG. 5.

VERTICAL
PLANE.

ELEVATION.

SECOND
QUADRANT

VERTICAL
TRACE

PLAN VIEW.

HORIZONTAL
TRACE

HORIZONTAL
PLANE.

PICTORIAL REPRESENTATION.

ELEVATION.

VERTICAL TRACE

HORIZONTAL TRACE.

FIG. 6.

PLAN

NOTE
LINE A B INTERSECTS THE
HORIZONTAL PLANE IN THE
SECOND QUADRANT THEREFORE
BOTH TRACES APPEAR ABOVE THE XY LINE.

ORTHOGRAPHIC REPRESENTATION.

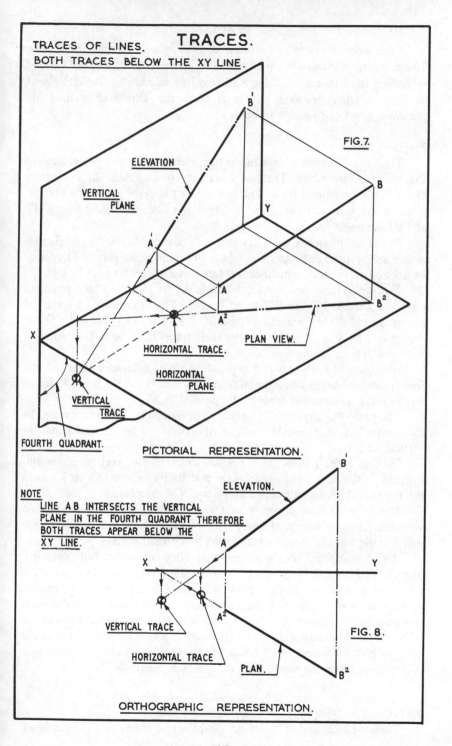

TRACES OF LINES.
BOTH TRACES BELOW THE XY LINE.

TRACES.

FIG.7.

ELEVATION

VERTICAL PLANE

B'

B

Y

A'

A

A²

B²

X

HORIZONTAL TRACE.

PLAN VIEW.

HORIZONTAL PLANE

VERTICAL TRACE

FOURTH QUADRANT.

PICTORIAL REPRESENTATION.

NOTE
LINE A B INTERSECTS THE VERTICAL
PLANE IN THE FOURTH QUADRANT THEREFORE
BOTH TRACES APPEAR BELOW THE
XY LINE.

ELEVATION.

B'

A'

X   Y

A²

VERTICAL TRACE

HORIZONTAL TRACE

PLAN.

B²

FIG. 8.

ORTHOGRAPHIC REPRESENTATION.

Four worked examples on traces of lines follow on pages 187 to 189. These examples involve the points set out above. In addition, the method of finding the true angles of inclination of the line to the principal planes by using auxiliary views is shown in each case. This is revision of the principles given on page 118 in **Book 1**.

Traces of Planes

The lines in which a plane meets the principal planes of projection are the traces of the plane. The line where the plane meets the horizontal plane is the horizontal trace. The line where the plane meets the vertical plane is the vertical trace. As with traces of a line, the abbreviations HT and VT are usually used.

Planes are of two main types, perpendicular or oblique. Perpendicular planes are perpendicular to one or both of the principal planes. They may be horizontal, vertical or inclined, as shown in Figure 9 on page 190.

Figure 9(A) shows a plane P which is perpendicular to both principal planes. Its traces VT and HT meet on XY. This is true for all traces of planes provided they are not parallel to XY. The lines AB and CD are drawn on the plane P and therefore their traces must lie in the traces of the plane. This is always true.

In Figure 9(B) the plane P is parallel to the horizontal plane. Therefore it cannot have any horizontal trace and neither can the line AB drawn on the plane. The vertical trace of P is parallel to XY.

The plane P in Figure 9(C) has no vertical trace because it is parallel to the vertical plane. Similarly the line AB contained by the plane has no vertical trace.

In Figure 9(D) plane P is perpendicular to the vertical plane and inclined to the horizontal plane. Note that its traces intersect on XY, and the traces of lines AB and CD lie in the traces of the plane.

It will be see from Figure 9 that with all perpendicular planes at least one view (plan or elevation) is an edge view of the plane and that this view will give the true inclination of the plane to a principal plane.

An oblique plane, illustrated in Figure 10, is inclined to both principal planes. It can only be represented satisfactorily in orthographic projection by its traces as shown in Figure 11. With an oblique plane neither trace is an edge view of the plane, so the angles between the traces and XY are not the true inclinations of the plane to the horizontal and vertical planes. As with the perpendicular planes in Figures 9(A) and 9(D), the traces of the oblique plane intersect on XY and the traces of the sides of the triangle ABC, which lies in the plane, lie in the traces of the plane.

To Convert an Oblique Plane to an Inclined Plane

Figure 12 on page 193 shows the principal planes of the first quad-

TRACES.

EXAMPLES OF TRACES OF LINES.

EXAMPLE 1.

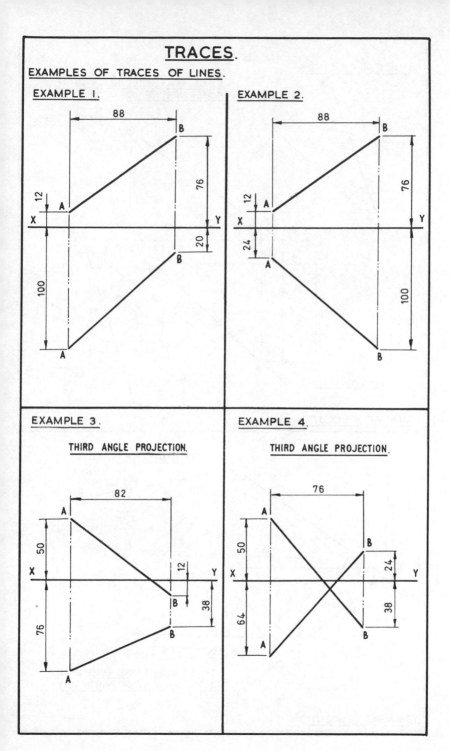

EXAMPLE 2.

EXAMPLE 3.

THIRD ANGLE PROJECTION.

EXAMPLE 4.

THIRD ANGLE PROJECTION.

187

TRACES.

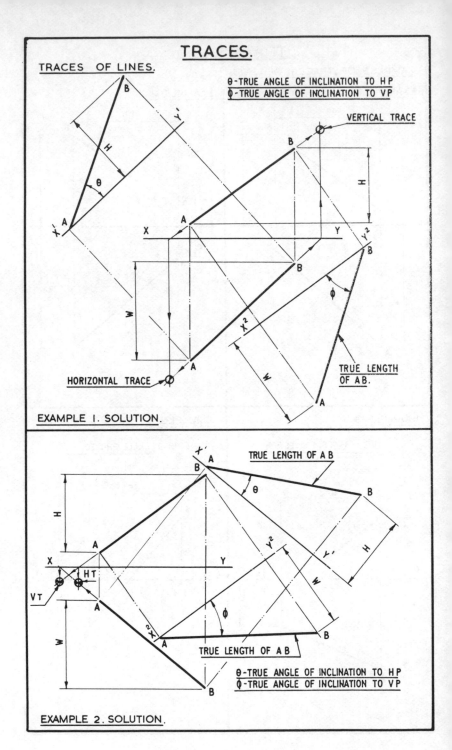

TRACES OF LINES.

θ - TRUE ANGLE OF INCLINATION TO H P
φ - TRUE ANGLE OF INCLINATION TO V P

VERTICAL TRACE

HORIZONTAL TRACE

TRUE LENGTH OF A B.

EXAMPLE I. SOLUTION.

TRUE LENGTH OF A B

TRUE LENGTH OF A B

θ - TRUE ANGLE OF INCLINATION TO H P
φ - TRUE ANGLE OF INCLINATION TO V P

EXAMPLE 2. SOLUTION.

TRACES.

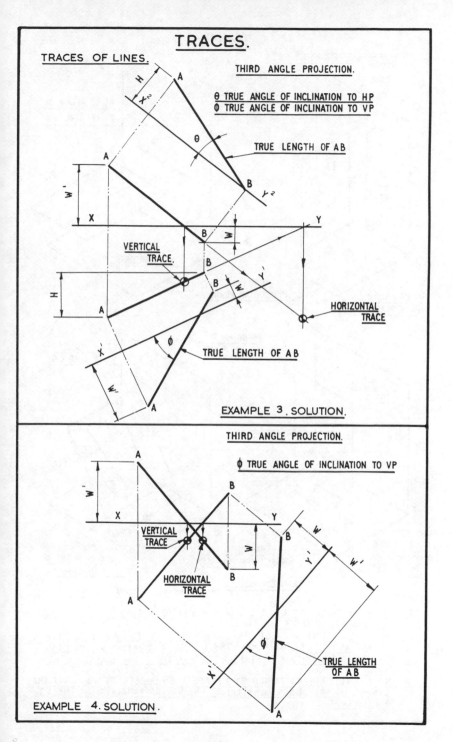

TRACES OF LINES.

THIRD ANGLE PROJECTION.

θ TRUE ANGLE OF INCLINATION TO HP
Φ TRUE ANGLE OF INCLINATION TO VP

TRUE LENGTH OF AB

VERTICAL TRACE.

HORIZONTAL TRACE

TRUE LENGTH OF AB

EXAMPLE 3. SOLUTION.

THIRD ANGLE PROJECTION.

Φ TRUE ANGLE OF INCLINATION TO VP

VERTICAL TRACE

HORIZONTAL TRACE

TRUE LENGTH OF AB

EXAMPLE 4. SOLUTION.

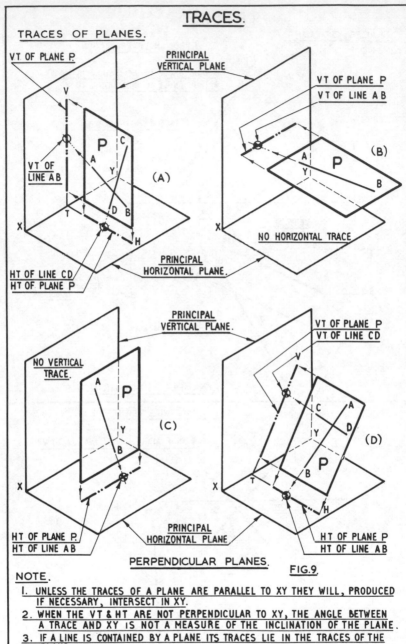

TRACES.

TRACES OF PLANES.

(A), (B), (C), (D)

VT OF PLANE P.

PRINCIPAL VERTICAL PLANE

VT OF PLANE P
VT OF LINE A B

VT OF LINE A B

(A)

(B)

NO HORIZONTAL TRACE

HT OF LINE CD
HT OF PLANE P

PRINCIPAL HORIZONTAL PLANE.

PRINCIPAL VERTICAL PLANE.

VT OF PLANE P
VT OF LINE CD

NO VERTICAL TRACE.

(C)

(D)

HT OF PLANE P.
HT OF LINE A B

PRINCIPAL HORIZONTAL PLANE.

HT OF PLANE P
HT OF LINE A B

PERPENDICULAR PLANES.

FIG.9

NOTE.

1. UNLESS THE TRACES OF A PLANE ARE PARALLEL TO XY THEY WILL, PRODUCED IF NECESSARY, INTERSECT IN XY.

2. WHEN THE VT & HT ARE NOT PERPENDICULAR TO XY, THE ANGLE BETWEEN A TRACE AND XY IS NOT A MEASURE OF THE INCLINATION OF THE PLANE.

3. IF A LINE IS CONTAINED BY A PLANE ITS TRACES LIE IN THE TRACES OF THE PLANE.

4. HORIZONTAL LINES CONTAINED BY A PLANE ARE PARALLEL TO THE HT OF THE PLANE. SIMILARLY, LINES PARALLEL TO THE VP ARE PARALLEL TO THE VT OF THE PLANE.

TRACES

TRACES OF PLANES.

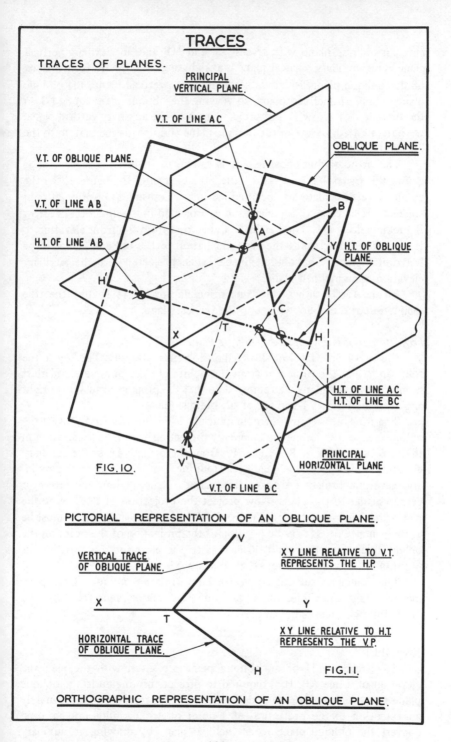

PRINCIPAL VERTICAL PLANE.

V.T. OF LINE A C

OBLIQUE PLANE.

V.T. OF OBLIQUE PLANE.

V

V.T. OF LINE A B

B

H.T. OF LINE A B

A

Y H.T. OF OBLIQUE PLANE.

H'

X

T

C

H

FIG. 10.

V'

H.T. OF LINE A C
H.T. OF LINE B C

PRINCIPAL HORIZONTAL PLANE

V.T. OF LINE B C

PICTORIAL REPRESENTATION OF AN OBLIQUE PLANE.

VERTICAL TRACE OF OBLIQUE PLANE.

V

X Y LINE RELATIVE TO V.T. REPRESENTS THE H.P.

X

Y

T

HORIZONTAL TRACE OF OBLIQUE PLANE.

X Y LINE RELATIVE TO H.T. REPRESENTS THE V.P.

H

FIG. 11.

ORTHOGRAPHIC REPRESENTATION OF AN OBLIQUE PLANE.

191

rant, an oblique plane with traces VT and HT and an auxiliary vertical plane. This auxiliary vertical plane is at right angles to the horizontal trace of the oblique plane. Relative to the auxiliary vertical plane, the oblique plane is only an inclined plane, so viewing the oblique plane along HT in the direction of arrow R and projecting on to the auxiliary vertical plane, we obtain an edge view of the oblique plane and its true inclination to the horizontal plane.

The orthographic construction is shown in Figure 13. Figure 13(A) shows the traces VT and HT of the oblique plane. In Figure 13(B) the auxiliary vertical plane has been added in any convenient position at right angles to HT. An auxiliary elevation is projected in the direction of arrow R looking along HT. The height L, transferred from the front elevation to the auxiliary view, fixes the true inclination of the oblique plane to the horizontal plane. The oblique plane, when projected into the auxiliary elevation, is an inclined plane.

Figure 13(C) shows the same principle applied to finding the true inclination of the oblique plane to the vertical plane.

Projection of a Point on to an Oblique Plane

Figure 14 on page 194 shows the problem pictorially. The key to the solution is that the projector from the point P to the oblique plane must be normal to the plane. It follows then that the projector must be at right angles to the traces VT and HT of the oblique plane.

The method is shown orthographically in Figure 15. First convert the oblique plane into an inclined plane by projecting an auxiliary elevation in the direction of arrow R. Project P^1 from the plan to P^3 in the auxiliary elevation and transfer the height H^2 from the front elevation to the auxiliary elevation. Project P^3 on to the inclined plane, making the projector perpendicular to the plane. Now project the projection of P^3 back to the plan view. The projector from P^1 to the oblique plane in this view must be at right angles to HT, so the position of the projection of the point on the oblique plane can be found. Project it to the elevation and, to find its position in this view, transfer H^1 from the auxiliary view.

The principles set out above for converting an oblique plane to an inclined plane and projecting a point on to an oblique plane are illustrated in the following worked examples.

EXAMPLE 5

The traces VTH of an oblique plane are given with the plan and elevation of a line AB. It is required to project this line on to the oblique plane and to draw the plan and elevation of the projection. This is merely an extension of the projection of a point on to an oblique plane. First convert the oblique plane to an inclined plane by drawing an auxiliary

TRACES

<u>METHOD OF CONVERTING AN OBLIQUE PLANE TO AN INCLINED PLANE.</u>

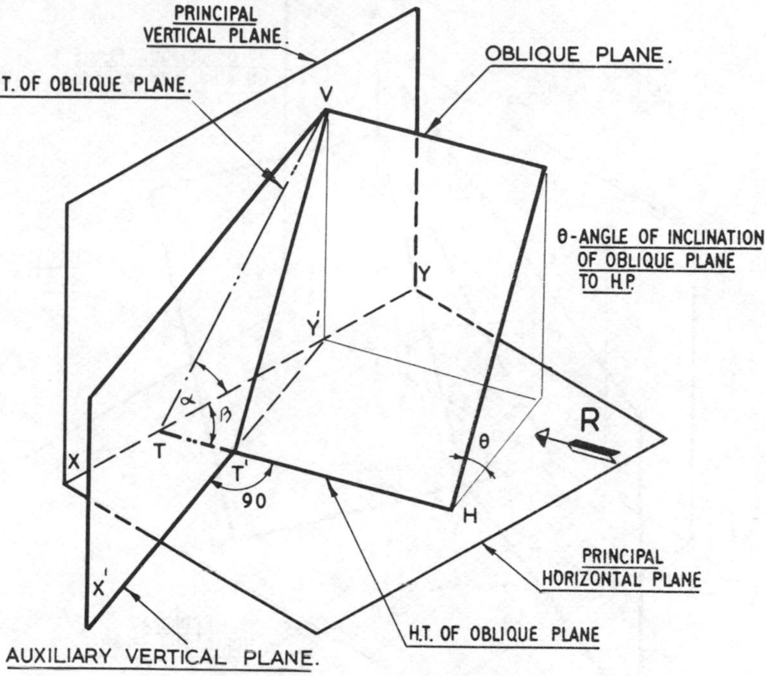

PRINCIPAL
VERTICAL PLANE.

OBLIQUE PLANE.

V.T. OF OBLIQUE PLANE.

V

θ-ANGLE OF INCLINATION
OF OBLIQUE PLANE
TO H.P.

Y

Y'

α β

R

θ

X

T

T'

90

H

X'

PRINCIPAL
HORIZONTAL PLANE

H.T. OF OBLIQUE PLANE

AUXILIARY VERTICAL PLANE.

<u>PICTORIAL VIEW SHOWING AUXILIARY PLANE. FIG.12.</u>

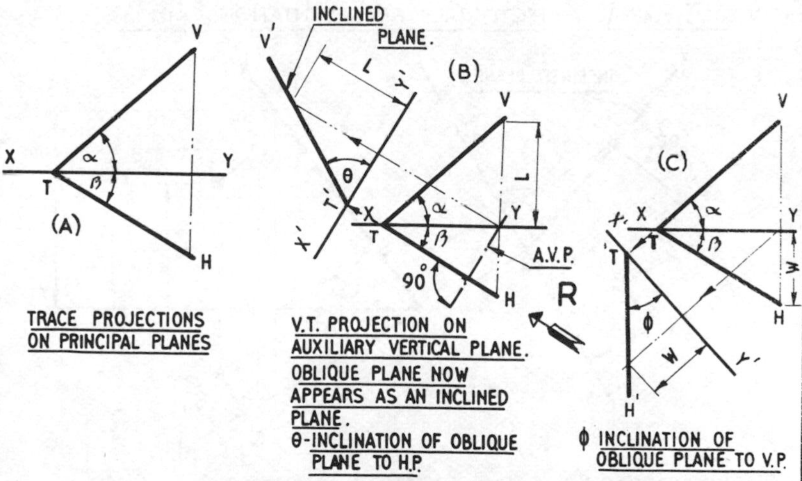

V

INCLINED
PLANE.

V'

L

(B)

V

L

X

Y

α

β

A.V.P.

θ

T'

X'

T

90°

H

R

(A)

X

Y

α

T

β

H

<u>TRACE PROJECTIONS
ON PRINCIPAL PLANES</u>

(C)

V

X

α

Y

T

β

W

φ

H

W

Y'

H'

<u>V.T. PROJECTION ON
AUXILIARY VERTICAL PLANE.
OBLIQUE PLANE NOW
APPEARS AS AN INCLINED
PLANE.</u>
θ-INCLINATION OF OBLIQUE
PLANE TO H.P.

φ INCLINATION OF
OBLIQUE PLANE TO V.P.

<u>ORTHOGRAPHIC REPRESENTATION. FIG.13.</u>

TRACES

PROJECTION OF A POINT ON TO AN OBLIQUE PLANE.

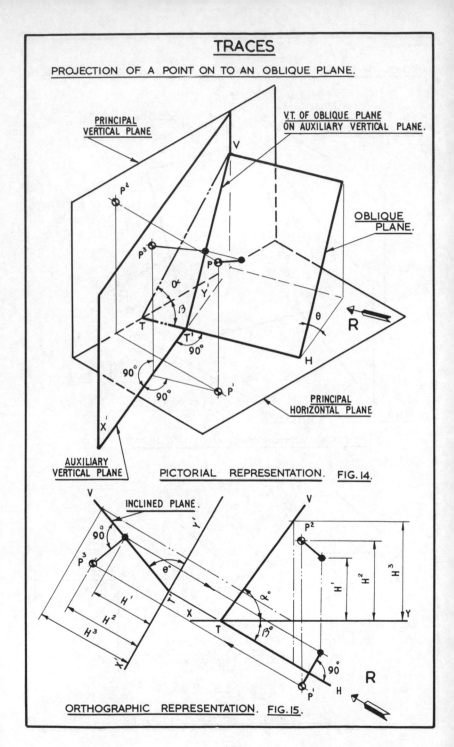

PICTORIAL REPRESENTATION. FIG. 14.

ORTHOGRAPHIC REPRESENTATION. FIG. 15.

194

elevation and project the line into this view. Project the ends of the line on to the inclined plane and project these points back to the plan. Points C and D on the plan of the line on the oblique plane can be found by projecting from A and B in the given plan to cross HT at right angles. The same principle may be applied to find C and D on the elevation of the line on the oblique plane.

EXAMPLE 6

Here the triangle ABC lies in the oblique plane VTH. The plan of the triangle is given. The elevation and true shape of the triangle are required. Start by converting the oblique plane to an inclined plane, and project the corners A, B and C of the given plan of the triangle on to the inclined plane. The true shape of the triangle is found by projecting a second auxiliary plan viewing the inclined plane normally. The elevation of the triangle is drawn by transferring the heights P, Q and R from the auxiliary elevation to the front elevation.

EXAMPLE 7

The plan and elevation of a triangle ABC are given with the traces VTH of an oblique plane. The plan and elevation of the triangle after it has been projected on to the oblique plane are required. Convert the oblique plane to an inclined plane by projecting an anxiliary elevation. Project the triangle into this view and project the corners on to the inclined plane. Project these points back to the plan and fix A^1, B^1 and C^1 in the projected plan by projectors at right angles to HT from the corners of the given plan. Project A^1, B^1 and C^1 to the elevation and find them by transferring heights P, Q and R from the auxiliary elevation to the appropriate projector.

Two examples are now given of solids cut by oblique planes. These can be solved using the principles already given.

EXAMPLE 8

The plan and elevation of a square prism are given with the traces VTH of an oblique plane. This plane is to cut the prism, passing through point P. Determine the plan and elevation of the cut prism and the true shape of the section produced by the oblique plane. First convert the oblique plane to an inclined plane and project the prism into this auxiliary view. Move V^1T^1 parallel to itself, to pass through P on the auxiliary elevation of the prism. The plan of the cut prism can now be completed by projecting from the cut auxiliary elevation, and then the front elevation can be completed by projection from the plan. The true shape of the section is found by projecting a second auxiliary plan normal to V^1T^1 and transferring widths such as W from the normal plan.

TRACES.

EXAMPLES OF TRACES OF PLANES.

EXAMPLE 5.

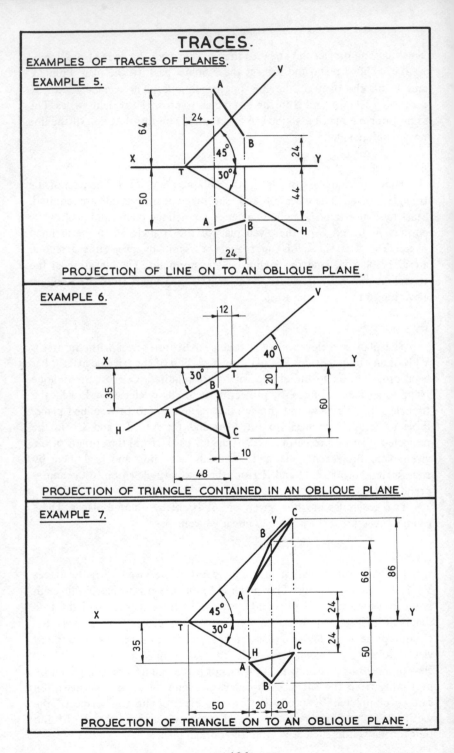

PROJECTION OF LINE ON TO AN OBLIQUE PLANE.

EXAMPLE 6.

PROJECTION OF TRIANGLE CONTAINED IN AN OBLIQUE PLANE.

EXAMPLE 7.

PROJECTION OF TRIANGLE ON TO AN OBLIQUE PLANE.

196

TRACES.

TRACES OF PLANES.

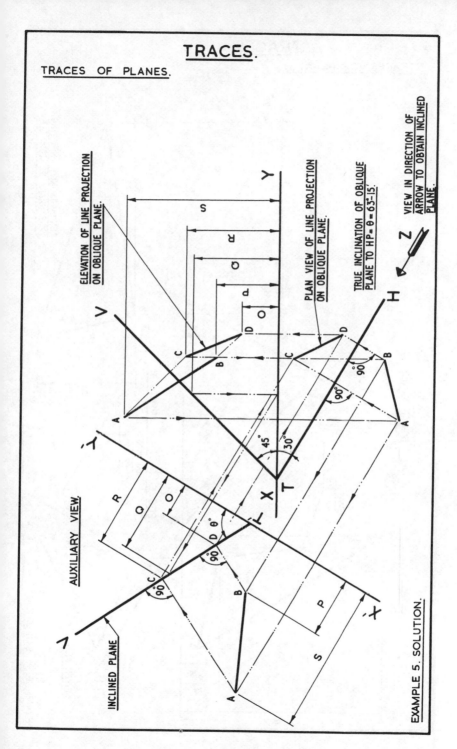

ELEVATION OF LINE PROJECTION ON OBLIQUE PLANE.

PLAN VIEW OF LINE PROJECTION ON OBLIQUE PLANE.

TRUE INCLINATION OF OBLIQUE PLANE TO HP = θ = 63°·15′

VIEW IN DIRECTION OF ARROW TO OBTAIN INCLINED PLANE.

AUXILIARY VIEW.

INCLINED PLANE.

EXAMPLE 5. SOLUTION.

197

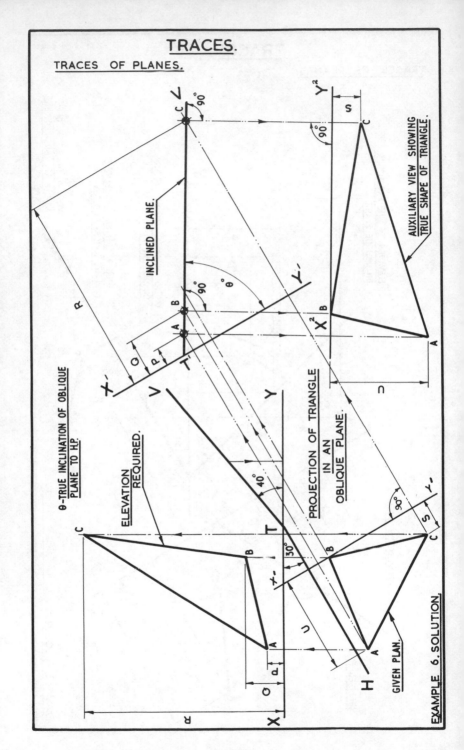

TRACES.

TRACES OF PLANES.

INCLINED PLANE.

θ—TRUE INCLINATION OF OBLIQUE PLANE TO H.P.

ELEVATION REQUIRED.

PROJECTION OF TRIANGLE IN AN OBLIQUE PLANE.

AUXILIARY VIEW SHOWING TRUE SHAPE OF TRIANGLE.

GIVEN PLAN.

EXAMPLE 6. SOLUTION.

TRACES.

TRACES OF PLANES

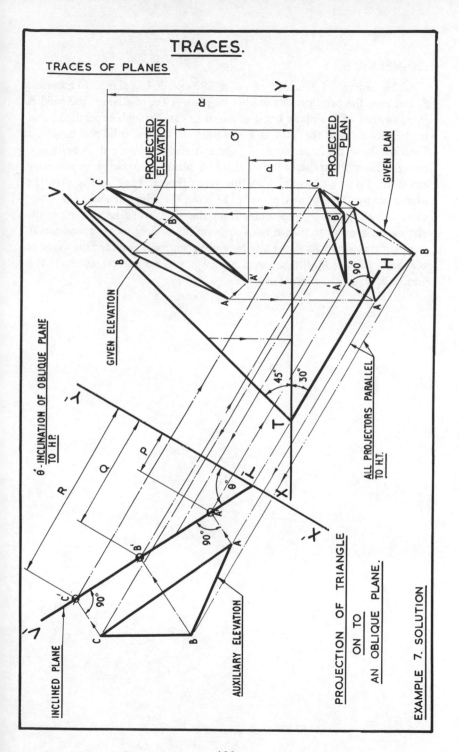

θ - INCLINATION OF OBLIQUE PLANE TO H.P.

PROJECTED ELEVATION

PROJECTED PLAN

GIVEN PLAN

GIVEN ELEVATION

INCLINED PLANE

AUXILIARY ELEVATION

ALL PROJECTORS PARALLEL TO H.T.

PROJECTION OF TRIANGLE ON TO AN OBLIQUE PLANE.

EXAMPLE 7. SOLUTION

199

EXAMPLE 9

This example, illustrated on pages 203 and 204, is similar to Example 8, but now the position of the oblique plane VTH relative to the solid is given instead of the plane being required to pass through a specified point on the solid. Find the plan and elevation of the cut solid and project a view to show the true shape of the cut surface. Proceed as before to convert the oblique plane to an inclined plane by drawing an auxiliary elevation. Project the solid into this view. Project back to the plan the points where the inclined plane V^1T^1 cuts the edges of the solid. Complete the elevation by projecting from the plan, using heights from the auxiliary elevation to locate the points on the projectors. A second auxiliary plan, projected from the auxiliary elevation, will give the true shape of the cut surface. Widths across this view are the same as corresponding widths W across the normal plan.

TRACES

SOLIDS CUT BY OBLIQUE PLANES.

EXAMPLE 8.

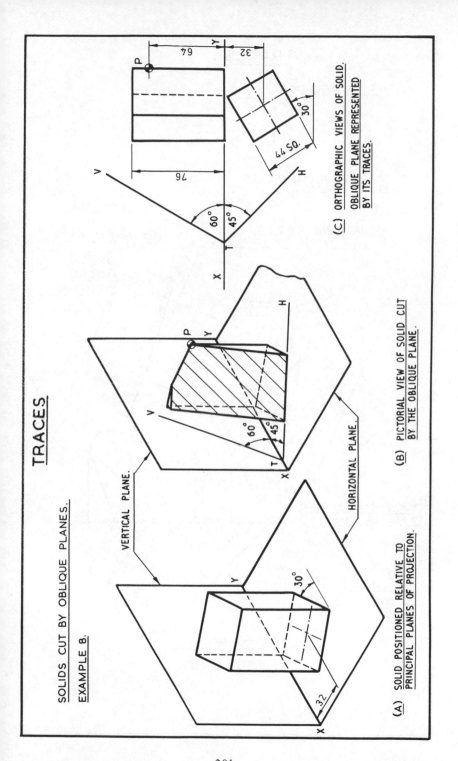

(A) SOLID POSITIONED RELATIVE TO PRINCIPAL PLANES OF PROJECTION.

(B) PICTORIAL VIEW OF SOLID CUT BY THE OBLIQUE PLANE.

(C) ORTHOGRAPHIC VIEWS OF SOLID. OBLIQUE PLANE REPRESENTED BY ITS TRACES.

TRACES.

EXAMPLE 8. SOLUTION.

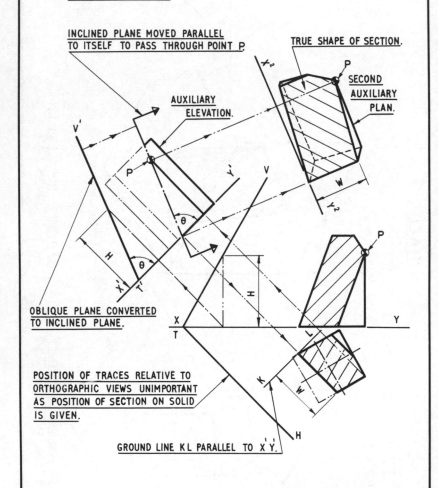

θ - TRUE ANGLE OF INCLINATION OF OBLIQUE PLANE TO H.P.

INCLINED PLANE MOVED PARALLEL TO ITSELF TO PASS THROUGH POINT P.

TRUE SHAPE OF SECTION.

AUXILIARY ELEVATION.

SECOND AUXILIARY PLAN.

OBLIQUE PLANE CONVERTED TO INCLINED PLANE.

POSITION OF TRACES RELATIVE TO ORTHOGRAPHIC VIEWS UNIMPORTANT AS POSITION OF SECTION ON SOLID IS GIVEN.

GROUND LINE K L PARALLEL TO X'Y.

TRACES.

SOLIDS CUT BY OBLIQUE PLANES.

EXAMPLE 9. NOTE—POSITION OF SOLID RELATIVE TO OBLIQUE PLANE GIVEN.

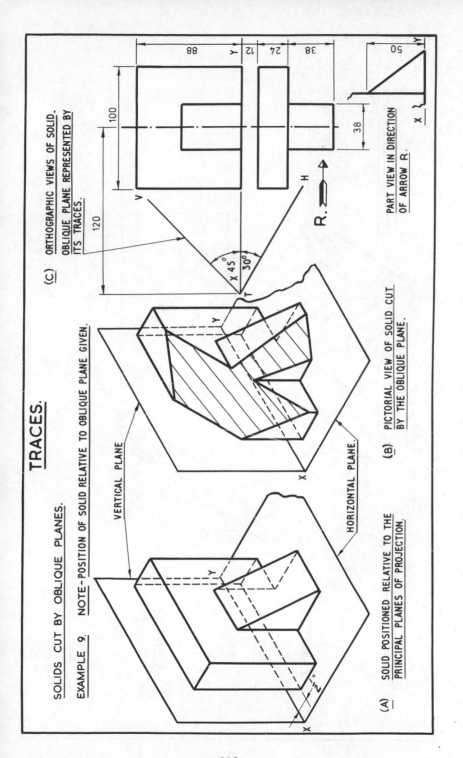

(A) SOLID POSITIONED RELATIVE TO THE PRINCIPAL PLANES OF PROJECTION.

VERTICAL PLANE

HORIZONTAL PLANE.

(B) PICTORIAL VIEW OF SOLID CUT BY THE OBLIQUE PLANE.

(C) ORTHOGRAPHIC VIEWS OF SOLID. OBLIQUE PLANE REPRESENTED BY ITS TRACES.

PART VIEW IN DIRECTION OF ARROW R.

203

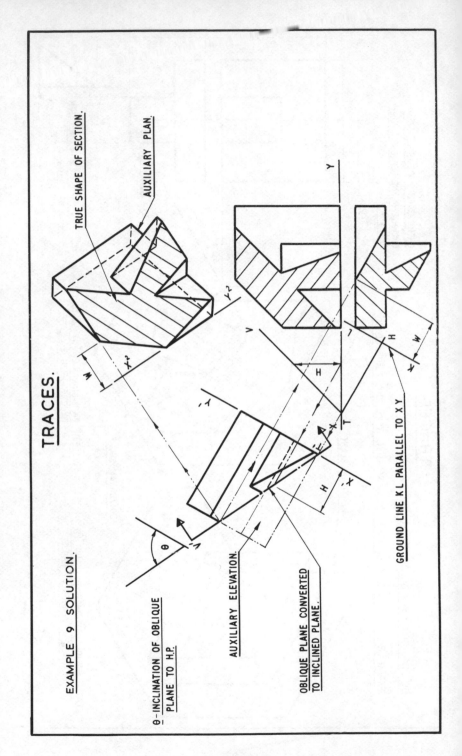

TRACES.

EXAMPLE 9 SOLUTION.

θ - INCLINATION OF OBLIQUE
PLANE TO H.P.

AUXILIARY ELEVATION.

OBLIQUE PLANE CONVERTED
TO INCLINED PLANE.

GROUND LINE K L PARALLEL TO X Y

TRUE SHAPE OF SECTION.

AUXILIARY PLAN.

PROBLEMS ON TRACES

Unless otherwise stated use First Angle projection and draw full size. Construction lines should not be erased. Hidden detail should be shown.

1—4. Draw the given views of the lines and determine their traces, true angles of inclination to the horizontal and vertical planes, and true lengths. Question 4 is to be drawn in Third Angle projection.

5. The elevation of a line AB is given. The end A is positioned in the plan. If the true length of the line is 118 mm, complete the plan, find the traces of the line, and its true inclinations to the principal planes. Use Third Angle projection.

6. The Figure shows the plan of a line AB with the position of B in the elevation. The line makes an angle of 30° with the horizontal plane, with A nearer the plane than B. Complete the elevation and find the true length of the line. Also find its traces and true inclinations to the principal planes. Use Third Angle projection.

7. The plan view of a line AB lying in an oblique plane VTH is given. Project the elevation of the line and find its true length. Also find the true inclination of the oblique plane to the horizontal.

8. A triangle is shown in plan and elevation in the Figure, together with its position relative to an oblique plane VTH. Produce the plan and elevation of the triangle when it is projected on to the oblique plane, and determine the true shape of the projection. Also find the true inclination of the oblique plane to the vertical plane.

9. The plan ABC of a triangle and the traces VTH of a plane containing it are given. Draw the plan and elevation of the triangle and find its true shape.

10.   The plan of a line AB, which lies in an oblique plane, is shown, together with the horizontal trace HT of the plane. The true inclination of AB to the horizontal plane is 55°. A second line CD lies in the same oblique plane and intersects AB at P. Determine the true lengths of both lines and the true angles between them.

11–12.   Both questions show the plan and elevation of a triangle ABC. The triangles lie in oblique planes. Determine the traces of these planes and their true inclinations to the vertical and horizontal planes.

13.   The triangle ABC shown in plan and elevation lies in an oblique plane. The same plane passes through the given hexagonal prism. Determine the traces of the oblique plane and project an elevation of the cut prism.

14.   The elevation and incomplete plan are given of a hexagonal prism which is inclined to both principal planes. The prism is 100 mm long and makes an angle of 30° with the horizontal plane. An oblique plane VTH, positioned as shown, cuts the prism. Draw an elevation of the cut prism and project from it a plan. State the true inclination of the oblique plane to the horizontal plane.

15.   Two views of part of a cylindrical strut are given. The strut is to be welded to a plate which lies in the oblique plane VTH. Find the true inclination of the plate to the horizontal plane. Draw the given views of the strut showing the strut end before welding to the plate. Also project a view to show the true shape of the strut end.

16.   The triangle ABC lies in an oblique plane. Find the traces of this plane and its true inclination to the horizontal plane. The same oblique plane cuts the hexagonal pyramid shown, passing through point P. Draw the plan and elevation of the cut pyramid showing the section produced.

17.   The traces HT and VT of an oblique plane are at 30° and 45° respectively to XY. Determine the true inclination of this plane to the horizontal plane. A triangle ABC has sides AB 50 mm, BC 70 mm, and CA 80 mm and lies in this oblique plane with BC parallel to and 20 mm from the vertical plane. B is the corner of the triangle nearest to XY in the

elevation. Draw the plan and elevation of the triangle. Determine the horizontal and vertical traces of a line from A to a point 20 mm from B along BC in the elevation.

PROBLEMS ON TRACES.

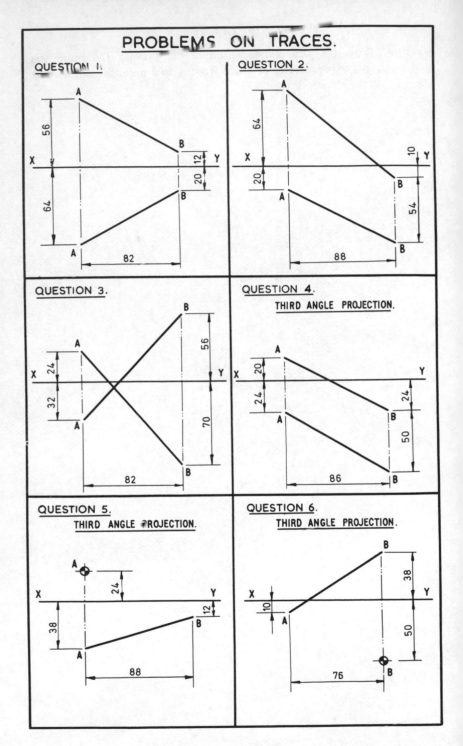

QUESTION I.

QUESTION 2.

QUESTION 3.

QUESTION 4.
THIRD ANGLE PROJECTION.

QUESTION 5.
THIRD ANGLE PROJECTION.

QUESTION 6.
THIRD ANGLE PROJECTION.

PROBLEMS ON TRACES.

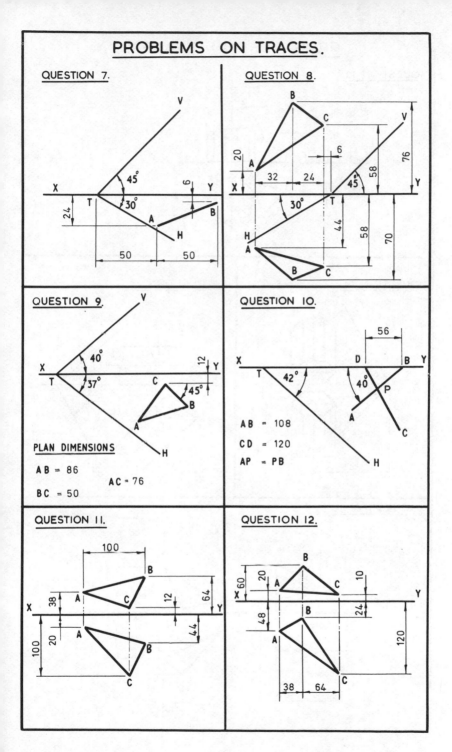

QUESTION 7.

QUESTION 8.

QUESTION 9.

PLAN DIMENSIONS

AB = 86

AC = 76

BC = 50

QUESTION 10.

AB = 108

CD = 120

AP = PB

QUESTION 11.

QUESTION 12.

PROBLEMS ON TRACES.

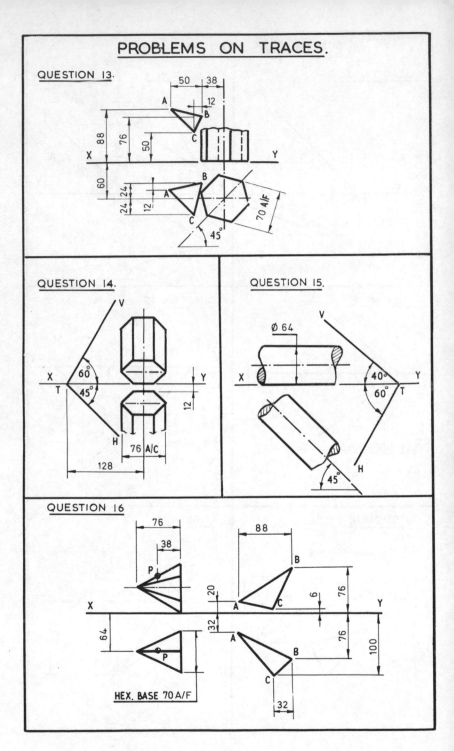

QUESTION 13.

QUESTION 14.

QUESTION 15.

QUESTION 16

HEX. BASE 70 A/F

MACHINE DRAWING

In the problems which follow, unless otherwise stated, the scale is to be full size, First Angle projection is to be used, and hidden detail and dimensions need not be shown.

BEARING ASSEMBLY

Details for a 76 mm diameter Bearing are shown on page 212. Draw half full size the following views of the complete assembly.

A sectional front elevation on BB.

A sectional plan view on AA.

An outside end view looking on the Bearing Cap.

Note: On the given drawing, tapped holes are either omitted or shown incompletely. They must be shown correctly on the solution.

AIRCRAFT BRACKET

Two views of this detail are given on page 213. Draw the given front elevation and project from it sectional end views on AA and BB and an outside plan view.

VALVE ASSEMBLY

Views of the details for a small Valve are given on page 214. Draw twice full size the following views of the complete assembly.

A half sectional front elevation corresponding to the given sectional elevation of the Body. The right hand half of the view is to be in section.

An outside end view in the direction of arrow A.

Gland packing is to be shown in the 12 mm diameter counterbore in the Spindle Guide

The Handwheel to fit the 6 mm square end of the Spindle has been omitted.

MACHINE DRAWING.

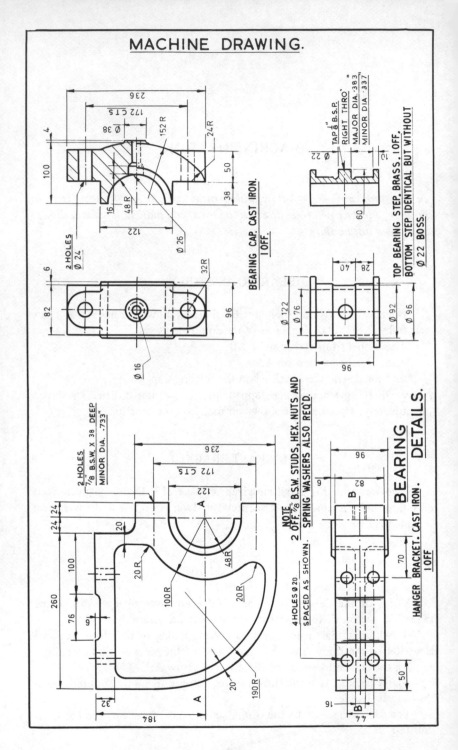

BEARING CAP. CAST IRON.
1 OFF.

Ø 38
Ø 26
152 R
24 R
48 R
50
38
100
4
16
236
172 CTS
122

2 HOLES Ø 24
6
82
96
32 R
Ø 16

TAP ½" B.S.P.
RIGHT THRO'
MAJOR DIA. ·383"
MINOR DIA. ·337"
Ø 22
60
40
28
TOP BEARING STEP, BRASS, 1OFF.
BOTTOM STEP IDENTICAL BUT WITHOUT Ø 22 BOSS.

Ø 122
Ø 76
Ø 92
Ø 96
96

BEARING DETAILS.

2 HOLES
⅞" B.S.W. X 38 DEEP
MINOR DIA. ·733"
24 24
100
260
76
9
32
184
236
172 CTS
122
A
20
20 R
100 R
48 R
20 R
20
190 R
A

NOTE
2 OFF ⅞" B.S.W. STUDS, HEX. NUTS AND
SPRING WASHERS ALSO REQ'D.

4 HOLES Ø 20
SPACED AS SHOWN.
96
6
82
70
50
16
B
B
44
HANGER BRACKET. CAST IRON.
1 OFF

212

MACHINE DRAWING.

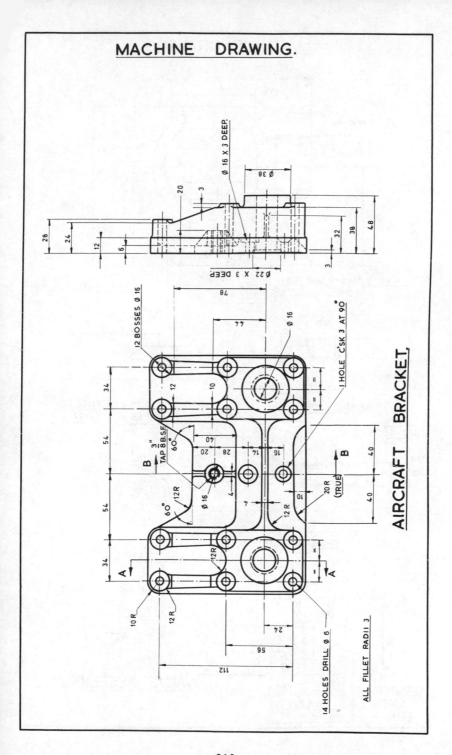

AIRCRAFT BRACKET.

213

MACHINE DRAWING.

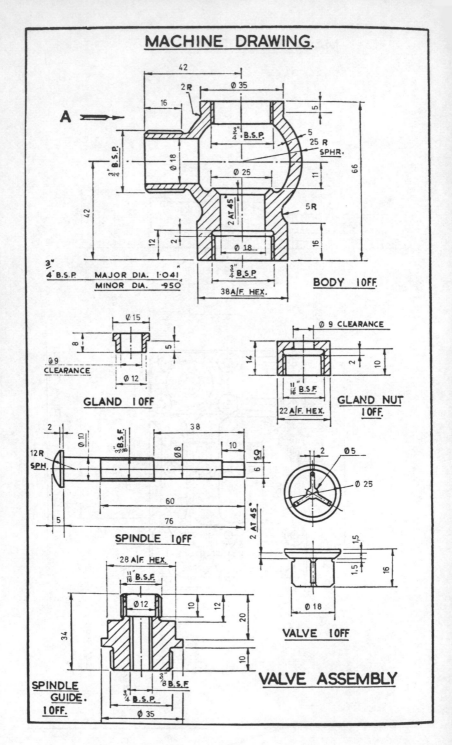

A

42

2 R

Ø 35

16

5

¾" B.S.P.

5

25 R SPHR.

Ø 18

¾" B.S.P.

Ø 25

11

66

42

5R

2 AT 45°

12

2

16

Ø 18

¾" B.S.P.

¾" B.S.P.   MAJOR DIA. 1·041"
            MINOR DIA. ·950"

38 A/F. HEX.

BODY 1OFF.

Ø 15

8

5

·9 9 CLEARANCE

Ø 12

GLAND 1OFF

Ø 9 CLEARANCE

14

2

10

11/16" B.S.F.

22 A/F. HEX.

GLAND NUT 1OFF.

2

Ø 10

3/8 B.S.F.

38

10

12 R SPH.

Ø 8

6

5·9

60

2 AT 45°

5

76

SPINDLE 1OFF.

2   **Ø 5**

Ø 25

1·5

1·5

16

Ø 18

VALVE 1OFF.

28 A/F. HEX.

11/16" B.S.F.

Ø 12

10

12

20

34

10

3/8 B.S.F.

¾" B.S.P.

Ø 35

SPINDLE GUIDE. 1OFF.

VALVE ASSEMBLY

MACHINE DRAWING
OIL PUMP COVER

Draw twice full size the following views of the Oil Pump Cover shown on page 216.
The given front elevation.
A sectional end view on QQQQ in place of the given end view.
A sectional auxiliary plan view on PP.

LATHE TAILSTOCK

Details for a small Lathe Tailstock are shown on page 217. Draw the following views of the assembled Tailstock, supply the missing details to fit hole B and lock the Sleeve.
A sectional front elevation corresponding to the given front elevation of the Body.
A half sectional end view corresponding to the given end view of the Body, with the left hand half in section and the section plane passing through hole B.

CARBURETTER BODY

The plan and elevation of a Carburetter Body are illustrated on page 218. Using Third Angle projection draw the following views of the component.
The given plan view.
A sectional front elevation on AAAA.
A sectional end view on BB.

CLAMP

On page 219 are shown the details for a Clamp. Draw the following views of the assembled componets.
A sectional front elevation corresponding to the given elevation of the Fixed Jaw, the section plane passing through the centreline.
An outside plan view.
An outside end view positioned on the right of the front elevation.
Show the jaws open 25 mm and the Tommy Bar vertical.

215

MACHINE DRAWING

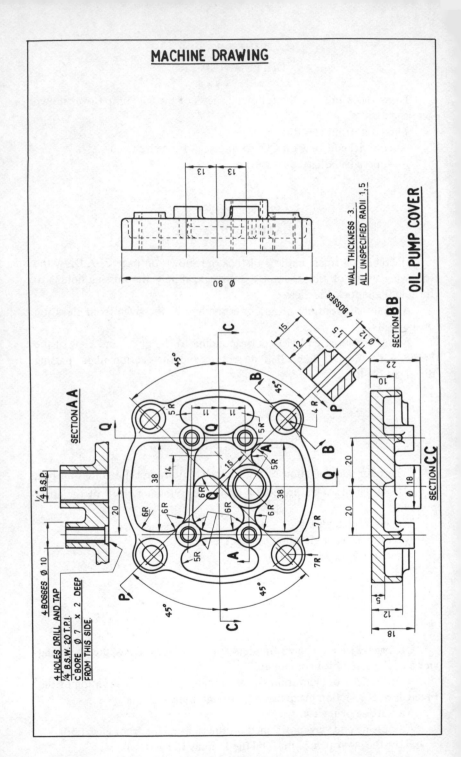

OIL PUMP COVER

SECTION A A

SECTION B B

SECTION C C

WALL THICKNESS 3.
ALL UNSPECIFIED RADII 1,5

4 HOLES DRILL AND TAP
¼" B.S.W. 20 T.P.I.
C BORE Ø 7 × 2 DEEP
FROM THIS SIDE.

216

MACHINE DRAWING.

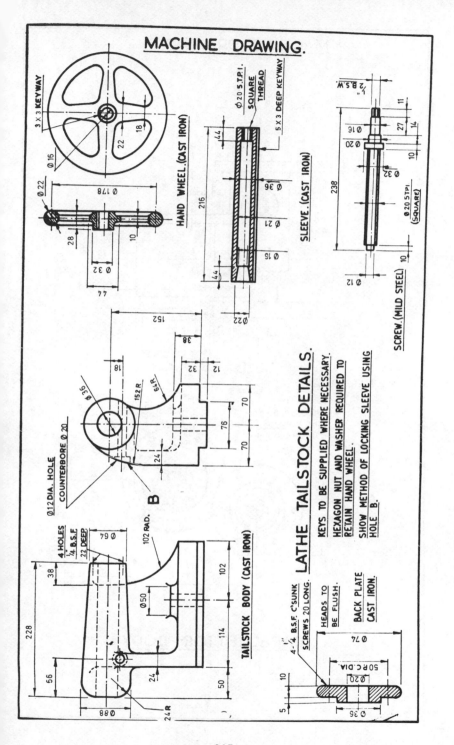

LATHE TAILSTOCK DETAILS.

KEYS TO BE SUPPLIED WHERE NECESSARY.

HEXAGON NUT AND WASHER REQUIRED TO RETAIN HAND WHEEL.

SHOW METHOD OF LOCKING SLEEVE USING HOLE B.

HAND WHEEL. (CAST IRON)

SLEEVE. (CAST IRON)

SCREW. (MILD STEEL)

TAILSTOCK BODY (CAST IRON)

BACK PLATE CAST IRON.

HEADS TO BE FLUSH.

4-¼" B.S.F. C'SUNK SCREWS 20 LONG.

217

MACHINE DRAWING.

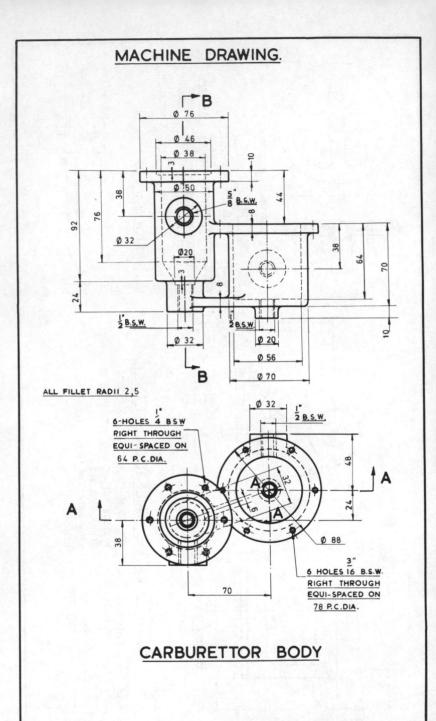

ALL FILLET RADII 2,5

CARBURETTOR BODY

218

MACHINE DRAWING.

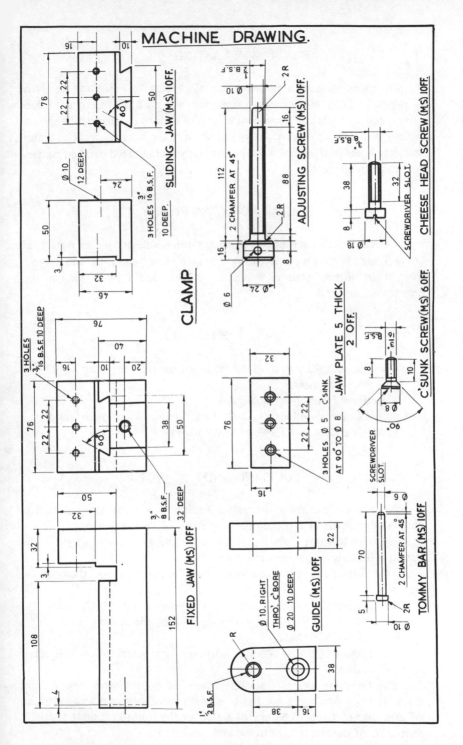

SLIDING JAW (M.S.) 10 FF.

3 HOLES 16 B.S.F.
10 DEEP.
Ø 10
12 DEEP
60°

CLAMP

ADJUSTING SCREW (M.S.) 10 FF.

2 B.S.F.
Ø 10
16
112
2 CHAMFER AT 45°
88
2 R
16
8
Ø 6
Ø 24

CHEESE HEAD SCREW (M.S.) 10 FF.

3/8 B.S.F.
38
32
SCREWDRIVER SLOT
8
Ø 18

FIXED JAW (M.S.) 10 FF.

3 HOLES
3/16 B.S.F. 10 DEEP
76
40
16 10 20
22 22
22
60°
50
38
3/8 B.S.F.
32 DEEP
50
32
32
3
108
152
4

JAW PLATE 5 THICK 2 OFF.

32
76
3 HOLES Ø 5
C'SINK
AT 90° TO Ø 8
C'SINK Ø 5
22
22
16

C'SUNK SCREW (M.S.) 60 FF.

B.S.F.
Ø 19
8
10
90°
Ø 8
SCREWDRIVER SLOT.

GUIDE (M.S.) 10 FF.

22

Ø 10. RIGHT
THRO' C'BORE
Ø 20 10 DEEP.
R
1/2 B.S.F.
38
38 16

TOMMY BAR (M.S.) 10 FF

Ø 6
70
2 CHAMFER AT 45°
5
2 R
Ø 10
SCREWDRIVER SLOT

ELBOW CASTING

The incomplete plan and elevation of a Steam Valve Casting are given on page 221. Draw these views, completing them with the interpenetration curves, and add a sectional end view on AA. Hidden detail must be shown in the front elevation but need not be shown in the other views. The 6 mm diameter holes in the branch flange need only be indicated by their centre-lines in the plan view.

ENGINE MOUNTING FITTING

A detail from an aeroplane engine mounting is illustrated on page 222. Using Third Angle projection draw the given front elevation and project from it an outside plan view and an outside end view looking in the direction of arrow B.

LOCATION FIXTURE

Draw the following views of the Fixture shown on page 223.
The given plan view.
A sectional front elevation on AA.
A half sectional end view on CC, the left hand half being in section.
Hidden detail is only required in the plan view.

COUPLING AND DISC CAM

A sectional elevation through a Coupling with an integral cam is shown on page 224. Draw the following views of the component.

An outside front elevation in place of the given sectional front elevation. This view is to show hidden detail.

Two outside end views, one looking on the coupling face, the other on the cam.

The motion given to the follower by the cam is to be:

$0°-90°$ Lift 38 mm with simple harmonic motion.

$90°-180°$ Dwell.

$180°-360°$ Fall 38 mm with uniform acceleration and retardation.

The Coupling rotates clockwise when the given view is viewed from the left. The Coupling flange has two part conical bosses running into the 86 mm diameter boss. The line of action of the follower is on the vertical centreline of the component in the end views.

MACHINE DRAWING.

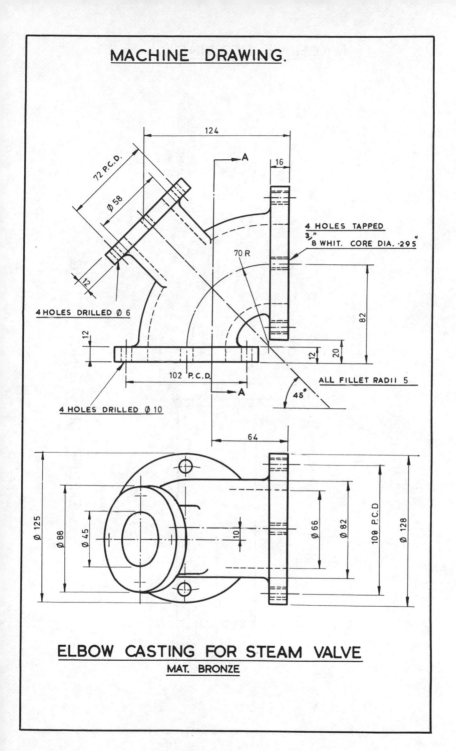

ELBOW CASTING FOR STEAM VALVE
MAT. BRONZE

MACHINE DRAWING.

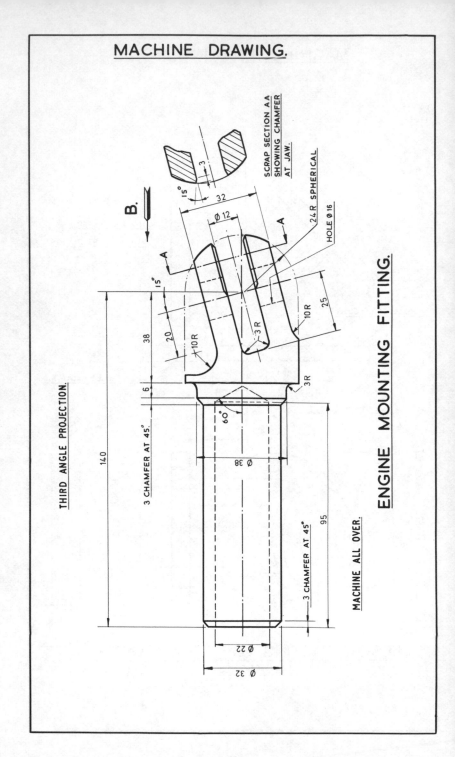

SCRAP SECTION AA
SHOWING CHAMFER
AT JAW.

B.

THIRD ANGLE PROJECTION.

MACHINE ALL OVER.

ENGINE MOUNTING FITTING.

15°
32
Ø 12
A
A
24 R SPHERICAL
HOLE Ø 16
25
10 R
3 R
15°
38
20
10 R
140
6
3 CHAMFER AT 45°.
60°
Ø 38
95
3 R
3 CHAMFER AT 45°
Ø 22
Ø 32
3

MACHINE DRAWING.

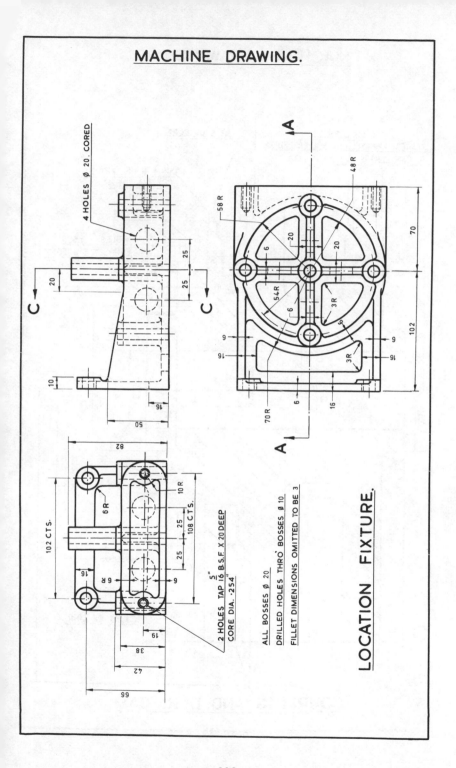

4 HOLES Ø 20. CORED

2 HOLES TAP 16 B.S.F. X 20 DEEP
CORE DIA. ·254″

ALL BOSSES Ø 20

DRILLED HOLES THRO' BOSSES Ø 10

FILLET DIMENSIONS OMITTED TO BE 3

LOCATION FIXTURE.

MACHINE DRAWING.

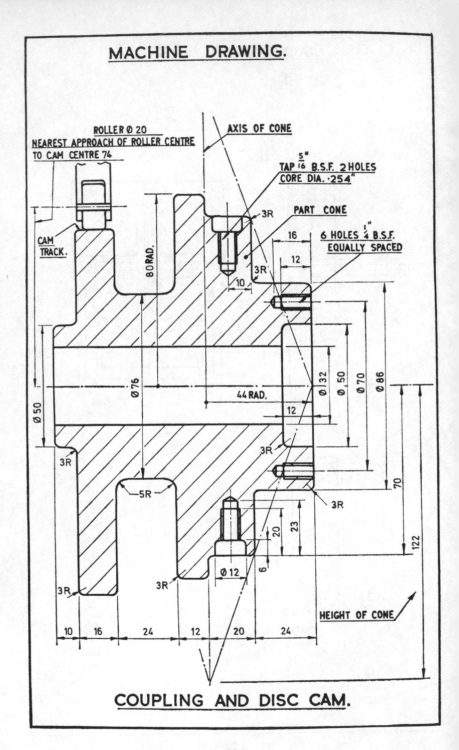

COUPLING AND DISC CAM.

PUMP BARREL

Draw half full size the following views of the Pump Barrel shown on page 226.

An outside front elevation in place of the given sectional front elevation.

A sectional plan view on BB in place of the given part plan view.

A sectional end view on AA.

WALL BRACKET

Views of a special Wall Bracket are shown on page 227. Draw the given plan view and complete the front and side elevations.

When the plan is viewed in the direction of arrow C, the 50 mm radius in the side elevation appears as its true shape.

Lines XX and YY should be positioned as shown to fit the required views on A2 metric paper.

Hidden detail is only required in the plan view.

DISTRIBUTION CASING

Two elevations of a Distribution Casing are given in Third Angle projection on page 228. Using Third Angle projection draw the following views of the Casing.

A front elevation obtained by viewing the given front elevation in the direction of arrow A.

In projection with the front elevation, a sectional end view on BB.

A sectional plan view through CC projected from the front elevation.

PULLEY BELT ADJUSTER

Details for a Pulley Belt Adjuster are shown on page 229. Draw the following views of the Adjuster with all the parts assembled.

A sectional front elevation with the edges XX and YY of the Base and Adjusting Bracket in line. The section plane is to pass through the centre of the Adjusting Screw.

An outside end view obtained by viewing the front elevation from the left.

225

MACHINE DRAWING.

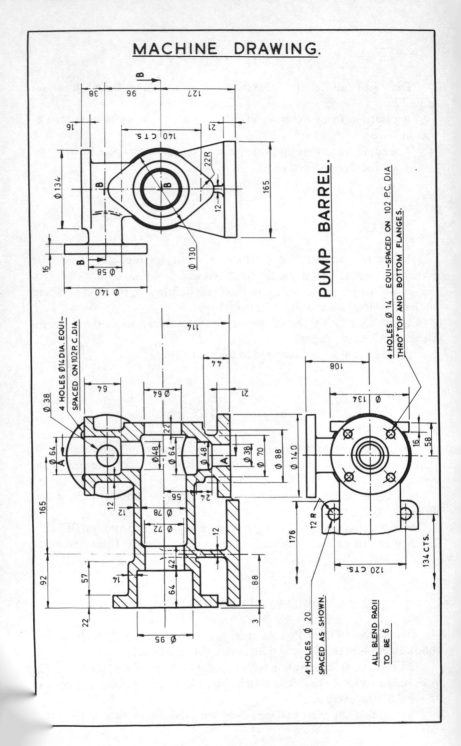

PUMP BARREL.

4 HOLES Ø 14 EQUI-SPACED ON 102 P.C. DIA
THRO' TOP AND BOTTOM FLANGES.

4 HOLES Ø14 DIA. EQUI-SPACED ON 102 P.C. DIA

4 HOLES Ø 20
SPACED AS SHOWN.

ALL BLEND RADII
TO BE 6

MACHINE DRAWING.

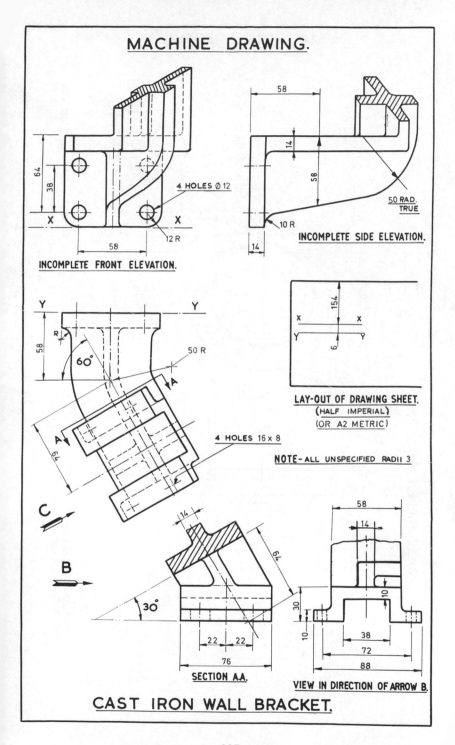

INCOMPLETE FRONT ELEVATION.

4 HOLES Ø 12

64

38

58

12 R

X — X

INCOMPLETE SIDE ELEVATION.

58

14

56

50 RAD.
TRUE

10 R

14

LAY-OUT OF DRAWING SHEET.
(HALF IMPERIAL)
(OR A2 METRIC)

154

6

X — X

Y — Y

58

R

60°

50 R

64

A — A

4 HOLES 16 x 8

NOTE – ALL UNSPECIFIED RADII 3

C

B

30°

14

64

22 | 22

76

SECTION A.A.

58

14

10

30

10

38

72

88

VIEW IN DIRECTION OF ARROW B.

CAST IRON WALL BRACKET.

227

MACHINE DRAWING

DISTRIBUTION CASING.

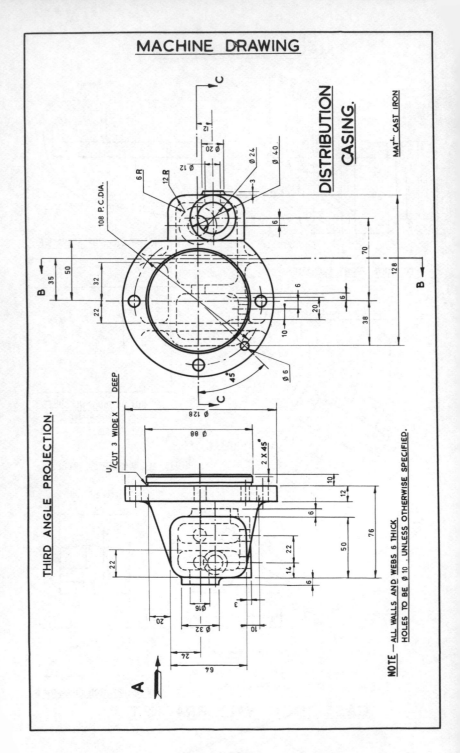

THIRD ANGLE PROJECTION.

MAT^L. CAST IRON

NOTE — ALL WALLS AND WEBS 6 THICK
HOLES TO BE Ø 10 . UNLESS OTHERWISE SPECIFIED.

228

MACHINE DRAWING.

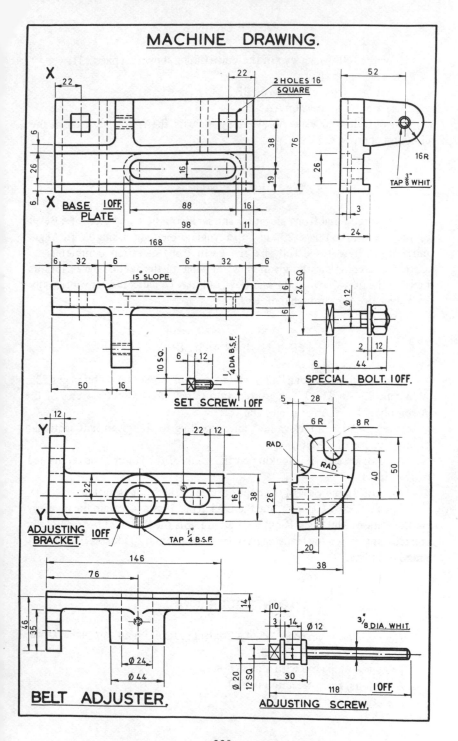

BASE PLATE. 1OFF.

2 HOLES 16 SQUARE

TAP ⅜" WHIT.

15° SLOPE.

SET SCREW. 1OFF

SPECIAL BOLT. 1OFF.

¼ DIA B.S.F.

ADJUSTING BRACKET. 1OFF.

TAP ¼" B.S.F.

RAD.

RAD.

BELT ADJUSTER.

⅜" DIA. WHIT.

ADJUSTING SCREW. 1OFF.

VALVE CASING

Draw the following views of the Valve Casing shown on page 231.
The given plan view.
A sectional front elevation on BB.
A sectional end view on AA.
An outside end view obtained by viewing the front elevation in the direction of arrow C.

BEVEL PINION

A part sectional front elevation and an incomplete end view of a Bevel Pinion are given on page 232 in Third Angle projection. Using Third Angle projection, draw twice full size the given front elevation completely in section and complete the given view showing all the teeth. The serrations need not be fully drawn in the end view, but may be indicated conventionally by a chain dot line through their tips.

PINION GEAR ASSEMBLY

The components for a Pinion Gear Assembly are detailed on pages 232, 233 and 234 in Third Angle projection. Draw the following views of the Assembly in Third Angle projection.
A sectional front elevation corresponding to the given half sectional front elevation of the Housing.
An outside end view looking on the teeth of the Pinion. The teeth need not be shown.
An outside end view of the opposite side of the front elevation.
The Lock Nut, Figure 3, and the Lock Ring, Figure 4, retain the Bearings on the Pinion. The Lock Ring, Figure 5, retains the Pinion Sub-Assembly in the Housing. When the Housing Bush is assembled in the Housing, the faces A are to be in line.

CONTROL BRACKET

Views are given on page 235 of a Control Bracket for an aeroplane. Draw the following views of the detail.
The given plan view with hidden detail.
A sectional front elevation on QQ.
A sectional end view on PP.

MACHINE DRAWING.

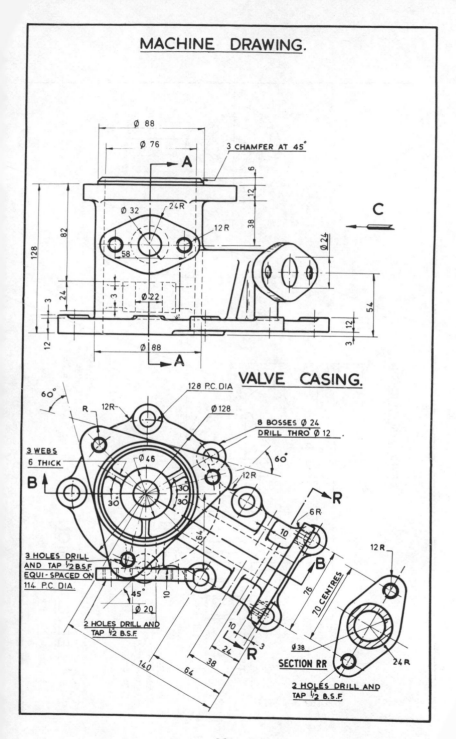

VALVE CASING.

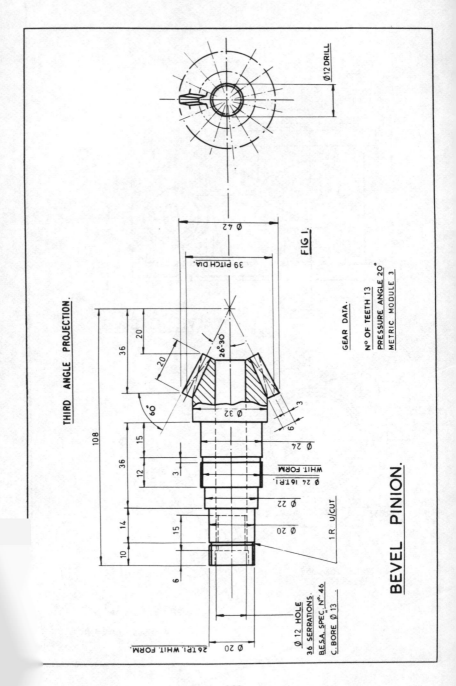

THIRD ANGLE PROJECTION.

FIG I.

GEAR DATA.

Nº OF TEETH 13
PRESSURE ANGLE 20°
METRIC MODULE 3

BEVEL PINION.

MACHINE DRAWING.

DETAILS FOR PINION GEAR ASSEMBLY.

THIRD ANGLE PROJECTION.

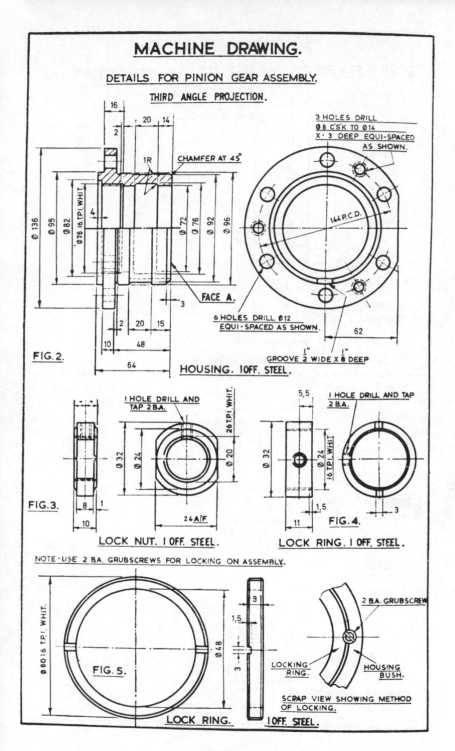

3 HOLES DRILL
Ø8 C'S'K TO Ø14
X · 3 DEEP EQUI-SPACED
AS SHOWN.

CHAMFER AT 45°

1R

144 P.C.D.

FACE A.

6 HOLES DRILL. Ø12
EQUI-SPACED AS SHOWN.

GROOVE ½" WIDE X ⅛" DEEP

FIG. 2.

HOUSING. 1 OFF. STEEL.

I HOLE DRILL AND
TAP 2 B.A.

26 T.P.I. WHIT.

FIG. 3.

24 A/F

LOCK NUT. 1 OFF. STEEL.

I HOLE DRILL AND TAP
2 B.A.

16 T.P.I. WHIT

FIG. 4.

LOCK RING. 1 OFF. STEEL.

NOTE · USE 2 B.A. GRUBSCREWS FOR LOCKING ON ASSEMBLY.

Ø 80 16 T.P.I. WHIT.

FIG. 5.

2 B.A. GRUBSCREW

LOCKING
RING.

HOUSING
BUSH.

SCRAP VIEW SHOWING METHOD
OF LOCKING.

LOCK RING.   1 OFF. STEEL.

233

MACHINE DRAWING.

DETAILS FOR PINION GEAR ASSEMBLY.

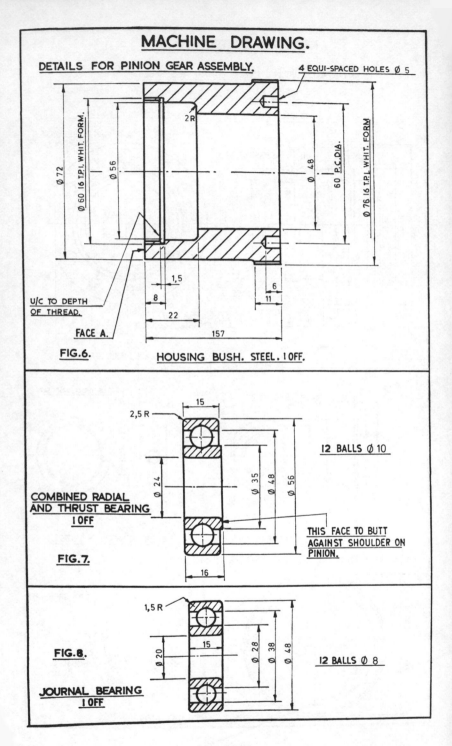

4 EQUI-SPACED HOLES Ø 5

Ø 72
Ø 60 16 T.P.I. WHIT. FORM.
Ø 56
2 R
Ø 48
60 P.C.DIA.
Ø 76 16 T.P.I. WHIT. FORM.

U/C TO DEPTH OF THREAD.

FACE A.

1,5
8
22
6
11
157

FIG.6.   HOUSING BUSH. STEEL. 1 OFF.

2,5 R
15

12 BALLS Ø 10

Ø 24
Ø 35
Ø 48
Ø 56

COMBINED RADIAL AND THRUST BEARING 1 OFF

THIS FACE TO BUTT AGAINST SHOULDER ON PINION.

FIG.7.

16

1,5 R

FIG.8.

15
Ø 20
Ø 28
Ø 38
Ø 48

12 BALLS Ø 8

JOURNAL BEARING 1 OFF

MACHINE DRAWING.

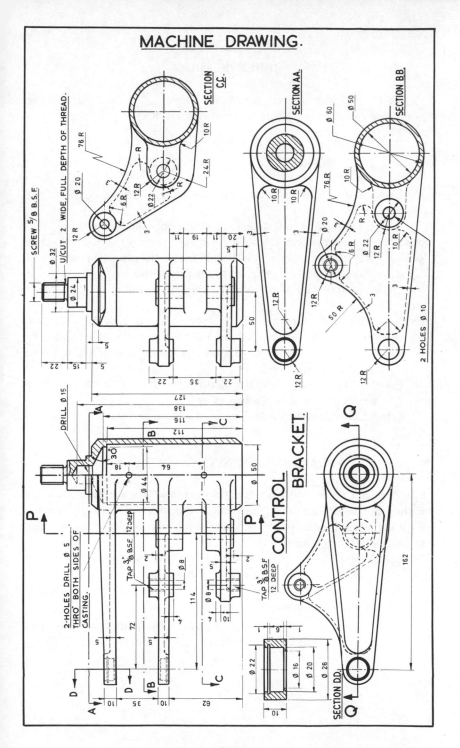

CONTROL BRACKET.

SECTION CC.

SECTION AA.

SECTION BB.

SECTION DD.

DRILL JIG BODY

Views of this component are shown on page 237. Draw full size the given front elevation and a sectional end view on QQQQ.

CONNECTING ROD END ASSEMBLY

The details for this assembly are shown on page 238 and consist of the following.

A steel connecting rod, item 1, of which only the end is shown; two brass bearing halves, item 2; a mild steel front plate, item 3; a mild steel locking plate, item 4; two steel bolts, item 5; two steel hexagon nuts, and a cap screw to secure the locking plate to the front plate.

Draw the following views of the complete assembly in Third Angle projection.

(a) A half-sectional front view, corresponding to view A of the connecting rod. The top half of the view is to be in section. The visible half of the intersection curve on the connecting rod is to be correctly projected.

(b) A sectional plan view, the section plane passing through the horizontal centreline of the front view.

(c) An outside end view looking on the hexagon nuts.

BRACKET AND CASTING ASSEMBLY

Page 239 shows the parts for this assembly. When assembled on the casting face, centreline CC on the bracket coincides with cutting plane AA. With the bracket in this position, draw the following views of the assembly in Third Angle projection.

(a) A plan view, corresponding to the given part plan view of the casting face, showing the bracket completely.

(b) A front view, obtained by viewing the plan view in the direction of arrow B, showing the bracket completely.

(c) An auxiliary sectional view on AA. The fixing stud dimensions are to be settled by the student.

MACHINE DRAWING.

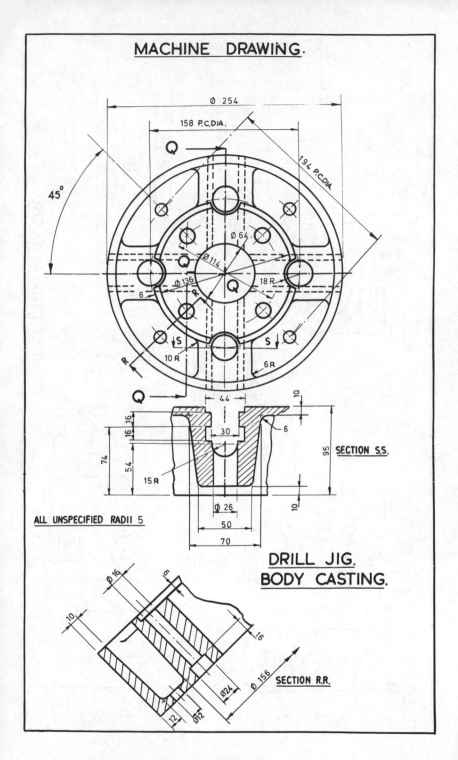

Ø 254

158 P.C.DIA.

194 P.C.DIA.

45°

Q

Ø 64

Ø 114

Ø 136

18 R

6

R

Q

S   S

10 R   6 R

R

44

10

16 16

30   6

74   54   95   SECTION S.S.

15 R

Ø 26

50

10

70

ALL UNSPECIFIED RADII 5

DRILL JIG.
BODY CASTING.

Ø 16   6

10   16

Ø 24   Ø 156   SECTION R.R.

12   Ø 12

237

MACHINE DRAWING.

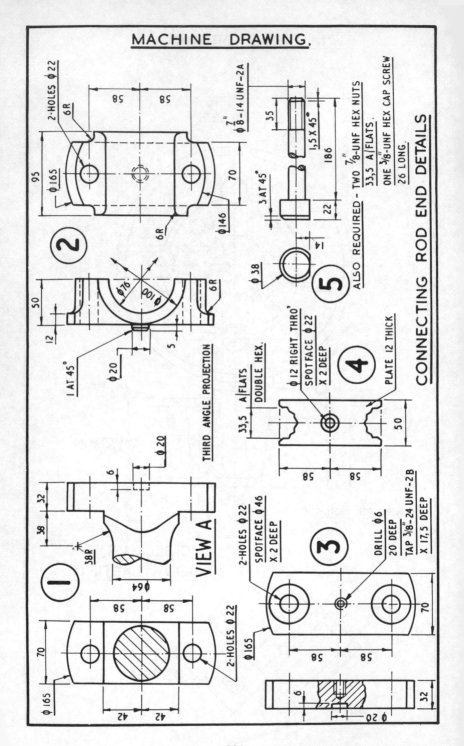

THIRD ANGLE PROJECTION

VIEW A

CONNECTING ROD END DETAILS

ALSO REQUIRED – TWO 7/8"-UNF HEX NUTS 33,5 A/FLATS.
ONE 3/8"-UNF HEX CAP SCREW 26 LONG.

238

MACHINE DRAWING

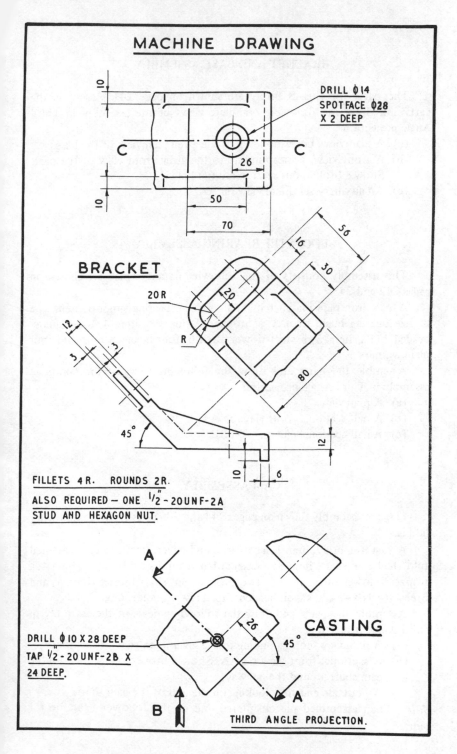

DRILL ⌀14
SPOTFACE ⌀28
X 2 DEEP

C ——— C

26

50

70

10

10

BRACKET

20R

R

56

16

30

20

80

12

3

3

45°

12

10   6

FILLETS 4R.   ROUNDS 2R.
ALSO REQUIRED — ONE ¹/₂″-20UNF-2A
STUD AND HEXAGON NUT.

A

A

26

45°

CASTING

DRILL ⌀10 X 28 DEEP
TAP ¹/₂″-20UNF-2B X
24 DEEP.

B

THIRD ANGLE PROJECTION.

BRACKET AND BASE ASSEMBLY

The parts for this assembly are shown on page 241. Assemble the parts and draw the following complete views of the assembly in Third Angle projection.

(a) A plan view, corresponding to the given plan view of the base.
(b) A front view, corresponding to the given front view of the base. Show a broken-out section around hole X.
(c) An auxiliary sectional view on AA.

FOOTSTEP BEARING ASSEMBLY

This assembly consists of the following details, which are shown on pages 242 and 243.

A cast iron base plate, item 1; a cast iron bearing support, item 2; a bronze bearing bush, item 3; a bronze bearing pad, item 4; four square-headed bolts, item 5; a steel dowel, item 6; four hexagon nuts and four plain washers.

Assemble the parts and draw the following views of the complete assembly in Third Angle projection.

(a) A plan view.
(b) A half-sectional front view on AA.
(c) A half-sectional end view on BB.

CAM ASSEMBLY

The cam assembly shown on pages 244 and 245 consists of the following details.

A cast iron body, item 1; a cast iron end cover, item 2; a casehardened mild steel cam shaft, item 3; a casehardened mild steel follower, item 4; a bronze follower bush, item 5; two bronze cam shaft bushes, item 6; and three—16UNF—2A hexagon headed cap screws, 20mm long.

Assemble the parts and draw the following views of the assembly in Third Angle projection.

(a) A plan view, corresponding to the given plan view of the body
(b) A sectional front view on AA. Show a broken-out section on the cam shaft around the keyway.
(c) An outside end view looking on the end of the cam shaft.

Note: When assembled the chamfered end of the follower bears on the cam.

MACHINE DRAWING

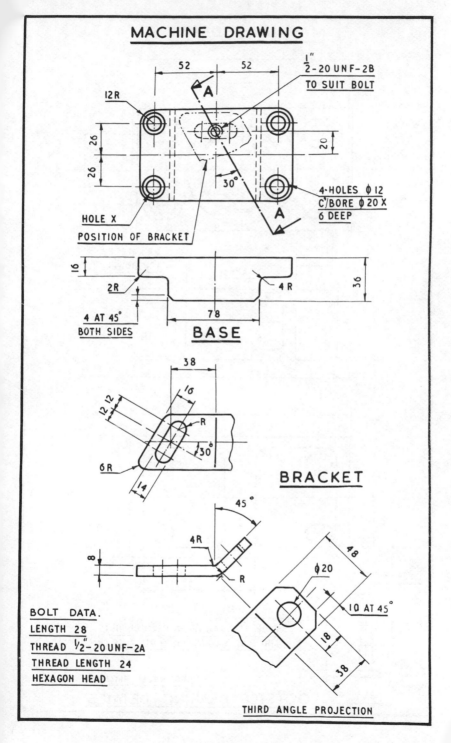

1/2"-20UNF-2B
TO SUIT BOLT

12R

52   52

26

26

20

30°

4-HOLES Φ12
C'BORE Φ20 X
6 DEEP

HOLE X
POSITION OF BRACKET

16

2R

4R

36

4 AT 45°
BOTH SIDES

78

BASE

38

16

12 12

R

30°

6R

14

BRACKET

45°

4R

8

R

Φ20

48

10 AT 45°

18

38

BOLT DATA.
LENGTH 28
THREAD 1/2"-20UNF-2A
THREAD LENGTH 24
HEXAGON HEAD

THIRD ANGLE PROJECTION

241

MACHINE DRAWING

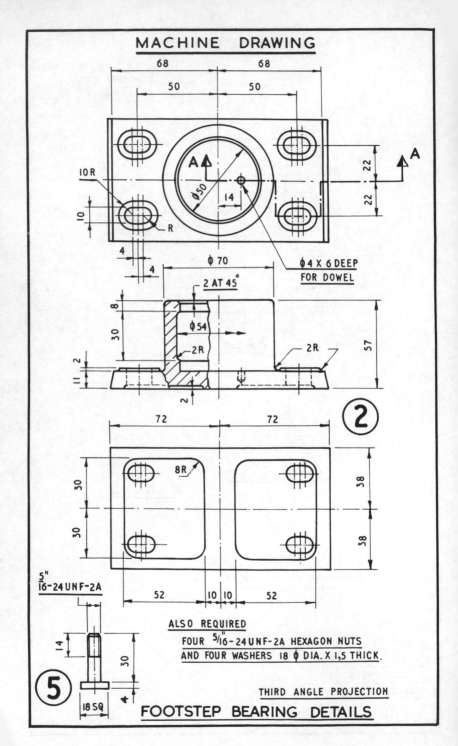

68   68
50   50

10 R
Ø50
14
R
10
4
4

A ↑   A ↑ A
22
22

Ø 4 X 6 DEEP
FOR DOWEL

Ø 70

2 AT 45°
8
Ø 54
30
2R   2R
2
11
2

57

(2)

72   72

8R
30
38
30
38

52   10 10   52

5"/16-24 UNF-2A

14
30
4

(5)

18 SQ

<u>ALSO REQUIRED</u>
FOUR ⁵/₁₆-24 UNF-2A HEXAGON NUTS
AND FOUR WASHERS 18 Ø DIA. X 1,5 THICK.

THIRD ANGLE PROJECTION

FOOTSTEP BEARING DETAILS

MACHINE DRAWING

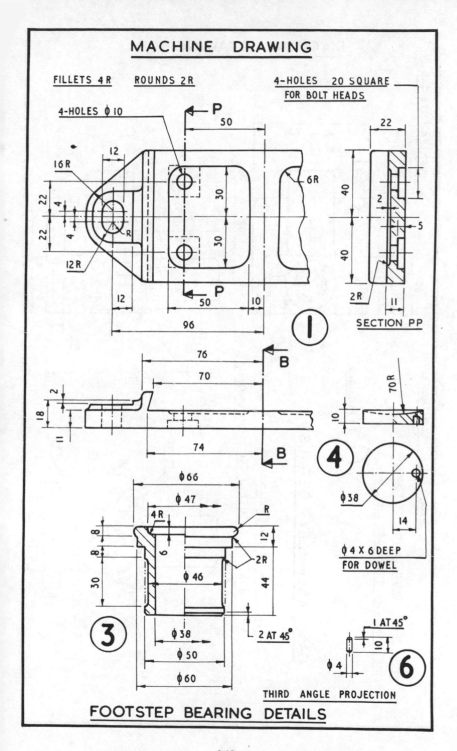

FILLETS 4R   ROUNDS 2R

4-HOLES Ø10

4-HOLES 20 SQUARE
FOR BOLT HEADS

P
50

16R

12

22
4
22
4
R

12R

30

30

6R

12

50   10

96

SECTION PP

22

40

2

5

40

2R   11

76

70

2

18

11

74

B

B

70R

10

Ø38

14

Ø4 X 6 DEEP
FOR DOWEL

Ø66

Ø47

4R

8

8

30

6

Ø46

R

12

2R

44

3

Ø38

Ø50

Ø60

2 AT 45°

1 AT 45°

10

Ø4

6

THIRD ANGLE PROJECTION

FOOTSTEP BEARING DETAILS

MACHINE DRAWING

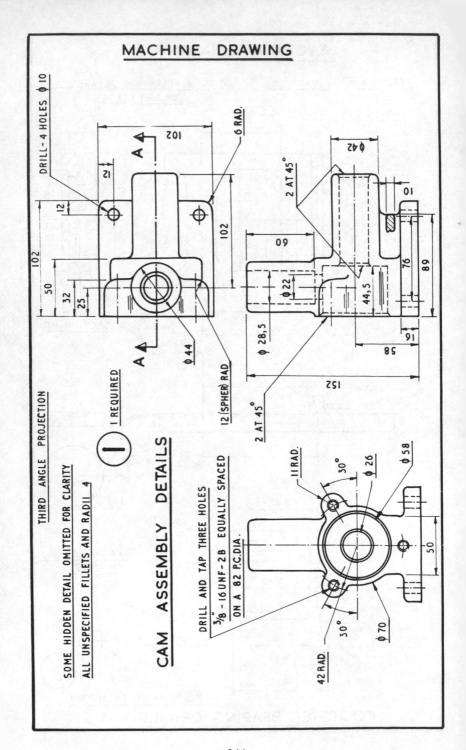

THIRD ANGLE PROJECTION

SOME HIDDEN DETAIL OMITTED FOR CLARITY

ALL UNSPECIFIED FILLETS AND RADII 4

I REQUIRED

CAM ASSEMBLY DETAILS

DRILL AND TAP THREE HOLES

³⁄₈" – 16 UNF – 2B EQUALLY SPACED
ON A 82 P.C.DIA.

DRILL – 4 HOLES ⌀ 10

102

12

12

12

102

102

50

32

25

⌀ 44

A

A

6 RAD.

⌀ 42

2 AT 45°

10

60

⌀ 22

44,5

⌀ 28,5

76

89

16

58

152

2 AT 45°

12 (SPHER) RAD.

11 RAD.

30°

⌀ 26

⌀ 58

30°

⌀ 70

42 RAD.

50

244

MACHINE DRAWING

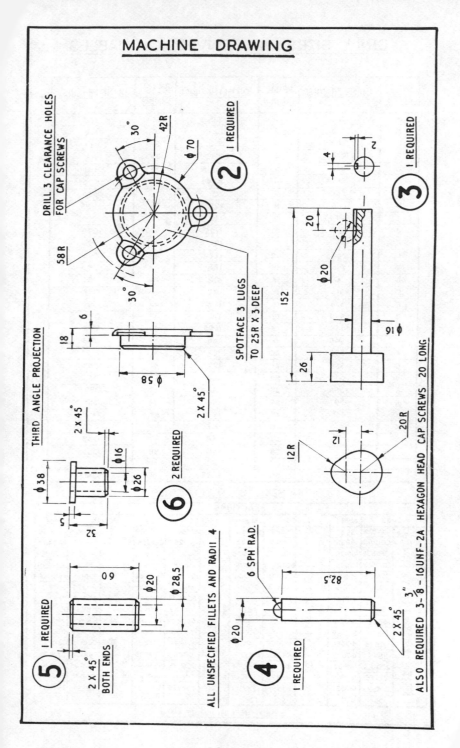

THIRD ANGLE PROJECTION

ALL UNSPECIFIED FILLETS AND RADII 4

ALSO REQUIRED 3-⅜-16UNF-2A HEXAGON HEAD CAP SCREWS 20 LONG

245

DRILL SIZES & CONVERSION TABLES.

DRILL LETTER	DIAMETER (INS)	DRILL NUMBER	DIAMETER (INS)	DRILL NUMBER	DIAMETER (INS)
A	·234	1	·228	31	·120
B	·238	2	·221	32	·116
C	·242	3	·213	33	·113
D	·246	4	·209	34	·111
E	·250	5	·2055	35	·110
F	·257	6	·204	36	·1065
G	·261	7	·201	37	·104
H	·266	8	·199	38	·1015
I	·272	9	·196	39	·0995
J	·277	10	·1935	40	·098
K	·281	11	·191	41	·096
L	·290	12	·189	42	·0935
M	·295	13	·185	43	·089
N	·302	14	·182	44	·086
O	·316	15	·180	45	·082
P	·323	16	·177	46	·081
Q	·332	17	·173	47	·0785
R	·339	18	·1695	48	·076
S	·348	19	·166	49	·073
T	·358	20	·161	50	·070
U	·368	21	·159	51	·067
V	·377	22	·157	52	·0635
W	·386	23	·154	53	·0595
X	·397	24	·152	54	·055
Y	·404	25	·1495	55	·052
Z	·413	26	·147	56	·0465
		27	·144	57	·043
		28	·1405	58	·042
		29	·136	59	·041
		30	·1285	60	·040

INCHES TO MILLIMETRES

FRACTIONS

INCHES	M.M.	INCHES	M.M.	INCHES	M.M.	INCHES	M.M.
1/64	·015625	17/64	·265625	33/64	·515625	49/64	·765625
	·3969		6·7469		13·0969		19·4469
1/32	·031250	9/32	·28125	17/32	·53125	25/32	·78125
	·7938		7·1438		13·4938		19·8438
3/64	·046875	19/64	·296875	35/64	·546875	51/64	·796875
	1·1906		7·5406		13·8906		20·2406
1/16	·06250	5/16	·3125	9/16	·5625	13/16	·8125
	1·5875		7·9375		14·2875		20·6375
5/64	·078125	21/64	·328125	37/64	·578125	53/64	·828125
	1·9844		8·3344		14·6844		21·0344
3/32	·09375	11/32	·34375	19/32	·59375	27/32	·84375
	2·3812		8·7312		15·0812		21·4312
7/64	·109375	23/64	·359375	39/64	·609375	55/64	·859375
	2·7781		9·1281		15·4781		21·8281
1/8	·125	3/8	·375	5/8	·625	7/8	·875
	3·175		9·525		15·875		22·225
9/64	·140625	25/64	·390625	41/64	·640625	57/64	·890625
	3·5719		9·9219		16·2719		22·6219
5/32	·15625	13/32	·40625	21/32	·65625	29/32	·90625
	3·9688		10·3188		16·6688		23·0188
11/64	·171875	27/64	·421875	43/64	·671875	59/64	·921875
	4·3656		10·7156		17·0656		23·4156
3/16	·1875	7/16	·43750	11/16	·6875	15/16	·9375
	4·7625		11·1125		17·4625		23·8125
13/64	·203125	29/64	·453125	45/64	·703125	61/64	·953125
	5·1594		11·5094		17·8594		24·2094
7/32	·21875	15/32	·46875	23/32	·71875	31/32	·96875
	5·5562		11·9062		18·2562		24·6062
15/64	·234375	31/64	·484375	47/64	·734375	63/64	·984375
	5·9531		12·3031		18·6531		25·0031
1/4	·25	1/2	·50	3/4	·75		
	6·35		12·7		19·05		

BASED ON 1 INCH = 25·4 M.M.

B.A. B.S.F. & B.S.P. THREAD SIZES.

THREAD SIZE	T.P.I.	MAJOR DIA. NOMINAL.	EFFECTIVE DIA. NOMINAL.	MINOR DIA. NOMINAL.
6 B.A.	47·9	·1102	·0976	·0850
4 B.A.	38·5	·1417	·1262	·1106
2 B.A.	31·4	·1850	·1659	·1468
1/4 B.S.F.	26	·2500	·2254	·2008
9/32	26	·2812	·2566	·2320
5/16	22	·3125	·2834	·2543
3/8	20	·3750	·3430	·3110
7/16	18	·4375	·4019	·3663
1/2	16	·5000	·4600	·4200
9/16	16	·5625	·5225	·4825
5/8	14	·6250	·5793	·5336
11/16	14	·6875	·6418	·5961
3/4	12	·7500	·6966	·6432
7/8	11	·8750	·8168	·7586
1	10	1·0000	·9360	·8720
1 1/8	9	1·1250	1·0539	·9828
1 1/4	9	1·2500	1·1789	1·1078
1 3/8	8	1·3750	1·2950	1·2150
1 1/2	8	1·5000	1·4200	1·3400
1/8 B.S.P.	28	·3830	·3601	·3372
1/4	19	·5180	·4843	·4506
3/8	19	·6560	·6223	·5886
1/2	14	·8250	·7793	·7336
5/8	14	·9020	·8563	·8106
3/4	14	1·0410	·9953	·9496
7/8	14	1·1890	1·1433	1·0976
1	11	1·3090	1·2508	1·1926
1 1/4	11	1·6500	1·5918	1·5336
1 1/2	11	1·8820	1·8238	1·7656
1 3/4	11	2·1160	2·0578	1·9996
2	11	2·3470	2·2888	2·2306

B.S.W. THREAD SIZES.

NOMINAL DIAMETER	NUMBER OF THREADS PER IN.	MAJOR DIAMETER	EFFECTIVE DIAMETER	MINOR DIAMETER
$\frac{1}{8}''$	40	·1250	·1090	·0930
$\frac{3}{16}$	24	·1875	·1608	·1341
$\frac{1}{4}$	20	·2500	·2180	·1860
$\frac{5}{16}$	18	·3125	·2769	·2413
$\frac{3}{8}$	16	·3750	·3350	·2950
$\frac{7}{16}$	14	·4375	·3918	·3461
$\frac{1}{2}$	12	·5000	·4466	·3932
$\frac{9}{16}$	12	·5625	·5091	·4557
$\frac{5}{8}$	11	·6250	·5668	·5086
$\frac{11}{16}$	11	·6875	·6293	·5711
$\frac{3}{4}$	10	·7500	·6860	·6220
$\frac{7}{8}$	9	·8750	·8039	·7328
1	8	1·0000	·9200	·8400
$1\frac{1}{8}$	7	1·1250	1·0335	·9420
$1\frac{1}{4}$	7	1·2500	1·1585	1·0670
$1\frac{1}{2}$	6	1·5000	1·3933	1·2866
$1\frac{3}{4}$	5	1·7500	1·6219	1·4938
2	4·5	2·0000	1·8577	1·7154
$2\frac{1}{4}$	4	2·2500	2·0899	1·9298
$2\frac{1}{2}$	4	2·5000	2·3399	2·1798
$2\frac{3}{4}$	3·5	2·7500	2·5670	2·3840
3	3·5	3·0000	2·8170	2·6340
$3\frac{1}{4}$	3·25	3·2500	3·0530	2·8560
$3\frac{1}{2}$	3·25	3·5000	3·3030	3·1060
$3\frac{3}{4}$	3	3·7500	3·5366	3·3232
4	3	4·0000	3·7866	3·5732

STANDARD HEXAGON SIZES.

BRITISH HEXAGONS.

NOMINAL SIZE ACROSS FLATS	ASSOCIATED SCREW THREAD B.A. & B.S.F.	WIDTH ACROSS CORNERS APPROX. MAX.
·193″	6 B.A.	·220
·248	4 B.A.	290
·324	2 B.A.	·370
·445	$\frac{1}{4}$	·510
·525	$\frac{5}{16}$	·610
·600	$\frac{3}{8}$	·690
·710	$\frac{7}{16}$	·820
·820	$\frac{1}{2}$	·950
920	$\frac{9}{16}$	1·060
1·010	$\frac{5}{8}$	1·170
1·100	$\frac{11}{16}$	1·270
1·200	$\frac{3}{4}$	1·390
1·300	$\frac{7}{8}$	1·500
1·390	$\frac{15}{16}$	1·600
1·480	1	1·710
1·670	$1\frac{1}{8}$	1·930
1·860	$1\frac{1}{4}$	2·150
2·050	$1\frac{3}{8}$	2·360
2·220	$1\frac{1}{2}$	2·560

UNIFIED HEXAGONS.

NOMINAL SIZE ACROSS FLATS	ASSOCIATED SCREW THREAD UNF OR UNC	WIDTH ACROSS CORNERS APPROX. MAX.
$\frac{1}{4}″$	N°6 (·138)	·290
$\frac{5}{16}$	N°8 (·164)	·360
$\frac{11}{32}$	N°10 (·190)	·400
$\frac{7}{16}$	$\frac{1}{4}$	·500
$\frac{1}{2}$	$\frac{5}{16}$	·580
$\frac{9}{16}$	$\frac{3}{8}$	·650
$\frac{11}{16}$	$\frac{7}{16}$	·790
$\frac{3}{4}$	$\frac{1}{2}$	·860
$\frac{7}{8}$	$\frac{9}{16}$	1·010
$\frac{15}{16}$	$\frac{5}{8}$	1·080
$1\frac{1}{16}$	$\frac{3}{4}$	1·230
$1\frac{1}{4}$	$\frac{7}{8}$	1·440
$1\frac{7}{16}$	1	1·660